AUG 07 – OcT. 07 = 1

D1551852

AUG 07 – OcT. 07 = 1

1117
8/10

PAUL T. FRANKL AND MODERN AMERICAN DESIGN

PAUL T. FRANKL
AND MODERN
AMERICAN
DESIGN

Christopher Long

GLEN ELLYN PUBLIC LIBRARY
400 DUANE STREET
GLEN ELLYN, ILLINOIS 60137

YALE UNIVERSITY PRESS   NEW HAVEN AND LONDON

Copyright © 2007 by Christopher Long.
All rights reserved.
This book may not be reproduced, in whole or in part,
including illustrations, in any form (beyond that
copying permitted by Sections 107 and 108 of the
U.S. Copyright Law and except by reviewers for
the public press), without written permission from
the publishers.

Designed by Baseman Design Associates
Set in Fiolosofia and Univers

Printed in China by Oceanic Graphic Printing, Inc.

Library of Congress Cataloging-in-Publication Data
Long, Christopher.
   Paul T. Frankl and modern American design/Christopher Long.
      p. cm.
   Includes bibliographical references and index.
ISBN: 978-0-300-12102-5 (clothbound : alk. paper)
1. Frankl, Paul T. (Paul Theodore), b. 1886. 2. Designers—United
States—Biography. I. Title.
NK1412.F73L66 2007
745.092—dc22   2006026780

A catalogue record for this book is available
from the British Library.

The paper in this book meets the guidelines
for permanence and durability of the Committee
on Production Guidelines for Book Longevity of
the Council on Library Resources.

10 9 8 7 6 5 4 3 2 1

Cover: (front) Paul T. Frankl, Skyscraper bookcase, c. 1927 (see fig. 59);
(back) Paul T. Frankl, woodweave chair, c. 1938 (see fig. 128)

Frontispiece: Paul T. Frankl, Speed sofa, mid-1930s.
Wood with pony-skin upholstery, 28 x 97 x 42 in. (71.1 x 246.4 x 106.7 cm).
Courtesy Sotheby's, New York

FOR GIA MARIE

Contents

Preface

The beginnings of this book extend back more than twenty years, to my early days as a graduate student at the University of Texas at Austin. In 1982, I attended a seminar, taught by Jeffrey L. Meikle, on twentieth-century American design. I was a student of Central European culture and ideas, so the course was outside my specialty, and for my final seminar paper I thought it would be interesting to explore the influence of Austrian émigré designers on the rise of modernism in the United States. After some diligent searching in the libraries, I decided to write about one of the most prominent of these figures, Viennese-born Paul T. Frankl.

I knew very little about Frankl at the time—only that he belonged to the generation of Viennese modernists who had been educated after the turn of the century and had come to New York around the time of World War I. The biographical sources I found were spotty and, in many instances, contradictory. Frankl's birth year was given variously as 1886 or 1887, and there was confusion about when and where he died. It was also unclear where he had been educated. In several published pieces from his later years, Frankl wrote that he had studied in Vienna, Berlin, and Paris—without offering any details. And I could find few biographical details concerning Frankl's early years in New York or his first experiments with modernism.

Given the short time I had to research and write the paper, I decided, more by force of pragmatism than scholarly logic, to concentrate on what I did know about Frankl and his work. I discovered a sizable body of articles, most of them published in *California Arts and Architecture*, documenting his furniture and interiors of the later 1930s and early 1940s in Los Angeles, where Frankl had moved in 1934, and I thought it would be best to focus on this period of his career.

I was never entirely satisfied with the piece. Once the course was over, I put it aside and eventually forgot about it. A few years later when I began work on my dissertation, a study of the Viennese architect Josef Frank, I kept stumbling onto records about Frankl in the various Austrian archives I visited. More often than not, because of the similarities between the two names, entries on Frankl followed immediately after those on Frank. I began to read and collect the records on Frankl and soon learned many details of his early life in Europe. Almost ten years later, after I finished revising my Frank book for publication, I began to think about my next project. I decided to revisit the Frankl material I had and see if it might yield an article or, perhaps, even a monograph. I had spent much of the preceding decade in Central Europe—in Graz, Munich, Vienna, and Prague—and I thought it would be an interesting experience to do research in U.S. archives, something I had done only on a few occasions up to that point. I located Frankl's daughter, Paulette Frankl, then living in Bolinas, California. She graciously allowed me to look through the papers and photographs she had preserved from her father's life and career and put me in touch with other relatives. Eventually, the story of Frankl's life emerged. And it turned out to be a remarkable one. I soon realized that the story was not confined to Frankl and his work. Of even more import was the role he played in the rise of modern American design. This book, then, is an attempt to explore the career of an eminent but still surprisingly little-known figure, and to reexamine the history of modern design in the United States—its genesis, rise, and triumph.

This work is also about the search for "Americanness" in American design culture. In the course of a single decade, from the mid-1920s to the mid-1930s, designers in the United States fashioned a novel and vibrant aesthetic, one decidedly different from that of the European avant-gardes. Not only was that new aesthetic closely adapted to American tastes and values, but it was conspicuously tied to American commercial realities and American modes of production. The United States was the first country to develop mass consumer marketing and sales institutions for mass-produced goods. Modernism in the United States, to a far greater extent than was the case in Europe in the years between the world wars, was a consequence of the culture of consumer capitalism. The making of modern American design was closely bound up with how the new aesthetic was popularized and sold; it is a story of the interrelationship of studio and store, and of how each influenced the other.

Frankl was among the leaders of this effort to forge a uniquely American design. He was the first to offer, in the form of his "Skyscraper" furniture, a stylistic idiom that stood resolutely apart from the language of those working in Europe—and, more than any of his fellow modernists in the United States, he assumed a leading role in preaching the gospel of modernism to the nation's merchants and consumers. Frankl was both artist and spokesman. He believed that, in the fight for the new, these two personae could not be segregated: modern design would find acceptance only when the marketplace was prepared for it.

One of the potent ironies of the history of modern American design is that Frankl and many of its other chief creators—from Eliel Saarinen and Kem Weber to Raymond Loewy and Walter von Nessen—were Americans by choice, not by birth or education. That so many immigrant Europeans were intimately involved with the forging of an American aesthetic is central to the story of how it came about: their striving to discover their own Americanness colored their interpretations of what a modern American culture should be. As outsiders, Frankl and the other European-born designers glimpsed truths about the American reality that remained indistinct to their American counterparts— and they exploited these insights in pursuit of what they believed was genuinely American.

Because the story of modern American design was never confined to what took place on the drafting boards of its creators, any inquiry into its rise and advance must search more broadly. This work, therefore, is only partly a design history. It is also a cultural and intellectual history, one informed by an examination of social and economic factors. Though focused on a single figure, it is about a complex set of relations—personal, historical, aesthetic, and commercial—all of which intersected to spawn modernism in its many guises.

Attentive readers will note that I avoid some commonly used stylistic terms, including *Art Deco*, *Zigzag Moderne*, and *Streamlined Moderne*. I have done so in part because these terms were not in use at the time Frankl was alive and working. *Art Deco* was the creation of the English art historian Bevis Hillier in 1968; *Zigzag Moderne* and *Streamlined Moderne* came into widespread use only after they were popularized in the writings of David Gebhard in the 1970s and 1980s. I chose to dispense with these stylistic labels not only because they are of later origin, but also because they confine us to the existing narrative about the design scene in the 1920s, 1930s, and beyond, making it difficult for us to envision an alternative one. My aim is to posit another, divergent history, based largely on sources from the time—a history that is now obscured to some degree by later accounts.

The term *Art Deco* has proven to be especially problematic in this regard. As a descriptor of style, it is unusually elastic and imprecise. But, more than that, it establishes distinctions that were not clearly perceived in the interwar years. In the exhibition catalog of the recent Art Deco exhibition at the Victoria and Albert Museum in

London, Charlotte Benton and Tim Benton (who, along with Ghislaine Wood, curated the show) present perhaps the best definition of Art Deco. It was, they write, a "complex" and "eclectic" style that drew from European crafts traditions as well as historical sources, such as ancient Egypt and the art of pre-Columbian Meso-America. They distinguish the Art Deco style from "Modernism" in large measure because it lacked, as they write, "the latter's stated aims, which were utopian and emancipatory." It was therefore a rival style to "Modernism," but a "pragmatic" one "not permeated by a belief in the redemptive value of art," in contrast to "the work of the designers of the Arts and Crafts movement, Art Nouveau, and Modernism."

This definition provides a useful description of the situation at the time, but it excludes much of Frankl's oeuvre. Only part of what he designed in the 1920s and early 1930s can be properly categorized as Art Deco; many of his designs of the early 1930s are closer formally to the works of the Bauhaus or De Stijl designers than they are to any of his American contemporaries. And Frankl's intentions—although he had strong commercial motives—were always wrapped up with his vision of design as a liberating force. In his writings, Frankl articulated a fervent belief in the struggle for modernism, and he saw little distinction between his own work (or that of his American colleagues, for that matter) and the design ideas of the European avant-garde. All of these approaches, he was convinced, were strands of a larger search for an aesthetic that would be consonant with the industrial age. For a time, Frankl used the terms *Moderne* and *Modernistic* to describe his work; by the early 1930s, however, he had cast them off, convinced that he was contributing to the broader advance of modernism. It is the story of that vision that I have tried to tell in this book.

A work of this sort is, perforce, always something of a collective enterprise, and I would like to thank some of the many people who have aided me with my research. For assisting me with locating information and photographs, I want to acknowledge John Axelrod (Boston), Claire

Bonney (Basel), Denis Boses (Los Angeles), Barbara Bradac (Rock Island, Ill.), Amy Ciccone (Los Angeles), Linda Congdon (Waukesha, Wis.), Jane Creech (New York), David Deatherage (St. Louis), Barbara Dee (Avalon, Calif.), Ric Emmett (Coral Gables, Fla.), Kathleen Ferres (Grand Rapids, Mich.), Christopher Fillichio (Boca Raton, Fla.), Janice Flinchum (New York), Russell Flinchum (New York), Jeannine Folino (Boston), Leigh Fried (New York), Marilyn Friedman (New York), Denis Gallion (New York), Claire Gunning (New York), Kateřina Hanzlíková (Prague), Thomas S. Hines (Los Angeles), Jennifer Howe (Cincinnati), Michael Jefferson (Chicago), Erich Jiresch (Vienna), Chris Kennedy (Springfield, Mass.), Pat Kirkham (New York), Gerhard von Knobelsdorff (Berlin), William Krisel (Los Angeles), Markus Kristan (Vienna), Marianne Lamonaca (Miami Beach), Alfred Lechner (Vienna), Martha Drexler Lynn (Los Angeles), Juliane Mikoletzky (Vienna), Lyz Nagan (Chicago), Wilfried Nerdinger (Munich), Jennifer Komar Olivarez (Minneapolis), Dan Oliver (Phoenix), Janet Parks (New York), Erika Patka (Vienna), Renée Prosperi (Chicago), David Rago (Lambertville, N.J.), Renate Reiss (Hudson, N.Y.), Jeff Ross (New York), Anne-Sophie Roure (New York), Clive Russ (Woonsocket, R.I.), David Ryan (Minneapolis), Chris Sala (New York), Sarah B. Sherrill (New York), Barry Shifman (Indianapolis), Julius Shulman (Los Angeles), Suzanne Slesin (New York), Anna Smorodinsky (Los Angeles), Vincent Snyder (Austin), John Sollo (Ft. Collins, Colo.), Jewel Stern (Miami), Michael Stier (New York), Anna Stuhlpfarrer (Vienna), Barbara Sykes (New York), Christoph Tepperberg (Vienna), Otto M. Urban (Prague), Steven Van Dyk (New York), Charles L. Venable (Cleveland), Filip Wittlich (Prague), and Richard Wright (Chicago).

In addition, I want to extend my thanks to the librarians, archivists, and staff members of the following institutions: Avery Architectural and Fine Arts Library, Columbia University, New York; Baupolizei (MA 37), Vienna; Bernice Bienenstock Furniture Library, High Point, N.C.; Brooklyn Museum, New York; Cincinnati Art Museum;

Grand Rapids Public Library, Grand Rapids, Mich.; Library of Congress, Washington, D.C.; Library of the Cooper-Hewitt National Design Museum, New York; Los Angeles Public Library; The Metropolitan Museum of Art, New York; Museum of Fine Arts, Boston; New York Historical Society; New York Public Library; Österreichische Nationalbibliothek, Bildarchiv, Vienna; Österreichisches Staatsarchiv—Kriegsarchiv, Vienna; Springfield Art Museum, Springfield, Mass.; Technische Universität, Hochschularchiv, Berlin; University of California, Los Angeles, Library; University of California, Santa Barbara, Library; University of Southern California Library, Los Angeles; Wiener Stadt- und Landesarchiv, Vienna; Wiener Stadt- und Landesbibliothek, Vienna; and the Wolfsonian Museum, Florida International University, Miami Beach. I am especially indebted to Janine Henri and Daniel Orozco, of the Architecture and Planning Library at the University of Texas at Austin, for their help over many years.

I owe a special debt to Elana Shapira, who very ably assisted me with finding documents in Vienna related to the Frankl family and their businesses, and to Jennifer Scanlan, who helped me to uncover Frankl's traces in New York. Over the years, a number of my graduate students have aided me with the research for this book. I want to acknowledge Barbara Ellen Brown, W. Owen Harrod, Jenny Wah Ko, Danielle Langston, Laura McGuire, Ely Merheb-Emanuelli, Zarina Saidova, and Byonghoon Yoo. As always, Anthony Alofsin, Richard Cleary, and Danilo Udovicki-Selb, my colleagues in the School of Architecture at the University of Texas at Austin, offered the stimulus of their ideas and suggested possible avenues of research. I remain deeply grateful to them for their insight and support. I would also like to acknowledge my students Vladimir Kulić and Monica Penick, who read the entire manuscript carefully and made a number of valuable suggestions for its improvement. During my prolonged work on this project, I have also benefited a number of times from the counsel and assistance of John C. Waddell, to whom I am deeply grateful.

I also want to express my appreciation to those at Yale University Press who, with patience and skill, helped to make this book a reality, in particular, Frank Baseman, Patricia Fidler, Kristin Henry, Jessie Hunnicutt, Michelle Komie, John Long, and Mary Mayer.

A summer research grant from the University of Texas at Austin generously supported my research in Los Angeles, and grants from the Hogg Research Fund and the Martin S. Kermacy Fund of the School of Architecture, University of Texas at Austin, helped to offset the costs of the photographs and allowed me to undertake several research trips. I am especially grateful to Frederick Steiner, Dean of the School of Architecture, for his continued support. The printing of the book was made possible by generous gifts from Mr. John Axelrod (Boston, Mass.), Mr. John C. Waddell (New York), and Mr. Richard Wright (Chicago); and a grant from the Martin S. Kermacy Fund. I also want to thank John Carrico, Brian Morrison, and Ruth A. Weaver at Austin Prints Photo Lab for the superb prints they prepared from the original negatives in the Frankl archive.

My writing of this book has been greatly facilitated by the generous cooperation of the Frankl family. Jane Boulton (Palo Alto, Calif.), Michael Boulton (Mill Valley, Calif.), Nicholas Koenig (Corralitos, Calif.), and Cis Zoltowska (Los Angeles) all enthusiastically shared with me documents, photographs, or memories that were crucial in piecing together the events of Frankl's life and career. I am especially indebted to his two children, Peter Boulton and Paulette Frankl, who gave me complete access to the materials in their possession and patiently answered my incessant queries. The many hours I spent with Paulette discussing her father and his world were among the most memorable and pleasant I have spent during my many years of research. I feel singularly fortunate to have had her cooperation. This book is, in myriad ways, the product of her gracious collaboration.

I remain deeply grateful to my father, Harry C. Long, who never wavered in his belief in my chosen career path. My final debt is to my wife, Gia Marie Houck, who, as always, gave me her unflagging support and love.

Prologue

On a chill, rainy Wednesday evening in New York in November 1925, a small group of designers and artists met in a midtown gallery to discuss the state of modern design in the United States. Among those present were Lee Simonson, creator of numerous modern stage sets for the Theater Guild (one of the city's experimental "little theaters"), and graphic artist Lucian Bernhard, recently arrived from Germany. Also in attendance were Polish-born painter and book illustrator Witold Gordon, who had come to New York after fleeing the German advance on Paris in 1914; Robert Leonard, a budding graphic artist; and Donald Deskey, a young furniture designer, fresh from a brief teaching stint at a small art school in Pennsylvania.

The organizer of the meeting was Paul T. Frankl. Thirty-nine years old, Frankl was the owner of one of the tiny handful of galleries in the United States offering modern decorative objects. Trained in his native Vienna and, later, in Berlin, he had arrived in Manhattan shortly after the eruption of World War I. He established himself as a furniture and interior designer and ran a successful gallery for two years. He returned to Europe during the late stages of the war, then moved back to New York in early 1920. A few months later, he opened a shop on East Forty-eighth Street, just around the corner from Fifth Avenue. The Frankl Galleries soon earned a reputation for its promotion of cutting-edge European design. By 1925, Frankl was also producing his own modern furniture. His initial attempts bore the impress of contemporary French, German, and Austrian design. But Frankl soon fashioned his own distinctive idiom—one that betrayed his belief in the importance of expressing American life and conditions.

Frankl's quest for a distinctive modern American design faced considerable opposition. Most Americans in the early 1920s were still zealously committed to historic revivalism, and there were widespread misgivings about the latest European design trends. Frankl knew that he could not win his struggle alone. He sought out like-minded artists and designers to form a common front in the battle for the new. The small group began convening regularly at the Frankl Galleries, discussing strategies for putting modern design before the public.

After their meeting, the men decided to go to a French restaurant to have a late dinner and continue their conversation. They all climbed into a taxicab for the ride downtown. On the way, the driver skidded around a corner on two wheels. Frankl, who was sitting in the rear, leaned forward and cautioned the cabbie to be more careful: "Listen, old man, if you spill this bunch there will be no modern art in America!"[1]

Frankl's warning to the driver was only a small exaggeration. The little group pressed into the car that dreary night represented a sizable segment of the committed modernist designers in the country; their untimely demise may not have halted the rise of modernism, but it would surely have slowed its progress.

When the taxi abruptly came to rest again on all four wheels, it set into motion events that would alter the course of American design and transform the way almost every American lived.

Opposite:
Frankl at his desk in
Woodstock, mid-1920s
(detail of fig. 39)

CHAPTER ONE

Vienna

Paul T. Frankl was born in Vienna and spent his formative years there. The experience of growing up in the Austrian capital left its mark on him far beyond the trace of a German accent that he retained to the end of his life. It molded his personality, his attitudes, his ideas of style, and, above all, his belief in the cause and rightness of modern design.

In an unpublished autobiography written near the end of his life, Frankl recalled the Vienna of his youth: an "enchanting and thriving metropolis" where "music filled the air" and "the Viennese crowded the famous cafés" each afternoon. Theodor Billroth, Ernst Brücke, Sigmund Freud, and others had made the Habsburg capital one of the world's centers for medicine. And because Vienna was the seat of government of a great polyglot empire, its streets teemed with "Germans, Hungarians, Czechs, Italians, Poles, Dalmatians, Serbs, and many Mohammedan Turks."[1]

Vienna was also at the epicenter of a revolution sweeping through art, architecture, and design. "In Vienna," Frankl recorded, "the modern movement found a fertile soil and a ready acceptance.... Klimt and Kokoschka stirred turbulent tempers to fiery heights," and Joseph Maria Olbrich's Secession Building became a "modern shrine." The critic and writer Berta Zuckerkandl observed: "With few exceptions everything developed as if a simultaneous vision had modeled the style of our age. Mysterious links were forged connecting language, colours, forms, tones, and attitudes to life."[2]

All of these forces touched the young Frankl; together, they shaped his developing vision of modern design.

Paul Theodor Frankl was born on 14 October 1886, the third of four sons of wealthy Viennese real estate specula-

Opposite:
Fig. 1. Ringstrasse, Vienna, 1893

tor and developer Julius Frankl and his wife, Emma.[3] Julius Frankl belonged to the segment of Vienna's haute bourgeoisie who had made their fortunes during the heady years of the *Gründerzeit*, the period of spectacular economic boom and rapid urbanization that followed the abortive revolution of 1848. Born in 1852, Julius was the sixteenth of seventeen children of Wilhelm Frankl, a prosperous landowner who held property in the city of Preßburg, where the family resided, and in the nearby countryside. Preßburg, a border town on the Danube thirty miles downstream from Vienna, was situated at the edge of three distinct linguistic regions: Slovak, Hungarian, and German. In later years, the city, renamed Bratislava, would become the capital of the Slovak Republic. During Julius's youth, it was under Hungarian administration and all official business was conducted in Hungarian, though the Frankl family—like the majority of the town's Jewish inhabitants—spoke German at home and carried out their daily affairs in both German and Slovak. Julius and his many brothers and sisters were reared in comfortable circumstances, but, as the sixteenth of seventeen, he could hardly have awaited a large inheritance. And so, in the early 1870s, not long after completing his secondary schooling, he set off for Vienna to make his own way.

Years later, Julius Frankl was fond of regaling his sons with the story of how he had arrived in the Austrian capital "with only a few coins in his pocket."[4] In truth, though he arrived with little means, he was not without support. Several of his older siblings, as well as a number of aunts, uncles, and cousins, had already moved there and established themselves. They provided the young Julius with both lodging and work, greatly easing his transition to life in the capital.

Most of Julius Frankl's relatives were involved in banking and investment. His aunt, Charlotte Cohn, was the founder of the Merkur-Bank, one of the largest financial institutions in the monarchy. Not long after his arrival, Julius began what would be a brief but highly useful apprenticeship in the world of business, working in a variety of capacities in the Frankl clan's diverse firms. He learned his lessons well. With his first savings, he invested in land, buying an option on a small parcel on Vienna's periphery.

From the outset, Julius exhibited an uncanny capacity for turning his modest investments into impressive profits. He was aided in his financial dealings by the city's explosive growth. In 1860, Vienna, still a small town in comparison to Paris and London, had about half a million inhabitants; thirty years later, in-migration and the annexation of the surrounding towns and villages had increased the population to more than 1.4 million. The rate of expansion only accelerated during the early years of the new century. By 1910, the population had swelled to more than two million. Of the other major European cities, only Berlin grew faster. Barely two out of every five of Vienna's inhabitants at the turn of the century had been born there; large numbers poured in from the provinces, especially from neighboring Moravia, Bohemia, and Slovakia. The increased demand for housing pushed up land prices, and a law passed in 1892 that exempted owners of tenements in the outer districts from real estate taxes for thirty years spurred further speculation.[5]

The face of the city was also changing. In 1857, Emperor Franz Josef authorized the razing of the old city walls, and by the late 1860s, when Julius arrived in the city, the Ringstrasse, a broad boulevard lined with impressive new public buildings and elegant apartment houses, had already filled the resultant space (fig. 1). The older one- and two-story houses that once occupied the outer suburban districts had by then begun to give way to much larger five- and six-story apartment houses and tenement blocks. Farther out from the city center, what had been fields and pastures in the first half of the century were being transformed into residential districts for a rapidly expanding working class.

Within a decade of his arrival, Julius Frankl had acquired large parcels of land in and around the expanding metropolis, much of it in the outlying districts of Favoriten, Meidling, Hietzing, Ottakring, Döbling, and

Liesing. In the late 1880s, he began to develop his properties, constructing housing blocks, stores, and other commercial buildings. He registered his development firm under his own name, listing himself initially as a *Bauunternehmer*—a builder and contractor.[6] But it was as a real estate speculator that Julius made his fortune. He acquired a number of his properties in partnership with members of the wealthy and powerful Kuffner clan, who owned one of the city's largest breweries. They bankrolled many of Julius's speculative purchases, allowing him to buy land on margin by putting down only a small percentage of the total price in exchange for a high interest rate.[7]

In 1904, Julius also acquired a brick factory, allowing him to further increase his profits by reducing his costs for building materials.[8] He reinvested the income from his many ventures in additional land, often reselling it within a short time for a tidy profit. By the early years of the new century, he had become one of the wealthiest men in the city, described in official documents as a *Großgrundbesitzer*—a large landowner—a designation reserved for the tiny elite of great property owners.

Julius's wealth brought him newfound status.[9] He became an intimate of the populist mayor of Vienna, Karl Lueger. A self-proclaimed anti-Semite, Lueger had views on the "Jewish question" that were more pragmatic than ideological: his stock phrase, "Wer a Jud is, bestimm i!" (I determine who is a Jew!), in effect meant that he reserved the right to determine who would suffer from his public attacks, but he was genial with his Jewish friends in private. In 1902, Julius Frankl was made a Knight of the Order of the Austrian Emperor Franz Josef, in part through Lueger's agency, and in recognition of his donations of land and buildings for several schools and other philanthropic works.[10]

By then, Julius had also begun to erase some of the vestiges of his Jewish heritage. In 1881, he married Emma Friedmann, daughter of an old Viennese Jewish family that had converted to Catholicism.[11] Emma's father was a well-to-do merchant; he provided his daughter with a dowry of fifteen thousand gulden on the provision that

Julius invest it in his real estate firm. But there was a large obstacle to overcome before the couple could marry: marriage laws in the Habsburg lands prohibited the union of Jews and practicing Christians. A marriage between people of different religions required the conversion of one partner to the other's faith, and Julius, though nonobservant, was unwilling to convert to Christianity. A declaration that one was "without religious affiliation" (*Konfessionslos*), however, allowed a potential spouse to sidestep the law. After drawn-out discussions, Emma decided to make an official pronouncement that she was without religious affiliation, permitting the union to take place. (After Julius's death, she converted back to Catholicism.)[12] The couple decided, though, that each of

Fig. 2. Frankl family, c. 1900. *Clockwise from bottom left:* Wilhelm, Paul, Emma, Utto, Robert, Julius

their four sons, who followed in roughly two year inter-
vals—Otto (1882), Robert (1884), Paul (1886), and
Wilhelm (1889)—would be baptized in the Catholic faith,
a move that both parents knew would ensure their offspring the best possible prospects in a city where anti-
Semitism was endemic (fig. 2).[13]

Julius Frankl's increasing wealth and prestige was
reflected in the family's changing domestic quarters. At
the time of Paul's birth, the Frankls lived at Schwindgasse
20, in the city's fourth district, a respectable but hardly
exclusive area. In 1900, Julius bought a grand house in the
villa district of Hietzing at Auhofstraße 12, a short distance from Schönbrunn, the emperor's summer palace.[14]

The house on the Auhofstraße, a three-story neo-
Renaissance edifice built in 1865, was well suited to the
tastes of its new owner. Julius Frankl's aesthetic outlook
had been formed against the backdrop of Viennese his-
toricism. Like most of the *novi homines* who had risen
from more modest origins, he filled his house with the
trappings of late-nineteenth-century bourgeois culture:
dark, ponderous "Alt-Deutsch" furnishings, Oriental
rugs, "odd Chinese and Persian pieces," and paintings in
the then-popular Realist style.[15]

Julius believed in the aristocratic tradition of furthering culture and the arts. The family regularly attended the
theater and made the rounds of the art exhibitions and
galleries. "Both art and music were subjects of lively,
often stormy discussions," Paul Frankl would later
remember. Julius "was not creative himself, [but] he had
an artistic temperament and enjoyed the company of
artists in many fields."[16] He held regular soirees for
members of the Viennese art world, and over the years he
amassed an impressive collection of art and sculpture. Yet
one found little evidence in the Frankl home of the aesthetic revolution then taking place in Vienna; although
Julius was acquainted with Gustav Klimt and kept abreast
of the newest trends in painting, his collecting remained
centered on the art of the Old Regime—the works of Hans
Markart, Anton Romako, and other latter-day proponents
of academicism and Romanticism.[17]

Despite Julius's interest in art, it was music that stood
in the forefront of the family's cultural pursuits. The
operetta composer Oscar Straus was among the many
musicians who came regularly to the family's villa, playing
his newest compositions late into the night. Violin virtu-
oso Fritz Kreisler was another frequent guest, joining in
long evenings of chamber music. Kreisler sometimes
accompanied the family on their vacations to Sils, in
Upper Engadine, Switzerland, where he took young Paul
mountain climbing. Paul and his brother Robert absorbed
their father's love of music, and in their teens they
became "entranced" with Gustav Mahler's elaborate productions of Wagner's *Ring of the Nibelung*. They attended
every performance they could, following along with the
"voluminous musical scores."[18]

But Julius Frankl's enthusiasm for the arts and culture
did not mean that he desired to see his children enter
into artistic professions. One by one, he enrolled his four
sons not in one of the city's humanistic *Gymnasien* or art
schools but in the technically oriented *Realschulen*, in an
effort to prepare them to assume their roles in the family
real estate business. In 1897, the young Paul Frankl
entered the Imperial and Royal Staatsrealschule in
Vienna's fourth district. Julius intended for his third son
to become an architect: Paul would design buildings for
the family firm, and Julius would serve as developer and
finance their construction.

Ambitious, outwardly self assured, and intelligent, Paul
was nevertheless an indifferent student. The surviving
records reveal that he excelled at drawing and gymnastics,
but he demonstrated decidedly less aptitude for academic
subjects. No doubt one reason for his poor performance
was a fervent wish he had nurtured since early childhood
to become an artist. His father, sensing that it would be
better—at least for the time being—to indulge his son's
yearnings, allowed him to enroll in art school at night.
Every evening, following the end of his classes at the
Realschule, Frankl studied drawing and painting.

Frankl worked diligently to perfect his artistic skills.

He learned much, as he later recorded in his autobiography, "not from my teachers, to be sure, but from a fellow student who always sat next to me ... a cadaverous looking youth ... who looked like a younger brother of Dante whose plaster mask hung on the wall." That demonic presence was Julius Pincus, who later found fame under his adopted name, Jules Pascin. A year older than Frankl, Pascin first came to Vienna from Romania at the age of eleven to attend boarding school, but he was called back after a financial crisis to help in his father's grain brokerage firm. Miserable in the provinces, he ran away from home to pursue his art studies in the Austrian capital. Not long after his arrival he met Frankl. The two boys became inseparable, and Pascin lived with the Frankls for several months before moving to Munich in 1903.[19]

Pascin was already an accomplished draftsman by the time the two met. While working for his father in Bucharest, Pascin had befriended the madam of a local bordello; there he made some of his earliest drawings—quick sketches of prostitutes and their surroundings.[20] Within a year of his departure from Vienna, he was contributing drawings to *Jugend* and *Simplicissimus*, two of the leading publications of the new art movement. His open, light drawing style left an indelible impression on Frankl. From Pascin, Frankl learned to draw with great economy—and to invest his work with emotion: "Even in his early days in art school, [Pascin] never drew just for pure exercise; there always had to be a story expressed in every line he put on the paper. Like a good writer, he saw beyond and below the surface of what his exquisite drawings expressed."[21]

But Frankl's developing facility for drawing and painting did little to improve his performance in school. After a dismal year, he transferred to the provincial Realschule in nearby Wiener Neustadt, where he spent the 1898–99 school term. His grades improved just enough to allow him to return, in the fall of 1899, to his former school in Vienna. In 1902, he transferred once more, this time to a Realschule in Elbogen (today Loket, Czech Republic).

Perched on a steep hill above the Ohře River in south-

Fig. 3. Elbogen (today Loket, Czech Republic), c. 1905

western Bohemia, the picturesque little town is known today for its medieval castle and for its well-preserved nineteenth-century chain suspension bridge (fig. 3). Aside from the castle and parish church, the only other large structure in the town at the beginning of the century was the Realschule, housed in an imposing white neo-Renaissance building on the main square. The school enjoyed a reputation at the time as an excellent and progressive institution. But Julius Frankl apparently chose it less for its stature than for its isolation. By his sixteenth year, the young Frankl was not only underperforming at school; he had become a discipline problem. For carefree young men from affluent families, fin-de-siècle Vienna offered innumerable distractions: afternoons at the horse races or in the cafés; evenings at the opera, theater, or cabarets; dalliances with shop girls. The precise reason for Frankl's banishment to Elbogen is unclear. It may have been prompted by an episode a family friend related to Paul's son, Peter, decades later: after a night of drinking, Paul and his two older brothers reportedly picked up three prostitutes on the fashionable Kärntnerstraße. The next day they treated each woman to a new fur coat, charging the garments to their father's account.[22]

Whatever the immediate cause, Julius Frankl apparently decided that Elbogen, which offered far fewer temptations than Vienna, would force his son to focus on his studies. Paul Frankl spent his final two years of school there. His grades improved, though they were far from stellar. Not surprisingly, he received his highest marks in freehand drawing. He also excelled in gymnastics, a passion that remained with him throughout his life. In the early summer of 1904, he sat for his final *Matura* examination. Despite receiving the lowest possible passing score, he was presented with a certificate that would allow him to attend a university. [23]

But Frankl still aspired to become an artist. On his frequent visits home, he went to see exhibitions at the Secession, the center of the new art movement in Vienna. The building, designed by Joseph Maria Olbrich, served as the exhibition space for the Vereinigung bildender Künstler Österreichs—Secession (Association of Austrian Fine Artists—Secession) (fig. 4). A group of the city's progressive artists, architects, and designers led by

Fig. 4. Joseph Maria Olbrich, Secession Building, Vienna, 1897–98

Gustav Klimt had formed the organization in 1897 in an effort to liberate themselves from Vienna's conservative artists' establishment. During the first years of the group's existence, the Secessionists mounted an impressive array of exhibitions, showing their own works as well as those of Paul Gauguin, Ferdinand Hodler, Fernand Khnopff, Auguste Rodin, and other leading artists.

Frankl was especially taken with Klimt's paintings. The dynamic play of forms in Klimt's elegantly stylized portraits and landscapes and his bright coloristic effects—particularly his use of metallic paints—left a strong impression on him. Frankl was also able to see the furniture and interiors of many of the city's preeminent designers, including Olbrich, Leopold Bauer, Josef Hoffmann, and Jože Plečnik (figs. 5, 6).

But for Frankl, art still took precedence over design. Whenever he could, he made the rounds of Vienna's galleries. He was also a frequent visitor to the Galerie Miethke, the city's foremost private dealer in new art. He was particularly drawn to the paintings of the German artists' group Scholle, the Italian-Swiss pointillist Giovanni Segantini, and Vincent van Gogh. Intoxicated by their work, he aspired to become one of the *Maler-Fürsten*, the princes of painting, who would uncover a new secret language of art and thereby affirm the inner values of the modern age.

But in the end, filial obligation won out: after much anguished deliberation, he "abided by [his father's] wish" that he study architecture. [24] In the autumn of 1904, Frankl enrolled at the Vienna Technische Hochschule.

In the early years of the new century, the Technische Hochschule was the preeminent polytechnic university in the Austro-Hungarian monarchy. A degree from the school was almost a prerequisite for entering state service or the highest levels of the architecture profession. The faculty included some of the best-known practitioners of the day—Karl Mayreder, Alexander Wielemanns, and Max von Ferstel—and many of the country's foremost architects had passed through its portals at one time or another in their studies. The dean of the school was Carl König. In the 1880s and early 1890s, König had established the neo-Baroque as the city's dominant stylistic idiom, and he became one of its most celebrated practitioners. [25] But the mood was now changing. By the time Frankl entered the school, the tide of modernism had begun to sweep past König and most of the school's other professors. Many of Vienna's younger architects and designers embraced the new *Jugendstil*, the Central European version of Art Nouveau. Olbrich's Secession Building, erected while Frankl was still attending Realschule, was only the opening blow against architectural convention. By 1900, the avant-garde was in full

revolt. The fresh currents in architecture and design were felt throughout the profession, shifting away from historic revivalism toward an aesthetic founded upon simplicity and modern materials and technologies. Within a few years, the flowing, vegetal lines of the early Jugendstil began to give way to a novel language of purist geometry and formal reduction expressed most eloquently in the designs of Hoffmann and Koloman Moser.

For Frankl, who in his last years at Elbogen had followed the work and activities of the modernists, including the "illustrious Otto Wagner . . . and his young and gifted disciples," the atmosphere at the Technische Hochschule seemed oppressive and antiquarian. The professors, he wrote, were "elderly men, deathly afraid of every fresh wind. To them, architecture, denuded of ornate decoration, was as despicable as the bare feet of Isadora Duncan were to an era accustomed to hourglass shaped, short frocked ballet dancers." König, he thought, was a "capable, though stale and orthodox[,] architect eternally renaissancing in the styles of the past." [26]

The school's curriculum, virtually unchanged since the time when most of the faculty had studied there decades before, was heavily weighted toward the study of architectural history. Students were required to sign up for more than four hundred hours of history courses spread over four of the program's five years; in addition, they were required to spend an entire semester building models of classical Greek and Roman temples and other historical structures. [27] "Our architectural training in Vienna," Frankl would remember years afterward, "started with the art of ancient Egypt. From [there] our studies took us across the Mediterranean, this inland sea of classic culture, to ancient Greece, where art flourished at its height during the period of Perikles and the temples of the Acropolis." This stress on Greco-Roman classicism, he believed, was wholly misguided: "The first step in the wrong direction of teaching an art that should and must be alive is by starting at the wrong end. Architecture, like history, should start with the present, and the problems confronting us, and like a film in reverse, roll back

Fig. 5. Josef Hoffmann, bentwood side chair designed for J. and J. Kohn, c. 1906

Fig. 6. Leopold Bauer, living room ensemble, 1904

through previous civilizations, showing us the solutions
others have found, and in doing so have contributed to
the history of mankind." It was "in rebellion against this
early education" that "many of us have turned modern,
seeking a style that is our own, in preference to styles that
were Greek to us."[28]

Frankl's student records show that in his first term he
signed up for a course with Karl Mayreder, husband of
feminist Rosa Mayreder (though not specified in the documents, it was most likely Mayreder's course on perspective drawing), as well as a class in freehand drawing taught
by Eduard Veith. Frankl failed to finish the course with
Mayreder; Veith gave him a grade of *vorzüglich*, or excellent. It was the only course he completed during his two
semesters in the school.[29]

Frankl's disinterest stemmed in part from an incident
that took place in his first term. After awarding Frankl a
prize in a school competition, König revealed to his father
that the reason his son had won "was not due to the merit
of [his] entry but rather the low level of the other students."[30] It was a slight that went deep: Frankl's bitterness and hurt is still palpable in his autobiography, written more than five decades afterward.

By the end of his second term, Frankl had resolved to
leave the school and move to Berlin. The following
autumn, he enrolled at the Technische Hochschule
there.[31]

CHAPTER TWO

An Expression of Our Age

Frankl's decision to transfer to the Berlin Technische Hochschule in the fall
of 1905 was prompted only partly by his frustration with his education. He also
felt a growing need to wrest himself from his father's control. While attending
the Vienna polytechnic, Frankl had continued to live at home, and there
had been increasing friction between the strong-willed father and his equally
headstrong son.

Frankl was hardly alone in seeking refuge in Berlin.
In the years prior to World War I, a large number of young
Austrian artists and intellectuals fled north to escape the
conservative atmosphere of Vienna. In contrast to the
Habsburg capital, which seemed irreversibly tied to the
past, Berlin, as Frankl would later record, was a "vigorous
and young" metropolis. The possibilities there seemed
almost unlimited.[1]

Once little more than a Prussian garrison town,
the city had exploded with activity in the decades after
German unification. In less than forty years, the population had increased more than tenfold; by 1910, Greater
Berlin approached 3.5 million inhabitants, making it
almost a third larger than Vienna. Though not yet the

Opposite:
Paul T. Frankl, inglenook
for a library, c. 1913
(detail of fig. 11)

Fig. 7. Technische
Hochschule, Berlin,
c. 1905

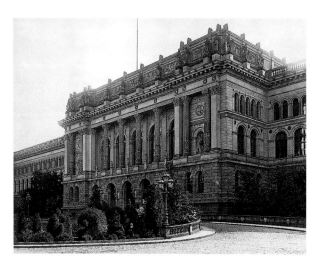

"Babel of the world" that novelist Stefan Zweig found in
the 1920s, it was already overflowing with portents of the
new. In nearly every sphere of artistic and intellectual life,
the city offered vitality unmatched elsewhere in
Germany.[2] Berlin was a magnet for those seeking escape
from Wilhelmine conformity—or for those simply wanting to soak in the atmosphere of change. For the talented
and ambitious youth of the German Empire, it held out
the promise of opportunity and adventure. To be there
was to reside at the middle of the cultural maelstrom.[3]

For a student of architecture, the German capital offered
a glance at a new type of building and design, one adjusted
to suit the requirements of mass production. In Vienna,
traditional crafts and artistic individualism still dominated.
Berlin, by contrast, was fast emerging as the center of a new
design ethos founded on simplicity, utility, and serial manufacturing.[4] The young Swiss architect Charles-Édouard
Jeanneret (the future Le Corbusier), who came to Berlin
not long after Frankl, was struck by the growing emphasis
on industry there: "If Paris is the capital of art," he wrote,
"Germany is the great production plant."[5]

The new "industrial culture" was expressed not only in
the anonymous consumer products of Germany's count-
less factories. It was apparent, too, in the works of a small
group of artists and designers—led by Peter Behrens,
Bruno Paul, and Richard Riemerschmid—who sought to

reshape the articles of the commercial market in accord
with artistic worth and quality. At the core of the new
movement in Germany was a concerted effort to educate
consumer taste and to reform education for arts and crafts
professionals.[6] The new design culture was also reflected
in the city's architecture.

It was in Behrens's office, more than anywhere else,
where these experiments were being carried out. In the
years Frankl spent in Berlin, Behrens attracted young
architects and designers eager to explore with him the new
spirit of building and design. Among those who found
temporary work in his studio were Le Corbusier, Walter
Gropius, and Ludwig Mies van der Rohe. Under Behrens's
employ, each of these young architects found ideas and
approaches that would guide their work in the future.[7]

Frankl was not as fortunate at the Berlin Technische
Hochschule (fig. 7). Although the school's curriculum was
less focused on the study of history than that of the Vienna
polytechnic, the professors were mostly older architects
who still practiced in the revivalist mode. Yet most also
stressed the importance of employing the most modern
methods of construction and the newest materials. The
Berlin Technische Hochschule, far more than its counterpart in Vienna, was a center for the investigation of recent
advances in architectural engineering—lessons that
would prove crucial to the young modernists.[8] But it was
not only the emphasis on the structural and material
aspects of architecture that set the Berlin school apart:
the curriculum offered instruction in modern art and
design and in the social aspects of architecture—courses
unavailable in Vienna.[9] There was, in addition, a greater
tolerance of ideas and novel experiments. Students in
Vienna often faced censure and criticism for unorthodox
designs; their fellow students in Berlin found greater
forbearance—even encouragement.

After settling into his studies in Berlin, Frankl fell into
his previous pattern: he managed to accomplish just
enough to earn solidly average marks. He was never in
danger of failing, but neither did he excel—except on a
single occasion. In his first year, Frankl entered a compe-

tition open to the entire student body. When the results were announced, he discovered that he alone had found the correct solution. "For weeks," he "walked on air." When the awards were finally presented, though, his name was not even mentioned. "Having an inscrutable flaw in its perspective it had been discarded," Frankl recalled. "Exactitude in Berlin was trump." Exasperated, Frankl resolved never again to enter a competition, a promise he scrupulously kept for the remainder of his life.[10]

Despite his easy grasp of the technical aspects of build-ing and his aptitude for drawing, Frankl's architectural studies were a trial. Still intent on studying art, he slipped away at every opportunity to sketch and paint or meet his artist friends in the cafés. He attended the required lectures and studios in building construction and design, but he found the whole experience unsatisfying. Each week, he looked forward only to the class in figure drawing from live models, taught by Professor Henseler on Wednesday afternoons (fig. 8). Upon completing his first year in Berlin, he was almost relieved when he was ordered to return to Austria to fulfill his military service.

As a university student, Frankl was assigned to officer's training. Because his father was still a Hungarian citizen, the younger Frankl was posted to a Hungarian cavalry unit—the Prince of Bulgaria, Ferdinand I, Hussar Regiment Number 11—as a one-year "volunteer," a genteel euphe-mism for well-heeled draftees.[11] As was customary for officer trainees, Frankl served "on his own costs"; he was expected to pay for his uniforms and for his own food and transportation. With little experience in horsemanship, he and his fellow cadets were put through a rigorous train-ing regimen to mold them into expert cavalry officers. Discipline was severe. The noncommissioned officers who provided most of the day-to-day instruction delighted in tormenting their young trainees. At barely five feet five in height, Frankl was hardly a commanding figure, and not infrequently he bore the brunt of their ire (fig. 9). "Brusque commands were shouted in shrill German," the language of the Austro-Hungarian army, "although the

men, Hungarians, understood no tongue but their own," Frankl later wrote. "There was no effort made to teach us their language." The experience, Frankl thought, was not without recompense—of a sort. "At the end of the term, I emerged as a second lieutenant. I had fallen off more horses than most people ever sat on and had acquired a rudimentary speaking knowledge of Hungarian, mostly slang badly blended with abominable swear words typical of a soldier's language."[12]

Frankl's military service records offer a more impar-tial assessment. His commander recorded that the young

Fig. 8. Paul T. Frankl, drawing of a seated woman, 1910. Pencil on paper. Collection Paulette Frankl

Fig. 9. Frankl (*foreground, third from left*) during army maneuvers, Groß-Meseritsch, Austria, 1909

officer was an "adequate horseman," with "some skill as a marksman," noting that he was also "cheerful, open, high-minded . . . obedient toward superiors." But he added that the young Frankl exerted "little influence" on those under him—in effect, that he was not particularly promising officer material, a judgment Frankl himself no doubt would have seconded.[13]

Frankl returned to Berlin in the autumn of 1907. He resumed his studies, but, as before, his interest was often fixed elsewhere. He found escape in the rich cultural life of the German capital. Almost nightly, he went to the theater or the opera, or carousing with friends in the cabarets and bars. When the weather permitted, he went motoring through the countryside in a racing car he had bought with his considerable allowance.[14]

In 1908, Frankl's halcyon days were suddenly interrupted: he received news from home that his father was dying of colon cancer. Shortly after Paul's return to Vienna, Julius Frankl died. Distraught by his father's passing, Frankl set to designing the gravestone. The simple marker, surmounted by a classical cornice with egg-and-dart moldings, became his first realized architectural work.[15]

More immediately, Frankl and his family had to face the

question of who would take over Julius's far-flung business interests. Paul and his two older brothers, Otto and Robert, were pressed into running their father's real estate firm. None of the sons had a solid knowledge of the business, and it soon was apparent that Paul had little facility for the finer dealings of real estate speculation. Robert, who at the time seemed to have the best head for business, took the lead; Paul, in order not to fall further behind in his studies, enrolled once more at the Vienna Technische Hochschule, in the winter of 1908–9. He registered for classes in utilitarian building, drawing, model making, and history. But, as before, he failed to complete any of the courses.[16]

The experience of his father's death had given Frankl new resolve, however. After spending part of the summer undergoing further mandatory training with his old hussar regiment, he returned to Berlin. There he resumed his studies with greater urgency, and over the next two years he completed most of the remaining required courses for his architecture diploma.[17] In the fall of 1911, he also married.

His new wife, Paula König, came from a middle-class German Protestant family. Born in Frankfurt am Main, she moved with her family to Berlin just after the turn of the century.[18] She studied piano with various private teachers, and by her early twenties, when she and Frankl met, she was an accomplished performer, specializing in the works of the moderns—Claude Debussy, Hugo Wolf, and Feruccio Busoni. Frankl's enthusiasm for music gave them a strong bond, but, as he later recalled, they also shared a fervent love of the theater: "Together we enjoyed the brilliant, sparkling, diversified musical, theatrical world of Berlin that in its day of glory had reached a supremely high level." They took in innumerable plays by the celebrated playwrights of the day—Oscar Wilde, Gerhard Hauptmann, Arthur Schnitzler, Ferenc Molnár, George Bernard Shaw, Maurice Maeterlinck, and Henrik Ibsen.[19]

At the end of the 1912 summer term, Frankl completed his last remaining classes at the Technische Hochschule. But his hope of becoming an artist still lingered. During his summer vacations in 1911 and 1912, he spent time away from Berlin studying art.

He went first, in the summer of 1911, to Munich. In later years, Frankl never revealed any details of the two months he spent there. It is doubtful that he formally registered at one of the city's many art schools; nor is there any record he did so. Most likely, he arranged instead for private lessons.

Munich had long been the preeminent center of art studies in Germany. Since the early 1890s, the city had been a magnet for the avant-garde, attracting students from throughout the German-speaking world and Eastern Europe.[20] In the time Frankl was there, Wassily Kandinsky was taking the last steps into total abstraction; the following year Kandinsky and his followers—Alexei von Jawlensky, Franz Marc, August Macke, and a few others—would form the Blaue Reiter group. But by the end of the first decade of the century, many of the older designers who had established the city as a hothouse for modernism—Behrens, Paul, August Endell, and Bernhard Pankok—had left, most of them for Berlin.[21]

It is unclear whether disappointment with Munich spurred Frankl's decision to spend the following summer in Paris. He may simply have been drawn to the even livelier art scene there. In Paris, Frankl arranged for private instruction with his old friend Julius Pincus, now sporting his gallicized name, Jules Pascin.[22] Pascin had arrived in Paris in 1905 and taken up station in Montparnasse. There he became part of an animated artists' circle that included Georg Grosz, William Howard, and Emil Orlik.

Frankl, liberated for the moment from the constraints of his studies, threw himself into the whirl of the Paris art world. In the early years of the century, Montparnasse had become home to a large population of foreigners, many of them from Central and Eastern Europe. Frankl became a regular at the Café du Dôme, the center of the new art scene, sitting and sketching for hours at one of the outside tables. He spent time each day with Pascin, and he met many other up-and-coming artists—including Elie Nadelman, Witold Gordon, and Tsuguharu Foujita, who would remain close friends for years.[23] The experience of Paris that summer left an indelible mark on Frankl and only strengthened his resolve to be at the forefront of the new art and design.

After the couple returned to Berlin at the end of the summer, Frankl found a position in the office of architect Otto Rudolf Salvisberg. Only four years older than Frankl, Salvisberg had moved to Berlin a few years earlier after studying architecture at the Technikum Biel, in his native Switzerland, and by the time Frankl commenced working for him, he already had a reputation for his progressive designs. Frankl later recorded that he sought out Salvisberg precisely because he admired his buildings "for being modern and advanced."[24] But more than that Salvisberg was already an experienced practitioner, and Frankl knew he could learn much from him about the finer points of building.

His choice, as it turned out, was an especially good one. Not only was Salvisberg keen on experimenting with modern building techniques, but, like Frankl, he had an avid interest in investigating the potential of steel, plate glass, aluminum, concrete, and other new materials.

Frankl left no record of his activities in Salvisberg's office. It is likely that he was involved with the design of a large villa in Zehlendorf and a commercial building, the Lindenhaus, in the center of Berlin—both works on the boards at the time.[25] The Lindenhaus was the first all-concrete commercial structure in Berlin, and it drew attention and praise from contemporary critics and observers of the architectural scene (fig. 10).[26]

While still in Salvisberg's employ, Frankl also began producing interiors and furniture under his own name, including work for the Hohenzollern Kunstgewerbehaus Friedmann and Weber, a respected Berlin firm specializing in handcrafted furnishings. Founded in 1879, the Hohenzollern Kunstgewerbehaus had, by the turn of the century, become the principal "outlet for the entire range of Berlin arts and crafts."[27] In 1899, Belgian designer Henry Van de Velde was appointed to head the studio and its allied workshops; in 1901, he designed the company's showrooms and offices. Many exhibitions of international arts and crafts—with works by Behrens, Josef Hoffmann, Koloman Moser, and René Lalique—filled the company's spaces, and agents from German and foreign museums regularly attended the shows to acquire objects for their modern collections.[28]

Frankl's inglenook for a library, executed in polished Italian walnut, was one of several designs he produced for the Hohenzollern Kunstgewerbehaus in January 1913, and it offers a first glimpse at his nascent modernism (fig. 11). The room's blending of historic eclecticism and contemporary English domestic style was consistent with the company's established look. But Frankl's introduction of simple planar moldings, box chairs, and sinuous Art Nouveau patterning pointed toward a novel aesthetic, a fusion of old and new that would come to define his early work. The decor was cozy and up-to-date. Yet it preserved an element of past civility fitting for the new urban bourgeoisie.

Frankl's display at the Hohenzollern Kunstgewerbehaus brought him notice within the ranks of the city's architectural and design circles. But he was unable to build on his first success. In the months after returning from Paris, Paula's health had become a concern. In the late winter of 1913, she began to exhibit symptoms of tuberculosis. Her doctor advised her to leave the city for a healthier environment. In late spring, Frankl, who had passed his final examination (*Diplom-Hauptprüfung*) at the university a short time before, took a position in an architect's office in Copenhagen so that Paula could spend time at the shore, breathing in the fresh air of the Baltic Sea.

Frankl, who quickly learned the rudiments of Danish, savored his simple life in Denmark; he knew, though, that it could not last. In early autumn, he and Paula relocated yet again on doctor's advice, this time south to Italy, where they intended to spend the winter.[29]

Frankl had never before ventured further south than Venice, and he was "anxious to take in with my own eyes the great works of art and architecture so familiar from books." He and Paula stopped first in Venice, then traveled on to Florence and Rome. They also visited Naples, where the couple toured the ancient ruins of Pompei and Herculaneum. Frankl found it all intoxicating. The "early medieval architecture of Florence in its stark simplicity,"

the "Botticellian beauty" of the Italian landscape, and the "incredibly blue Bay of Naples" left a powerful impression. He especially admired the vestiges of Roman architecture, which he thought spoke "most eloquently. . . . Sturdy bridges, their arches reflected in the rippling waters, buttressed against the stream, viaducts in perfect repair still serving their purpose, silent witnesses of the glory that once was Rome. In Herculaneum and Pompei [*sic*], there only partly laid bare, a few columns raising their venerable capitals above the protecting lava, were symbols of classicism in its purest form."[30]

But Frankl was having mounting doubts about whether the architecture of former times could offer a model for the present: "Why should we go on endlessly perpetuating what others had done, continue to use outmoded forms to express our time?" he asked. "We would have to find our own solutions as they have found theirs, our own forms and materials to fit our needs, typical of the rapidly changing times we live in, a live expression of our age, a record of our time, set down in the language that spells architecture."[31]

Frankl posed the same question in print. In an article titled, fittingly, "Der Stil unserer Zeit" (The Style of Our Time), which he wrote during his first month in Italy and published in the Berlin architectural journal *Der Baumeister* in November 1913, he denounced old ideas of aristocratic art. It was "not emperor, prince, or the Papacy," he wrote, who should determine the architectural forms of the new industrial age: "The decisive factor today is the idea of mass culture. It is the greatest problem of our time." Frankl argued that the most characteristic expression of this new culture was the work of the engineer. But to embrace technology alone was not enough; architects, artists, and designers, he insisted, needed to transform the language of mere practicality (*Zweckmässigkeit*) into a new art form that would establish "a new tradition."[32]

Frankl set out what form this new art might take in a second article for *Der Baumeister*, published in March 1914. The title of the piece, "Die Industrie als Kulturträger" (Industry as the Bearer of Culture), offered part of the answer. The decline of handicraft and the rise of modern industry, he

contended, required an aesthetic reorientation. The fundamental problem of modern times was not that industrially
produced goods were increasingly replacing handcrafted
objects, but that the quality of the new products remained
so low. Frankl questioned why that had to be the case: "It is
not evident why the products of our time should not have
the same legitimate claim to art and cultural value as those
of previous epochs. . . . Good forms are not a luxury; first,
they are not more expensive to produce than bad ones, and
second, they ensure greater marketability." To raise the
quality of manufactured objects, artists and designers needed to work directly with industry.[33]

It was a surprising assertion from a designer who up to
that time had produced handcrafted luxury works only.
But the divide between his actions and ideals reflected the
inherent contradictions of early modern design: the great

majority of the modernists were still, in fact, tied to older,
traditional modes of production—despite their stated
embrace of the idea of mass production.

Frankl's advocacy of the new industrial culture was
hardly novel: his two articles repeated—superficially at
least—the basic premises of the German Werkbund.
Founded in 1907, the Werkbund was an attempt on the
part of progressives to raise the quality of German manufactured goods through collaboration between designer
and producer.[34] Among its founding members were most
of the leading modernist architects and artists, including
Hoffmann, Olbrich, Van de Velde, and Behrens.

Frankl's *Baumeister* articles suggest that he was familiar with the Werkbund and its objectives and sympathetic
to its mission. But he never joined.[35] The reason may be
contained in the second article. Despite the Werkbund's

Fig. 10. Otto Rudolf
Salvisberg, attic,
Lindenhaus, Berlin,
1912–13

Fig. 11. Paul T. Frankl,
inglenook for a library,
c. 1913. Polished Italian
walnut. Executed by
Hohenzollern
Kunstgewerbehaus
Friedmann and Weber,
Berlin

emphasis on forging close bonds between the artistic
community and large producers, few industrially produced goods emerged; the great majority of the products
displayed at its annual exhibitions and in its publications
were expensive handmade goods. Many of the products,
as Frankl noted, represented "an astonishingly high
level" of achievement. Yet, as extraordinary as they were,
their impact was limited: they were available only to the
few patrons who could afford them. To be genuinely modern, he wrote, industry and artist had to make "products
for the masses, an art of our time." It was "erroneous and
pointless" to work only for "a small number of collectors"
who could afford the "aficionado prices."[36]

Frankl's implicit critique of the Werkbund—in neither
of the articles does he refer to it directly—echoed a vocal

internal debate about the organization's direction and
ideals that had already begun in the summer of 1912 at the
annual meeting of the Werkbund's German and Austrian
branches, held in Vienna. Several German members
charged that the Austrians' stress on expensive handcrafted items was symptomatic of a tendency within the
Werkbund to ignore the dictates of industrial production.[37]
The debate would erupt with renewed force at the 1914
meeting in Cologne, when Hermann Muthesius, one of
the Werkbund's founders, criticized the "artists" who
"protest against every suggestion for the establishment
of a canon and for standardization."[38] The solution,
however, was still years away: it was not until the 1920s
that Muthesius's call for *Typisierung* (the creation of
standardized types) would bear fruit.

Frankl himself, as he knew very well, was not immune to the charge of catering to the needs of wealthy collectors. But his article (which appeared several months before the 1914 meeting) extended Muthesius's argument in at least one important respect, by pointing to the need to design for the "broadest spectrum of society." Still, the piece drew little notice. Frankl was young and virtually unknown, and his critique was veiled behind a generalized affirmation of designers collaborating with industry—a position already widely accepted in modernist circles.

After returning to Vienna from Italy in late winter, Frankl was restless. "Having completed my studies [and] served my apprenticeship, I felt uncertain what to do next," he wrote. "I wished to look some more before deciding where to hang my shingle." He began to think about making a trip to the United States: "My late father, when he came back from America, regretted not to have seen it before. America, I knew, was where I should go."[39]

To make the long journey worthwhile, Frankl offered to report for *Der Baumeister* and several other Berlin-based architectural journals on the preparations for the Panama-Pacific International Exposition in San Francisco, slated to open in early 1915.[40] Paula, still recovering, would stay behind in her mother's care.

In the spring of 1914, six months before his twenty-seventh birthday, Frankl set sail on the luxury liner *Kaiser Wilhelm II* from the French port of Cherbourg.[41] What he thought would be a journey of only a few months became the beginning of a new life for him, and the start of a new era for American design.

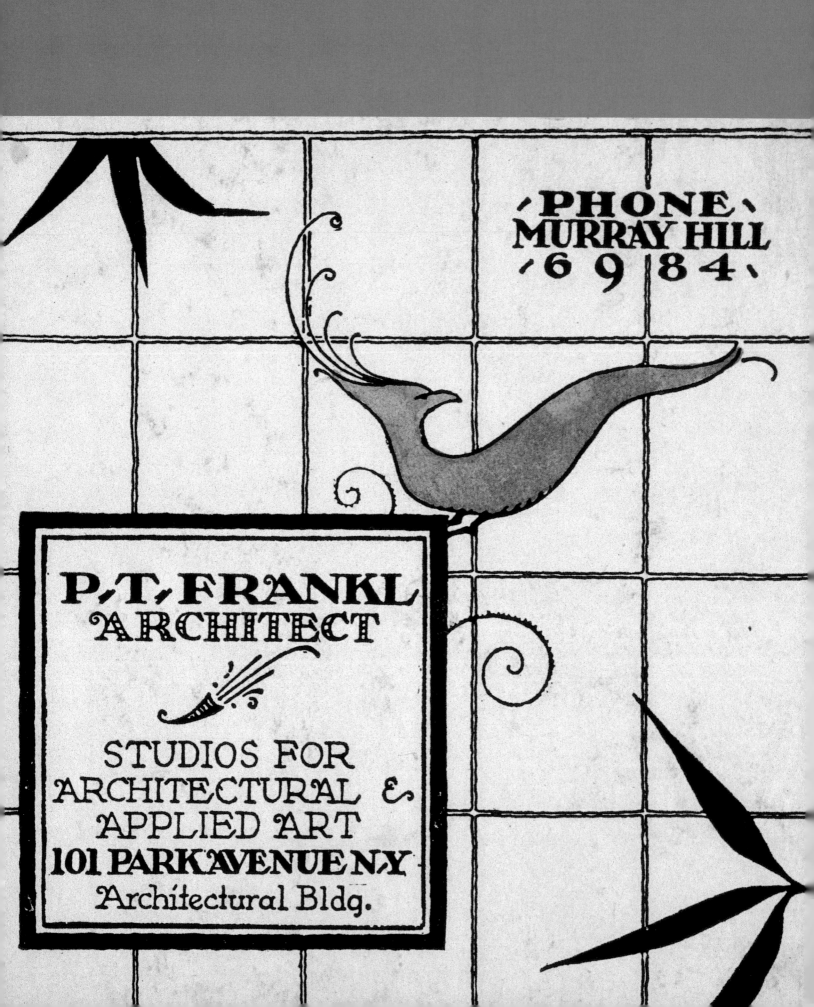

PHONE
MURRAY HILL
6 9 8 4

P. T. FRANKL
ARCHITECT

STUDIOS FOR
ARCHITECTURAL &
APPLIED ART
101 PARK AVENUE N.Y.
Architectural Bldg.

CHAPTER THREE

A Gentle Exit

When Frankl arrived in New York Harbor in late April 1914, he was greeted with a spectacular view of the city. "Spring was in the air," he remembered many years later. His first glimpse was of Manhattan "shrouded in a morning mist, slowly, majestically rising from a vapory haze."[1]

Opposite:
Paul T. Frankl, advertisement for Frankl's shop on Park Avenue, 1915 (detail of fig. 16)

At first, Frankl was enthralled with what he found after stepping ashore. From architectural journals published on both sides of the Atlantic, he was already "well acquainted with the large purely functional buildings of Detroit and other centers of industry" and with the massive grain elevators and silos of Kansas City, "circular structures of great height, broad in diameter, their pictures resembling prehistoric Egyptian temples." But Frankl was also "eager to see what place architecture retained in a young country, not hemmed in with traditions, not crammed full of monuments and palaces that belonged to another age."[2] He was especially excited by the prospect of seeing in person the buildings of Frank Lloyd Wright.

Frankl's initial elation soon turned to disappointment. In New York, he toured the recently completed Grand Central Station. He was stirred, he recorded, by its

Fig. 12. Panama-Pacific
International Exposition,
San Francisco, 1915

"tremendous scale and clear floor plan," which he thought
conveyed a decidedly modern effect—in spite of the building's classical detailing. Within a short time, though, he
realized not only that he had found little evidence of the
new, modern style in architecture that was beginning to
appear in Europe, but that there was no apparent excitement about its possibilities: "None of those I met were
interested in contemporary architecture."[3]

In Washington, D.C., where Frankl stopped next on
his cross-country journey, he visited the new Bureau of
Printing and Engraving. James B. Hill, the building's
designer, personally gave him a tour. Frankl was
impressed with the purity and simplicity of the design—
until he realized that he and his guide "had entered the
building from the rear, the employees' entrance[,] which
I mistook for the main entrance." His "enthusiasm gave
way to embarrassment" when Hill "proudly pointed at its
facade overwrought with Corinthian columns."[4]

Frankl's next stop was Chicago, where he hoped to
meet Wright. He had first encountered Wright's designs
in 1913, when a fellow student at the polytechnic showed
him the *Sonderheft*, a one-volume folio printed for Wright
by the Berlin publisher Ernst Wasmuth in 1911. It was one
of two publications Wright produced detailing, in photographs and plans, his recent Prairie Style houses and

other buildings. (The other was the larger, two-volume
folio *Ausgeführte Bauten und Entwürfe von Frank Lloyd
Wright* [1911], also published by Wasmuth and now usually
referred to as the Wasmuth portfolio.)[5] Examining the
book, Frankl was filled with a sense of clarity and purpose. He was fascinated by Wright's experiments with a
purified, rectilinear form language—and, even more, by
Wright's avoidance of historical motifs and his application of new materials and construction methods.[6]

Frankl was not the only Central European architect
of his generation to find creative stimulus in Wright's
Wasmuth publications: fellow Austrians Rudolph M.
Schindler and Richard Neutra and Czech architect
Antonin Raymond all made the pilgrimage to Wright's
studio in the years just before and after World War I.[7]
But Frankl, perhaps out of shyness, perhaps subcon-
sciously fearful of falling under Wright's spell, did not
write to him beforehand to arrange an appointment,
and when he arrived at Wright's office, he was informed
that Wright was away. Disappointed (but also, it seems,
a little relieved), he went to see Wright's houses and other
works in Oak Park. He was particularly impressed with
the all-concrete Unity Temple. But he found its severity
and its lack of applied ornament daunting; for all of his
professed allegiance to modernism, he was not yet
prepared for the full impact of Wright's asceticism.[8]

Frankl also spent hours in the Chicago Loop studying
the latest high-rises. He was struck by the scale and visual
force of the city's skyscrapers, but he was perplexed that
much of their detailing remained indebted to the past.[9]

After a few days in Chicago, Frankl continued his journey west. By the time he arrived in San Francisco in early
June, work on the Panama-Pacific fairgrounds was near-
ing completion.[10] Frankl toured the fairgrounds with
William B. Faville, the lead partner of Bliss and Faville,
who had devised the fair's neo-Mediterranean style.[11]
Frankl was unaffected by the buildings, but he found the
"stark simplicity" of the high walls enclosing the grounds
"moving" (fig. 12). Later, over lunch at the St. Francis
Hotel, he congratulated Faville on the walls' monumental

effect; to his dismay, Faville explained that the look had
been the result not of a deliberate design concept but of a
meager budget that had allowed only for the elaboration of
the broad Baroque gates.[12]

Seeing the Panama-Pacific Exposition only confirmed
Frankl's conviction that the United States, for all of its
potential and despite the efforts of Wright and a few others, lagged behind Europe in the search for a new architecture: "My visit to the States had been all I could have
wished for and a great deal more. My eyes beheld the
beauty that is America. I saw much and learned even
more, but my search for new expressions in architecture
was in vain. Instead I discovered the greatest country in
the world, unaware of its own greatness, copying the
meaningless outworn forms of architecture of bygone
days and bygone countries. A giant, slumbering, waiting
to be awakened."[13]

Though disheartened by the conservative cast of the
exposition, Frankl relished his time in San Francisco.
After nearly two weeks in the city, he made plans to return
to Austria. Instead of journeying back to Europe by way of
New York, however, he decided to extend his travels with
a trip through Asia. He exchanged his return ticket for
passage to Japan and was pleased to discover that the next
steamer would not depart until the following week, giving
him several more days in San Francisco.

In mid-June, Frankl sailed for Japan. His first stop was
Tokyo. He found lodging in a traditional inn not far from
the Imperial Palace and set out to explore the city.
Everything he saw intrigued him: the people, the landscape, the buildings, the simplest incidents of daily life.
He had done very little drawing during his journey
through the United States; now he felt compelled to
record "the vivid impressions that so strongly imprinted
themselves upon my mind."[14] His sketches, inspired by
the Japanese woodcuts he saw, took on a new delicacy, at
once open, subdued, and austere (figs. 13, 14).

Frankl was surprised that the large monumental
buildings he visited left less of an impression on him
than the humble dwellings and ordinary articles of daily

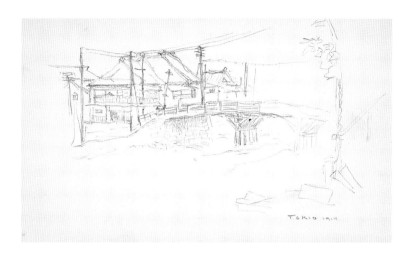

Above, top:
Fig. 13. Paul T. Frankl, sketch of Tokyo, 1914. Pencil on paper.
Collection Paulette Frankl

Above, bottom:
Fig. 14. Paul T. Frankl, drawing of a Japanese girl, 1914.
Pencil on paper. Collection Paulette Frankl

Fig. 15. Label designed by the International Art Service, 1914

use. He made careful note of even the most trivial details of living, their "refinement" and "dignity." [15] The Japanese "art of elimination" he saw everywhere seemed to him to pose a trenchant and fertile alternative to Western taste; he described it as "the distilled essence of beauty." [16] In the "plainness, this idealized conception of cleanliness, this simplicity of expression and [the Japanese people's] traditionally deep-rooted ability to use materials true to their nature," Frankl discovered a new aesthetic ideal that would become a vital element in his own design philosophy. [17]

He was particularly taken with the objects he saw in the shops. Wherever he went, he bought examples: painted scrolls, woodcuts, Sendai chests, grass mats, paper lanterns, lacquered bowls, handmade pottery, ordinary patterned fabrics, and antique Japanese screens. Within a short time, he had purchased so many items that he was forced to store them with a shipper in Yokohama until they could be sent back to Austria.

From Tokyo, he traveled south, making stops in Nagoya, the ancient capital of Nara, and Osaka. By late July, he was in Kyoto. It was there Frankl heard news of the outbreak of the World War. Unable to return to Austria or to remain in Japan, he made the decision to wait out the conflict—widely expected at the time to last only a few months—in New York. He booked passage to San Francisco, contracted with the trading company in

Yokohama to hold his purchases, and retraced his steps back to the East Coast.

Frankl had escaped the horrors of the war. When he left Paula in Europe a few months before, he wrote, "hers seemed the course of prudence, mine adventurous." The outbreak of conflict "had proved otherwise": her path had led to danger and panic, "whereas mine was a gentle exit from the bloody clutches of war." [18]

Frankl was back in New York by early September. With little money remaining, he needed a source of income to tide him over until he could return home. After some hasty inquiries, he found a job designing advertising posters for the International Art Service. As a young modernist in the making, he could not have chanced upon a better position. Established two years earlier by German and Austrian artists Arthur Wiener, Willy Sesser, and Harry Weissberger, the International Art Service, located on West Forty-second Street across from the New York Public Library, was one of the first design studios in the United States to apply modern ideas to advertising art. Not only did Wiener and his collaborators design numerous "flat" posters and print advertisements in the Jugendstil manner, but they introduced the idea of a unified design for their clients, creating a basic style for a company's advertisements, letterhead, packaging—even its business cards (fig. 15). [19]

Frankl adapted quickly to the new job. The International Art Service's style and design philosophy were already familiar to him from Vienna, and working in an office in which much of the day-to-day business was conducted in German provided a comfortable entrée into life in New York. He signed on for seventeen dollars a week. But the job would have far more important benefits. With little experience in graphic art, he relied on lessons from two fellow employees, Maud Fuller and her future husband, the Hungarian artist Miska Petersham, to learn the business.

Fuller, who later became famous as an illustrator and author of children's books, had joined the design department of the International Art Service after graduating from Vassar. In the company's drafting room she met Petersham, who had immigrated to New York two years before.[20] By the time Frankl began his tenure, both were already skilled designers in the modern manner. Their teachings would prove invaluable: he learned skills for graphic presentation that he would soon put to work in his own design practice, and, for the first time, he became fully aware of the power of advertising to shape the public's impressions and understanding.

Frankl's job with the International Art Service also brought him into contact with New York's developing art scene. When he first arrived in the spring, his impression was that, although the city was filled with portents of the new, the cultural scene seemed arrested.[21] Upon his return, he discovered a very different New York, now "thronged by polyglot refugees" from the war.[22] The many artists who found sanctuary in Manhattan from the war—Marcel Duchamp, Jean Crotti, Albert Gleizes, and Francis Picabia—had transformed it, almost overnight, into a center for the new art. For Frankl, who quickly found his own place in the city's avant-garde, it seemed a "new world was in the making." Shortly after his arrival, he was reacquainted with a number of his old friends from Europe, including Jules Pascin, who had fled France after the German invasion, and Fritz Kreisler, who had been seriously injured in the first weeks of the war and had come to the United States after his release from the Austrian army. Frankl also befriended dancer Isadora Duncan and her sister Elizabeth, Spanish cellist Pablo Casals, and Viennese designer Joseph Urban, who had come to New York by way of Boston that autumn.[23]

By November, it had become apparent that the war would not end quickly, so Frankl made arrangements for Paula to join him. He also sent a wire to his agent in Yokohama requesting that the rolls of silk, paper lanterns, and other goods he had acquired during his stay in Japan be shipped to New York. When the articles arrived, he intended to open an interior design studio.

Frankl's decision to enter into the interior decorating

field was in large part a response to necessity. After several fainthearted attempts, it was evident to him that it would be laborious and time-consuming to break into the ranks of the city's closed architectural profession. He had scant experience as an architect, and, cut off from home, he had little capital. Moreover, he knew of no architect in New York producing modern work. Not only would it be easier to establish his own practice designing interiors, he reasoned, but also it would allow him to produce the type of work he wanted without having to make compromises.

Paula arrived in early December 1914, traveling on an Italian steamer from Genoa.[24] The long crossing in rough winter seas had taken its toll on her delicate health. While aboard ship, she had contracted a serious bout of influenza. When she disembarked, she was so weak that Frankl feared her life would be in peril if she were forced to spend the winter in New York. Still awaiting the shipment from Japan, he decided to take her to Havana, where the warm climate would allow her to recover her strength. Frankl, meanwhile, would use the time to paint and to plan the launch of his gallery.

The couple stayed for the next two months at the Hotel Trocha in the Havana suburb of Velado. Frankl delighted in the lush tropical vegetation, and he spent time each day sketching and painting in the gardens or reading about the newest trends in art and design. He and Paula planned to remain in Cuba until the early spring, but their stay was cut short when he received a cable in late February informing him that the crates from Japan had arrived in New York and were being held by an appraiser pending customs inspection. They departed immediately, taking a boat the short distance to Key West, then transferring to an express train that took them to New York.[25]

After rescuing his Japanese goods from customs, Frankl found gallery space in the recently completed Architects Building at 101 Park Avenue, at the intersection of Park Avenue and Fortieth Street (fig. 16). The building, designed by two local architectural firms (Ewing and Chappell, and La Farge and Morris) and promoted as being "built by architects for architects," was the first

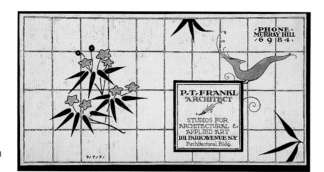

Fig. 16. Paul T. Frankl,
advertisements for
Frankl's shop on Park
Avenue, 1915. Collection
Paulette Frankl

Fig. 16. Paul T. Frankl,
advertisements for
Frankl's shop on Park
Avenue, 1915. Collection
Paulette Frankl

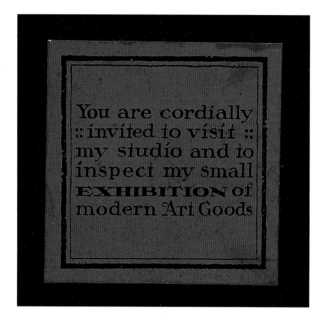

lost much of its impetus by the time the war erupted in
Europe. Gustav Stickley, the foremost American Arts and
Crafts furniture manufacturer, went out of business a year
after the war started, and *The Craftsman*, the principal
organ of the movement, ceased publication. Many of the
movement's other leaders had a hard time finding work.
Charles Sumner Greene moved to Carmel, California, in
1916 and lived in semiretirement; and Frank Lloyd
Wright, after completing the Midway Gardens in Chicago,
turned his sights toward Japan. [29]

Even before the war, the Arts and Crafts movement was
being supplanted by a growing conservatism in architecture and the decorative arts. By the time Frankl arrived in
New York, a renewed interest in period revival styles—
French Empire and Louis XV and XVI, English Tudor and
Queen Anne, Spanish Baroque, and American Colonial—
dominated the work of interior designers. "Interior decoration" was still a new field. In former times, architects or
tradesmen—cabinetmakers, upholsterers, drapers, or
shop owners— had advised home owners on the arrangement of interiors. But by the last years of the nineteenth
century, wealthy Americans had begun to engage professional decorators to reproduce Renaissance palaces or
French châteaux. The image of the profession thus became
closely associated with the idea of re-creating historical
interiors. Elsie de Wolfe, the most prominent of the new
"interior decorators," acknowledged in her trendsetting
book, *The House in Good Taste* (1913), the need for modern
heating and plumbing, but she emphasized the use of
antiques rather than "new" furnishings. [30] The interest in
period revivalism also reached into middle-class homes.
The leading American home magazines, *House Beautiful*
and *House and Garden*, advocated a more affordable means
of achieving the same look through the use of period
reproductions copied directly—or at least derived—from
historic prototypes.

Accompanying the renewed emphasis on period
revival furnishings was a growing renunciation of modern
forms. Helen Churchill Candee, a prominent decorator
and journalist in New York, expressed the attitude of most

modern office building on Park Avenue. It housed scores
of offices above the display rooms of the Architects'
Samples Corporation Office, which occupied the lobby
and mezzanine. [26]

With the limited means he had on hand, Frankl transformed the bare loft space into a showroom, using the
Japanese screens, scrolls, and bolts of material to cloak the
walls. [27] At first, his business consisted of selling the tea
sets, Sendai chests, decorative scrolls, and other objects he
had imported. But before long he began to offer his services
as an interior designer. One of his first advertisements for
the shop announced his intention to offer "artistic formes
[*sic*], good material, and first-class workmanship" to those
"looking for a modern home" (fig. 17). [28]

The idea of modern interior design was still new—or,
perhaps better, new again—in the United States in 1915.
The Arts and Crafts movement continued to influence the
American scene, especially on the West Coast, but it had

professional interior designers: "Modern developments," she declared, "are distrusted with reason. They are founded on the restlessness of taste, on the corrupting desire for novelty—a desire which trade encourages as being vulgarly 'good for business.'" Comparing modern furniture with "modern modes in dress," she declared that in either case, they "need only to pass out of fashion for the eye to discover their inherent ugliness."[31]

The position of interior design in 1915 stood in notable contrast to painting and sculpture. The New York Armory Show two years before had introduced the art of the European avant-garde to America, and the legions of artists who arrived after the beginning of the war only served to further invigorate and radicalize the art scene. At the front of the assault were Duchamp, Picabia, Crotti, and the young American Man Ray, who formed the New York branch of Dada. But they represented only the leading edge of a broader movement advancing American art. And it was not only foreign-born artists who came on the scene. Before the war, Alfred Stieglitz, who operated 291, the most important gallery for the new art, had promoted Rodin, Matisse, Picasso, and Brancusi (along with a small number of American painters and sculptors whose work was consistent with Continental Cubism and Expressionism). During the war years, however, Stieglitz refocused his attentions on a small group of native artists that included Marsden Hartley, Konrad Cramer, Andrew Dasburg, Max Weber, Walt Kuhn, Morris Kantor, Georgia O'Keeffe, Henry McLee, and William Zorach.[32]

Yet the same energy and vitality that inspired the works of the new émigrés and natives alike worked against the advance of modern interior design. New Yorkers, already long confronted with the coarse realities of the industrial age, from the urban landscape of skyscrapers and subways to the stresses of factory and office, sought release and comfort in more familiar, traditional surroundings at home.

Nonetheless, by the war years the impact of recent European interior design currents had begun to be felt in the city. The most conspicuous was the modular, geomet-

ric language of the Viennese Secessionists and their German counterparts. Americans had first encountered the new style in the Austrian and German pavilions at the St. Louis World's Fair in 1904.[33] The first Secessionist-inspired interiors appeared in the United States in the fair's immediate aftermath. Within a few years, the Secessionist mode had made a sufficient impact on American architecture and design that the word was sometimes used as a synonym for "modern."[34] Interest in

Fig. 17. Paul T. Frankl, advertisement for Frankl's shop on Park Avenue, 1915. Collection Paulette Frankl

Fig. 18. Paul T. Frankl, bathroom for an unknown New York client, 1915. Black and white marble

the *Secessionsstil* was further stimulated by a large travel-ing exhibition of the latest German and Austrian designs that toured the East Coast and several Midwest cities in 1912-13.[35] By the eve of the war, several galleries selling Viennese- or German-inspired designs had sprung up in Manhattan, including the Austrian Workshop, operated by Rena Rosenthal (sister of architect Ely Jacques Kahn); the Zimmermann Studios, owned by Paul Zimmermann, who had studied architecture and design with Peter Behrens at the Düsseldorf Kunstgewerbeschule before immigrating to the United States; and the Ascherman Studio, run by Edward Ascherman and his wife, Gladys, who made and sold modern "box furniture" inspired by contemporary Viennese designs.[36]

Frankl thus joined a small group of designers and gallery owners already advancing the idea of a mod-ernism based on contemporary Central European models.[37] But unlike them, Frankl offered his clients an aesthetic based not only on the Secessionist mode but also on other, more recent European design trends. One can see this in a bathroom he produced for an unknown client in New York in the spring of 1915 (fig. 18). It repeated the black-and-white geometric style Josef

Hoffmann and Koloman Moser had popularized just after the turn of the century.[38] But the room—especially the tub surround—exhibits, too, the influence of the con-temporary neo-Baroque. In Austria in the years after 1903, the Jugendstil began to give way to a revival of his-toricism. The leaders of this movement included many of the original Secessionists, among them Hoffmann and Joseph Maria Olbrich.[39] Their interest in the past repre-sented a departure from late-nineteenth-century period revivalism: rather than reproducing earlier styles, they used older elements in piecemeal fashion, blending forms and ideas from various cultures and eras. The resulting mélange suggested associations with historical styles—even though their exact sources were often no longer discernible. This new eclecticism found especially strong acceptance among the designers of Frankl's gen-eration, who had been educated after the turn of the cen-tury when the influence of the Secession was waning. They no longer subscribed to the "pure" modernism of the Jugendstil; instead, they appropriated some of its for-mal vocabulary, as well as "quotations" from a much larg-er repository of historical forms—from Renaissance and Baroque to Biedermeier and Rococo.

All of this was still quite exotic for most New Yorkers, and Frankl had a difficult time finding willing clients. His attempts to promote modern design were further hindered by his status as both a foreigner and an outsider: he had few connections to potential patrons and a shop at what was then an unfashionable address. He and the other German-speaking gallery owners also had to con-front a rising swell of anti-German sentiment, especially after the sinking of the passenger ship *Lusitania* by a German submarine in May 1915 tipped American public opinion against the Central powers. A few "enthusiasts," Frankl remembered years later, found their way to his shop, but his business, as before, continued to rely on selling his Japanese imports and "modern" decorative arts objects, especially lamps and pillows.[40]

Frankl's first important commission came instead by way of Polish émigré sculptor Elie Nadelman, an old acquaintance from Paris, whom he had met up with again not long after his return to New York.[41] Nadelman arranged for Frankl to design the interiors for a new "maison de beauté" that was opened in the spring of 1915 by another recently arrived Polish émigré, Helena Rubinstein. The salon, though still quite traditional (at Rubinstein's request), caused a considerable stir in the press and design circles and brought Frankl several other jobs, including a commission from Rubinstein's competitor, Elizabeth Arden, who asked him to design her new salon on Fifth Avenue (fig. 19).[42]

In spite of the publicity he received from the Rubinstein and Arden commissions, Frankl's showroom in the Architects Building was not a success. "Few people went that far East [to Park Avenue]," he recalled. "Helena's salon attracted crowds, but no one ever came from there. I was to find out the hard way that it is as detrimental to be too far ahead as to lag too far behind time."[43] Frankl realized that Americans would first have to be persuaded that modern design was the appropriate expression for the new age. In May, he made his first effort, publishing an article on the "modern art of interior decoration" in *Arts and Decoration.*

The piece called for, in Frankl's words, a "harmonious adjustment between the needs of mankind" and the "artistic and scientific development" of the modern age.[44] Advances in science, he argued, "reach deep into our daily family life, and have made a notable change in our customs." Contemporary interiors, he insisted, must respond to the challenges of the new age: "It is nonsense to constrain electric light to the form of old wax candles when that form was not originally designed for this manner of lighting." In the same way, "it is evidence of a complete misunderstanding when an artist covers an electric heater with the drapery of a Renaissance fireplace and believes he has complied with the style of his time if he illuminates wooden logs with electricity."[45]

But Frankl rejected the guiding idea of the Art Nouveau movement—that a wholly original modern interior design language had to be created: "We can, indeed, already

speak of a new culture in dwellings, the necessity and right of existence of which has sufficiently been proven. It is evident that we had not only to find a new form for factories and skyscrapers, department stores and railway stations, but above all for the dwelling-place of the well-to-do."[46] The new living culture, he contended, resulted directly from the striving "to unite the demands for convenience and appropriateness with the principles of beauty." The reliance on period furniture "is an acknowledgement of a poverty of ideas" in the present: "Period furniture has no justification in our time; it originated in a strange and different time; it was planned for other people of other times."

Frankl understood that a new style could not be arbitrarily imposed: "Art in general and especially the art of interior decoration," he reminded his readers, "depends not alone on the artist, but largely on the public. Therefore interior decoration as an art can only grow where artist and public work hand in hand, and where society is aware of its duty to cultivate further art."[47]

Frankl based his appeal on what he thought was common sense, but his views found limited acceptance. At the end of the article was a rebuttal from Guy Pène du Bois, editor of *Arts and Decoration:* "Despite the feeling

Fig. 19. Paul T. Frankl, Elizabeth Arden Salon, 1915

Fig. 20. Paul T. Frankl, advertisement for the Frankl Gallery on Fifth Avenue, c. 1915. Collection Paulette Frankl

expressed by the author . . . that the furniture of the great decorative periods has no place in the art of to-day, it would appear that interest in it is still distinctly alive."[48]

The cool reception Frankl found among professional decorators notwithstanding, he was able to secure several other important commissions. One was the Voisin, a restaurant operated by two Austrians, Otto and Alfons Baumgarten, at Park Avenue and Fifty-fourth Street.[49]

He also designed an apartment for fashion designer Lady Duff-Gordon in the same building, and he contributed sets and decorations for a number of charity affairs, arranged by the Austrian ambassador in Washington, Count Constantin Dumba, to collect money for refugees in war-torn Austria-Hungary.[50]

In the summer of 1915, in a bid to increase his visibility, Frankl gave up his gallery in the Architects Building and moved to a studio at 425 Fifth Avenue on the corner of Thirty-eighth Street (fig. 20). He also began to branch out in other directions. Through Isadora Duncan and other acquaintances in the Greenwich Village bohemia, he became involved with several experimental theater groups, designing sets for their productions.[51]

Frankl was thrilled with the opportunity to be active in the theater world. He also saw the work as a chance, as he described it, to "put modern decorative art before a broad audience."[52] His guide and partner was stage designer Lee Simonson.

A native New Yorker, Simonson had attended Harvard and later spent time studying in Paris. Not long after his return to the United States in 1912, he designed his first production, *Love of One's Neighbor*. The sets were among the first examples of the "New Stagecraft" in New York. Inaugurated in Europe a few years earlier, the New Stagecraft movement sought to abandon realism in theater scenery and replace it with simple and suggestive settings. Its aim was to present a mood, a time, and a place— without resorting to conventional pictorial means. One column might suggest a temple, a single tree, a forest.[53]

Frankl met Simonson through mutual friends in Greenwich Village, and the two men soon formed a close friendship.[54] By the fall of 1915, Simonson had become the principal designer for the Washington Square Players; he asked Frankl to contribute sets for several one-act plays.

The productions of the Players, one of the most visible "little theater" groups in the Village, offered the two men a perfect field for investigating the possibilities of modern design. The company, founded just a year before to introduce new American and European plays of "artistic merit," had a stated mission to "reach a higher standard" through "experiment and initiative."[55] Simonson took that charge seriously. Working with a few basic ideas he had assimilated from the Russian and European avant-gardes, he developed a radically stripped-down design style that dispensed almost entirely with traditional scenography. He encouraged Frankl to do the same; within a short time, both men found themselves at the forefront of New York stage design.

Frankl created five sets for the Players in 1915 and 1916, among them works by German-language playwrights Arthur Schnitzler and Frank Wedekind. He also designed the green room at the Bandbox Theatre, where the company was in residence.[56] His first sets in 1915, which included *Fire and Water*, by Hervey White, and *Helena's Husband*, by Philip Moeller, relied to some extent on standard pictorial ideas. But his design for *Bushido*, by Takeda Izumo, which premiered the following year, presented a new level of spareness, an effect he enhanced

through the dramatic use of spot- and backlighting (fig. 21). [57] By paring down the set to a few emblematic elements, Frankl was able to evoke the impression of a historical Japanese interior, but his reliance on straight-forward geometries and clear, bold lines offered a clarion image of incipient modernism.

Frankl applied many of these same ideas to the back-drops he created for several of Isadora Duncan's dance recitals. He made extensive use of theatrical gauze in a wide range of colors to evoke mood and rhythm, and he experimented with various lighting ideas to animate the space.

Frankl found the work and the attention he received rewarding. More important, the theater provided an opportunity to test unconventional aesthetic approaches. By the middle of 1916, Frankl was also experiencing

mounting success with his interior design practice. He executed several complete interiors in new residential buildings along Park Avenue, then just developing into a residential area for the upper middle class—among them, apartments for Robert J. F. Schwarzenbach, president of the Swiss textile firm Schwarzenbach, Huber, and Company, at 471 Park Avenue, and for Alfred de Liagre, who operated the textile import company A. de Liagre and Company, further up the avenue. [58] But Frankl's largest and most elaborate commission was an apartment for German textile magnate Hans E. Stoehr, president of Botany Worsted Mills, and his wife, Lotte, at 330 Park Avenue. [59]

The Stoehrs had taken out a long-term lease on the upper two floors of the new twelve-story building

Fig. 21. Paul T. Frankl, set design for *Bushido*, by Takeda Izumo, produced by the Washington Square Players at the Bandbox Theatre, New York (first performed 30 August 1916)

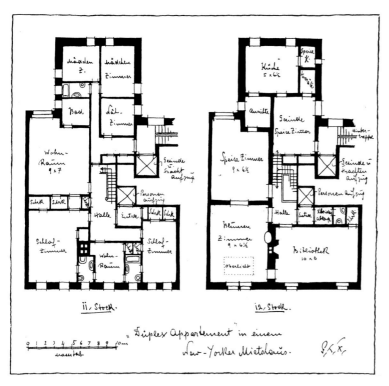

Fig. 22. Paul T. Frankl, Stoehr Apartment plans,
New York, 1916

Fig. 23. Paul T. Frankl, "modern Biedermeier room,"
Stoehr Apartment, New York, 1916

before construction began, allowing Frankl to configure the spaces and to direct all of the interior detailing. Following their wishes, he placed the bedrooms, the servants' rooms, and the two living rooms on the lower floor; on the upper floor, he arranged the principal public spaces: the dining room, a sizable library, and a conservatory (fig. 22).

The spaces, later extensively documented in the Central European design journals *Die bildenden Künste/Der Architekt* and *Innen-Dekoration*, reveal his developing inclinations and his continuing allegiance to modern Central European design.[60] Also evident, however, are Frankl's borrowings from Biedermeier neoclassicism. Biedermeier, the middle-class style of the *Vormärz* (literally, "before March," referring to the period before the revolution of 1848), was later derided by the artists and architects of the second half of the nineteenth century as a manifestation of bourgeois unimaginativeness and sobriety. For the young Viennese modernists who came on the scene after the fin de siècle, though, the unadorned facades of Biedermeier buildings and the austere forms of its furniture seemed to have inaugurated a modern tradition, one cast off by the historicists but now to be reclaimed. By the time of World War I, the moral and aesthetic authority of neo-Biedermeier was well established: awakened by Joseph Folnesics, Joseph August Lux, and Bruno Paul just after the turn of the century, it was taken up by many of the leading reformers in Austria and Germany, among them Hoffmann and Richard Riemerschmid.[61] For Frankl, as for many of his generation, the understated simplicity of Biedermeier buildings and furniture suggested not only a means to graft the language of the present onto the past but a way to overcome the artificiality of the Jugendstil.[62]

Frankl's debt to the Biedermeier revival in his design of the Stoehr Apartment is most patent in the "modern Biedermeier room," the smaller of the two living areas on the lower floor (fig. 23). The wall fabric and sofa cushions repeated modern ornamental patterning, but he took the forms of the settee, chairs, and table directly from early-nineteenth-century models, altering only slightly their proportions and arrangement.

For the apartment's other rooms, Frankl adopted a less literal approach, recasting the Biedermeier formal lexicon in a more manifestly modern spirit. In the sitting corner of the daughter's bedroom, he smoothed the contours of the individual pieces, removing the most explicit references to the historical originals (fig. 24). Yet the entire ensemble, completed with multi-patterned cushions, folk objects, and an Oriental rug, preserved the essence of Biedermeier rooms, not only in a formal sense but also in spirit.

The sitting corner of the daughter's room makes clear the importance of contemporary German design for Frankl. Having spent most of the previous decade in Germany, he was still under the influence of the leading German designers—especially Paul, Riemerschmid, Karl Bertsch, and Paul Mebes—who had developed their own interpretations of the updated early-nineteenth-century interior. His designs, however, exhibit a tendency—which became even more conspicuous in the 1920s and 1930s—to use heavier and more robust forms to make a forceful statement.

Frankl's lavish conservatory for the Stoehr Apartment encapsulated all of these early formative influences (fig. 25). The design and arrangement of the furniture disclose the impact of Biedermeier neoclassicism and the example of the German progressive designers, while his application of the multiple frame panels and thin moldings framing the walls give evidence of his continuing debt to the Viennese Secessionists.

But the surviving black-and-white photographs of the room fail to convey what is perhaps its most striking feature: Frankl's bold use of color. Set against the pearl-gray walls and Cipollino marble floors accented with black moldings was a seating group executed in gray lacquer with black and gold details and violet and cherry-red cushions.[63] Frankl's penchant for coloristic effects is manifested further in his design for the room's wall foun-

Fig. 24. Paul T. Frankl, sitting corner in a young woman's bedroom, Stoehr Apartment, New York, 1916

tain, which combined a shimmering gold faience mosaic with green verd-antique marble (fig. 26). The geometric patterning of the tile points once more to the ordering principles of the Jugendstil, but—no doubt inspired by his recent travels—he added several explicit Japanese references: a sweeping flower arrangement and a basin with small goldfish.

Despite Frankl's desire to introduce modern decorative art to America, the look of the Stoehr Apartment was still decidedly Central European. Indeed, the interiors showed little accommodation to their setting: aside from his extensive use of built-in closets and cabinets—still uncommon at the time in Austria and Germany—there were few other allusions to contemporary American life.[64] That the Stoehrs, like almost all of Frankl's early clients, were recent arrivals from Europe doubtless had much to do with the absence of specific American references in his designs. Dagobert Frey, a well-known commentator on the Austrian design scene who reported on Frankl's New York designs for *Die bildenden Künste*, immediately recognized that they represented a development of a dis-

Fig. 26. Paul T. Frankl, wall fountain in the conservatory, Stoehr Apartment, New York, 1916

tinctive Viennese aesthetic (*Wiener Eigenart*), relocated to the United States.[65]

In spite of Frankl's unique position in the New York design world, his efforts to move away from period revivalism were part of an incipient American modern movement in interior design. In an article in *House and Garden* in April 1917, B. Russell Herts, one of the principals of Herts Brothers Company Decorators on West Fifty-seventh Street and a recent convert to the modernist cause, described Frankl as a leader in the trend toward an American modern interior design: "Mr. Paul Frankl, an architect from Germany, is strongly imbued with the continental art of the secession, but his designs are, in a measure, personal, and must therefore become more and more impressed with the growing American spirit."[66]

But Frankl's attempts to fashion a new modern aesthetic for the American context were cut short. A few weeks after Herts's article appeared, the United States entered the war on the side of the Allies. Suddenly, Frankl found himself confronted with very different challenges.

Fig. 25. Paul T. Frankl, conservatory, Stoehr Apartment, New York, 1916

CHAPTER FOUR

Return to Europe

During Frankl's first years in New York, the war had seemed far away. Like most Americans, he followed the events in the newspapers, though with many friends and relatives—including all three of his brothers—serving in the Austrian army, he read the accounts with great interest. The sinking of the *Lusitania* in 1915 had threatened U.S. neutrality, but the country remained out of the war, as President Woodrow Wilson had pledged in his reelection campaign. The situation changed abruptly in February 1917, however, when the German government announced that it would resume unrestricted submarine warfare. In protest, the United States broke off relations with Germany; soon thereafter, Austrian ambassador Count Dumba and his staff were recalled.

With the impending American entry into the war, Frankl faced a difficult decision. Unsure whether his future was in the United States and uncertain about his status as an enemy alien, he made plans to return to Austria. Frankl's choice was not an easy one; he knew very well that upon his return he would be sent to rejoin his old reserve cavalry regiment at the front. But in 1917, he had not yet resolved to remain in New York: the idea of setting up an architectural practice in Vienna was still in his

Opposite:
Fig. 27. Paul T. Frankl, vanity and chair, Stoehr Apartment, New York, 1916

thoughts. Reluctantly, he and Paula prepared for the journey. Determined to give up interior decoration and dedicate himself to architecture if and when he returned to New York, Frankl hastily sold off the shop's remaining stock. What the couple could not sell, they simply gave away. In late February, they, along with a large contingent of German and Austrian officials and their families, boarded a Norwegian passenger ship for the voyage.

The winter crossing was long and uncomfortable. To avoid the German submarine blockade, the ship took a northerly route, sailing first to Halifax, Nova Scotia, then following a course between Iceland and the Faeroe Islands, well above the Arctic Circle. After eighteen days and many sleepless nights of worry about a possible torpedo attack, the ship landed at the port of Bergen, Norway. The Frankls continued their journey by rail, arriving in Vienna nearly a month after setting out. [1]

Their homecoming proved much less joyous than they had hoped. Frankl discovered that one of his brothers lay in the hospital seriously wounded. His mother, whose other two boys were still at the front, was stunned to see the only one of her sons who had been safely out of the country now standing before her. The mood in Austria was bleak. Despite the collapse of the old regime in Russia, the war continued unabated. The Austrian and German generals were still ordering offensives, but trench warfare, the machine gun, and massed heavy artillery had long since rendered such efforts bloody and futile. The war, everyone now understood, was one of attrition. "Defeatism," Frankl recalled, "filled the air." The pessimism issued not only from the sense of futility and stalemate: "The Austrians felt cheated, fighting on the wrong side when their sympathies were with the Allies." The fate "of the Habsburg monarchy, they knew, was sealed." [2]

When he reported to the War Ministry a few days later, Frankl was told that his former regiment, already at the front for three long years, had been nearly obliterated. The military authorities upbraided him for not having returned when the war broke out. "Officially" he was ordered to report to the headquarters of his unit in western Hungary

until he could be reassigned—but "privately" he "was told to have [his] head examined" for coming back. [3]

After a few weeks at the base, Frankl learned of a request from army headquarters for officers with engineering or architecture degrees who wanted to volunteer for service in Turkey. He applied immediately and was accepted. In November, while awaiting orders, Frankl delivered a lecture on his experiences in the United States to the Österreichischer Ingenieur- und Architektenverein (Austrian Engineers and Architects Association) in Vienna. [4] He also arranged for photographs of the Stoehr Apartment to be published (fig. 27), and he wrote an essay, "Wie wohnt man in Amerika?" (How Do Americans Live?), for the design journal *Innen-Dekoration*. A few weeks later, he joined a group of twenty technical advisers on the Orient Express bound for Constantinople. [5]

Frankl was assigned to oversee the construction of several narrow-gauge railways in Anatolia. The Turkish authorities knew nothing of the plans, however, and ordered the men to remain in the capital while they deliberated over how to deploy them. Frankl found himself with little to do, so he explored the city, walking endlessly through the bustling markets and the ancient, winding streets. He was pleased to meet up again with the former German ambassador to the United States, Count Johann Heinrich von Bernstorff, and his American wife, Jeanne Luckemeyer. Frankl had been introduced to them in Washington while attending a function at the Austrian embassy, and the Countess Bernstorff had visited his New York studio several times. She liked Frankl's work and commissioned him to design the couple's retirement home on Lake Starenberg near Munich.

The countess had in mind an American-style country place facing the lake. With little else to occupy his time, Frankl threw himself into the task. Over several days, he produced a design for a rambling villa, with continuous French doors opening out to the water. The detailing, like his interiors for the Stoehr Apartment, borrowed from

Biedermeier neoclassicism, but in a decidedly pared-down form: Frankl reduced the various elements, fashioning a straightforward, direct work. The house never proceeded beyond the conceptual phase—the count and countess became increasingly preoccupied with the flagging war effort and deterioration of the German government and had little time for consultations—but the experience bolstered Frankl's determination to return to the practice of architecture after the war.[6]

In late 1917, Frankl was ordered to report to the president of the Turkish National Bank. He learned that he and the other Austrian advisers were to assist the bank in a series of urban renewal and civil engineering projects. Frankl, though younger than most of the others, impressed his superiors with his maturity and leadership, and he was placed in charge of the group. He chose as his assistant the Viennese-trained architect Oskar Wlach.[7]

Five years older than Frankl, Wlach had already made a name for himself in Vienna as a designer of modern buildings and interiors. In 1908, he had formed a partnership with another rising young Viennese architect, Oskar Strnad; within a year, Josef Frank, who had just completed his studies at the Technische Hochschule, joined them.[8]

The three architects undertook an array of commissions, including several remarkably prescient modernist villas on the city's outskirts. When the war began, Wlach was stationed in Albania. He contracted malaria, and after a long convalescence, he was transferred to Polish Galicia. His illness recurred in 1917, and he was removed from the front and reassigned, along with Frankl and the others, to Constantinople.[9]

Frankl and Wlach collaborated on a diverse group of projects. They devised a plan to rebuild the Stambul and Galata quarters of Constantinople, which had been destroyed by a fire the year before, and they designed a central slaughterhouse for the city and an urban regulation plan for nearby Smyrna (now Izmir). But, Frankl remembered, "little of the work" they did "ever got out of the blueprint stage. There was neither money, nor material, and very little inclination [on the part of the Turkish authori-

ties] to have things done; also, there was a war going on."[10]

Dealing with the Ottoman bureaucracy proved frustrating, but Frankl could count his blessings in other ways. Aside from occasional British air raids, he was safe, and his army salary, supplemented with money from home, allowed him to live comfortably. He attended functions at the Austrian and German embassies, and he was able to travel throughout western Anatolia. His work for the bank was hardly taxing; throughout most of 1918, he literally kept bankers' hours, which in Turkey, Frankl discovered—equally to his delight and consternation—amounted only to a four-day work week, further abbreviated by frequent holidays. As the head of the technical group, it was Frankl's responsibility to coordinate with the various government ministries, although, as the war wound down, the officials grew increasingly disinterested and uncooperative. Nonetheless, he reveled in the opportunity to design large-scale architectural projects. Wlach's experience proved invaluable, and Frankl was able to put his knowledge into practice and to learn much in the process.[11]

Frankl's wartime idyll ended abruptly in mid-October, when he received a cable from Vienna informing him that Paula was gravely ill with diphtheria. He applied for leave, which was immediately granted, but in the turmoil of the war's waning days he discovered that direct trains to Vienna were no longer running. Desperate to return, he found passage on a steamer bound for Crimea. On the morning of 14 October, his thirty-second birthday, he set off northward across the Black Sea. Once more, Frankl made a well-timed escape. Only a few days later, the British forced the Ottomans to surrender. Wlach and the other Austrian technical advisers were interned by the victorious Allies; they would not return home until the middle of 1919.

After what seemed to Frankl an interminable five-day journey, his ship finally docked in Odessa. The situation in revolutionary Russia under the new Bolshevik regime was even more chaotic than in Turkey. Train service was sporadic at best, and food and other essentials were in scarce supply. He waited at the station in Odessa for several days before managing to find a train headed for the Polish border. When he arrived in the Austrian Empire, he discovered that the trains were still running despite a severe coal shortage, but they were unheated and packed with soldiers and refugees. After three days of changing trains repeatedly, he arrived in Vienna, exhausted and half-frozen. [12]

In the intervening days, Paula's condition had worsened. Never robust, even in the best of times, her health had deteriorated during the last months of the war as food and fuel had become ever harder to find. By October, there was virtually no coal to be had in Vienna, and rationing had reduced the diet of most of the city's inhabitants to near starvation levels. Already weakened by years of deprivation, thousands of Viennese fell victim to the Spanish influenza that raged throughout the war's closing months. Eventually, more than fifteen thousand Viennese would succumb to the illness. Schools, theaters, and other public venues were closed periodically to prevent the spread of infection.

When Frankl departed for Constantinople, he left Paula with his mother at the villa on the Auhofstraße, but she missed her independence and soon moved out, leasing a small apartment at Rosenbursengasse 4 in the inner city. Frankl found her there in a terrible state with double pneumonia. He moved her to the Imperial Hotel, the finest in the city, which still had heat and food. But his attempts to nurse her back to health were in vain; she died a few days later, on 30 December 1918. [13]

Paula's death left Frankl deeply depressed, and the deteriorating political and economic situation did little to bolster his mood. The armistice in early November had brought a cessation of hostilities on the front, but they were soon replaced by pitched battles between radical and reactionary militants in the streets. Even before the peace declaration, the process of dismantling Austria-Hungary had commenced. Shortly before Frankl's return from Constantinople, Hungary and Czechoslovakia had declared independence and sealed their borders, cutting off all food and fuel shipments to the capital. On 11

November, Emperor Karl, who had succeeded Franz Josef only two years before, renounced the throne and a new Austrian Republic was declared. "The terms of the Armistice left Vienna a sad, melancholic city, the seat of a government whose lands were insufficient to feed its population," Frankl recorded. [14] Not only had Austria lost most of its outlying provinces, but most of the country's industries were now in foreign territory. The middle class, in their patriotic zeal, had bought government bonds to finance the war effort; the bonds were now worthless and most found themselves in much-reduced circumstances. By early 1919, the food shortage was so severe that Sigmund Freud, whose family had lost most of their savings, asked the Hungarian publisher of one of his articles to pay him in potatoes instead of cash. [15] It seemed that only the war profiteers and those who ran the city's burgeoning black market had benefited from the disintegration of the monarchy.

Early in 1919, Frankl began to contemplate his future. Paula's passing had severed his last ties with his homeland. He was no longer close to his brothers, whom he considered spoiled ne'er-do-wells. More than ever, he was anxious to free himself from his family bonds. He found the general atmosphere oppressive: "The more I saw of Europe and the hatred that motivated all and every action there the stronger grew my longing to return to America at the earliest possible moment." [16]

His timing, though, could not have been worse. The collapse of the Habsburg Empire and the punitive measures leveled against Austria by the Treaty of St. Germain brought on a spiraling, devastating inflation. By the autumn of 1919, the Austrian krone, which had been exchanged at a rate of five to the dollar before the outbreak of the war, was worth less than a penny and was falling steadily in value. Frankl had received a sizable inheritance after his father's death, but as he waited for a reentry permit to the United States, his assets began to dissolve away. Desperate, he disposed of his share of the family business, selling what remained to his three

brothers for cash. To conserve as much of the proceeds as possible, he made a hasty trip to Denmark, exchanging his Austrian currency for the more stable Danish krone.

Before he departed for America, Frankl also remarried. In the summer of 1919, while waiting for his visa to be granted, he had met a young woman, Isabella Dorn (fig. 28). Isa, as she was known to family and friends, was ten years younger than Frankl and possessed striking good looks. She was slim and tall, with blonde hair bobbed in the newest mode, and always immaculately dressed—"stylish," as Frankl's cousin Cis Zoltowska recalled, "in ways that had nothing to do with fashion." [17] Born in 1896 in Bregenz, on the shore of Lake Constance, she had moved with her family while still a young girl to a country house just outside Vienna, which her father, a career army officer, had purchased with a small pension. Later, she moved to the city and found work in a dress

shop. She and Frankl fell in love not long after meeting, and they were married in Salzburg in early March 1920. [18]

Isa shared Frankl's fervent desire to leave Europe. But they were otherwise dissimilar in personality and outlook. Despite his upper-class upbringing, Frankl cared little for the trappings of wealth. Fastidious in appearance and gentlemanly in manner, he nevertheless loathed affectation and snobbery. Though Isa's family was not as well to do as Frankl's, she too had grown up in comfortable circumstances; her father had even received a title of nobility for his service in the military. But she was far more concerned than her new husband with the pursuit of wealth and with outer material success. And while she possessed a flair for design, she never fully understood, or sympathized with, his artistic yearnings or sense of mission. [19]

Those differences would remain concealed for years. At the time, both were eager to leave Europe and find a new life in America. In mid-1920, only a few months after their wedding, Frankl and Isa departed on a steamer bound for Canada. After a brief stay in Toronto, the couple made their way to New York. [20] The day after their arrival they applied for permanent residency in the United States.

Fig. 28. Isa Frankl (née Isabella Dorn), early 1920s

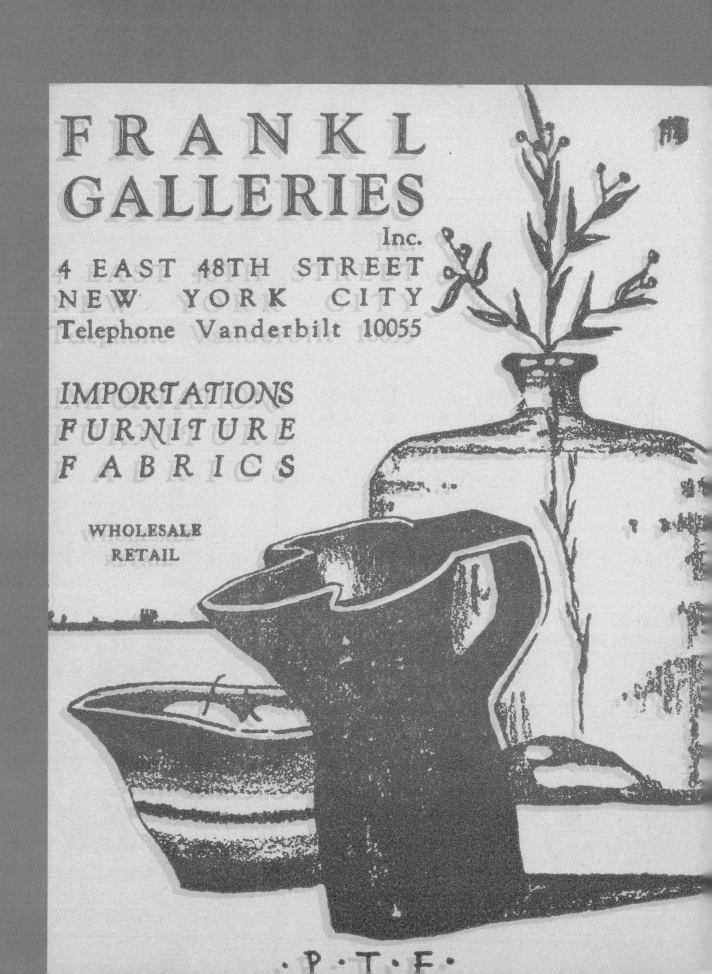

FRANKL
GALLERIES
Inc.
4 EAST 48TH STREET
NEW YORK CITY
Telephone Vanderbilt 10055

IMPORTATIONS
FURNITURE
FABRICS

WHOLESALE
RETAIL

· P · T · F ·

New Beginnings

Frankl's first years in New York after World War I were a time of frustration and search. For European exiles like Marcel Duchamp or Jules Pascin who had remained in the city, the last period of the conflict had offered a chance to explore new directions. But for Frankl, the experience brought only an interruption to his career and his quest for modern design. After an absence of nearly four years, he was forced to start his life there anew, painstakingly reestablishing contacts and building a new clientele.

The task proved much more daunting than during his first stay: in 1920, the fortunes of modernism in the United States were at a low ebb, and Frankl struggled for several years to make a living. But the early 1920s were not only a time of new beginnings for him personally; they also marked a new start for the modern movement in American design—and Frankl was determined to play a part in its making.

He discovered a New York very different from the city he had left in 1917. In the war's aftermath, the mood had changed. The conflict had interrupted the connections with modern European design. The pervasive anti-German sentiment spawned during the war led to a rejection of Germanic culture—including the new aesthetic currents arriving from Central Europe.[1] Frankl, like his fellow German and Austrian émigré designers, felt the backlash; for the first several years after his

Opposite:
Paul T. Frankl, advertisement for the Frankl Galleries, c. 1923 (detail of fig. 33)

return, he faced a decidedly adverse climate of opinion.

But it was not only anti-German feeling that he confronted: though many Americans exhibited a willingness to adopt new fashions and social customs in the wake of the war, they remained less open to experiments in art and design. The postwar *retour à l'ordre* (return to order) brought with it a period of cultural and artistic retrenchment that was felt throughout Europe and the United States.

In Europe, however, the end of the war also released fresh energies: with the dissolution of the old political system came an invigorated interest in reshaping long-established values and norms. The situation was very different on the other side of the Atlantic. At the very moment the European avant-garde was loudly affirming its commitment to a radical modernity, Americans sought sanctuary in the past, in the tried forms and aesthetic ideals of history. Most American architects remained wedded to the principles of the École de Beaux Arts and historical revivalism. The same held true for art and design. There was little sympathy, and less understanding, for modern painting and furniture. The new European art of "extreme simplification . . . produced 'according to mathematical principle'" and "strictly proletarian mood," as one American critic put it, left the public and most professionals cold.[2]

American business, sensing the mood, was reluctant to explore modern design ideas. By the early 1920s, many of the companies producing Arts and Crafts objects had folded. W. Frank Purdy, then the foremost American authority on industrial design, placed much of the blame for the new conservatism with the manufacturers, who had failed, in his words, to "give the public full confidence in American talent."[3] But others, including Richard F. Bach, curator of decorative arts at The Metropolitan Museum of Art, were convinced that, in the interest of economic and cultural development, the government should encourage manufacturers.[4] Bach acknowledged, though, that it would take more than governmental fiat to stimulate the development of American

design: the attitudes of industrialists, middlemen, and the buying public, he believed, all had to change.[5]

If American businesses, educators, and bureaucrats were slow to respond to the challenges of the postwar era, the tiny handful of German and Austrian designers and shop owners in New York quietly promoted the cause of modernism. Rena Rosenthal continued to operate her small shop on Madison Avenue (now renamed the Rena Rosenthal Studio).[6] And Edward Ascherman and Paul Zimmermann, who had also helped introduce Central European modernism to New York, continued to make and sell modern works.

They were now joined by others as well, most of whom had come from Europe on the eve of the war. One of the new arrivals was German artist and designer Winold Reiss. The son of one of Germany's most prominent portrait and landscape artists, Reiss had studied art in Munich before moving to the United States in 1913 to pursue his dream of painting American Indians. With little money to finance an expedition to the West, he settled in New York and soon earned a reputation as a teacher and designer.

Also among the new immigrants was Ilonka Karasz, who had arrived from Hungary in 1913. Trained at the School of Applied Arts in Budapest and influenced by contemporary Viennese design, Karasz settled in Greenwich Village and within a short time was contributing graphic works and illustrations to *The Masses*, *Bruno's Weekly*, *Playboy: A Portfolio of Art and Satire*, and other avant-garde publications.[7]

In late 1914, she and Reiss, together with several others, founded the Society of Modern Art. Their aim, as they wrote in a pamphlet announcing the society's creation, was "to advance the cause of the new art and graphic design." They established an office to "give gratuitous information on any phase of Modern Art and Design" and invited modern artists to exhibit and sell their work in the society's gallery. They also launched a magazine, *The Modern Art Collector*, devoted to contemporary European and American art and graphic design. But the enterprise was short-lived: the "resentment of German influence" effectively ended the

Fig. 29. Winold Reiss, Crillon Restaurant, New York, 1919–20

experiment in 1918. By the early 1920s, Reiss and Karasz found themselves, like most of the Central European modernists in New York, struggling to eke out a living.[8]

Reiss's only major commission of the early 1920s was for the Crillon Restaurant, at 15 East Forty-eighth Street (fig. 29). It employed the bold colors and radically simplified forms of the German and Austrian Jugendstil, though in a manner, as critic Edwin Avery Park declared, that was "in decidedly modern and thoroughly American taste, using flat surfaces [and] broad and colorful painted decoration based on patterns found in Navajo blankets and Indian pottery."[9] The restaurant's strident gold, red, and white color palette and clean lines were a stunning counterpoint to the traditional, historically inspired interiors that continued to dominate the New York scene. It gave an early glimpse of what was to come. But the Crillon, completed in 1920, remained an isolated example of the new design. Reiss managed to find a small number of private commissions, but it would be several years before he

or anyone else would have the opportunity to create a comparable work in the public eye.

The most conspicuous and successful of the new émigrés was Joseph Urban. Urban had been one of the leaders of the Viennese avant-garde at the turn of the century, cultivating his own personal version of the Jugendstil, one that combined the flowing lines and vegetal forms of French and Belgian Art Nouveau, the decorative patterning of Japonisme, and indigenous peasant art. After questions arose over his alleged financial mismanagement of the 1908 Imperial Jubilee, he moved to Boston where he took over as the chief set designer for the opera.[10] He remained there until 1915, when he was lured to New York to work as the stage designer for the Metropolitan Opera.

As the war dragged on, Urban began to produce designs for Florenz Ziegfeld's elaborate musical spectaculars, the Ziegfeld Follies.[11] His vibrant, colorful sets were based on the forms and decorative patterning of the Jugendstil—"a ritual of sumptuousness," as Lee Simonson described the

Fig. 30. Paul T. Frankl, advertisement for the Frankl Galleries on East Forty-eighth Street, 1921. Collection Paulette Frankl

results. The Ziegfeld Follies became hugely popular and, like Urban's fantastical sets for the Met, won much critical praise.[12] Urban was also able to put modernism before the American public in a series of sets designed for the International Film Service, a motion picture production company owned by newspaper magnate William Randolph Hearst. The films, most of which were vehicles for Hearst's mistress Marion Davies, were forgettable, but Urban's extraordinary backdrops evoked new worlds entirely unfamiliar to most Americans. Yet, like Frankl's prewar stage designs, what was acceptable to the public in the realm of make-believe was very different from that of ordinary life; in the end, Urban's efforts were confined almost entirely to the world of entertainment.

After the war, others arrived from Europe, including Swiss-born William Lescaze, who moved first to Cleveland before resettling in New York; and Walter von Nessen, who had trained with Bruno Paul in Berlin and spent time in Sweden before emigrating to the United States.[13] In the postwar years, modernism also found a champion on the West Coast—Kem Weber. Weber had come to the United States in 1914 to supervise the completion of the German pavilion at the Panama-Pacific International Exposition.

Like Frankl, he was stranded when the war broke out in Europe. He taught art in Santa Barbara for a time before moving, in 1921, to Los Angeles, where he began working for Baker Brothers, a progressive furniture manufacturer; eventually, he became chief designer for the company, responsible for creating the look of its furniture as well as the store's interiors and packaging.[14]

Frankl, upon his return to the United States in 1920, thus joined a small but determined group of immigrant designers seeking to overturn the old order and introduce the new aesthetic. His dream during his three-year-long hiatus in Europe had been to go back to New York and set up an architectural practice. But the task proved much more formidable than he had imagined. He had little capital and few potential clients; moreover, he discovered that the economy had not yet fully recovered from the war. Most of the established architectural firms, he later recalled, were "laying off employees, not hiring them."[15] With mounting bills and no income, Frankl accepted an offer from Lee Simonson to design sets for the production of *Sonya*, a play staged by the Theater Guild in the spring of 1921.[16]

Frankl was happy to be active once more in theater, but he was wary of trying to make a living in the unpredictable world of stage design. Throughout the late winter, he scoured the city for opportunities, hoping to land the right client or commission that would provide a proper launch for his new career. The problem of finding a job became even more acute when he learned in early spring that Isa was expecting their first child.[17]

With savings dwindling, Frankl was relieved when an old client from before the war called and asked him to design the interiors of his expansive new house on Long Island. Frankl rented a loft in the city for a studio and, with the client and his wife, began making all the necessary purchases to decorate the house. Because his credit had lapsed during his absence, he paid for all of the furnishings and fabrics with what cash he had on hand. After the couple failed to show up one day for an appointment, Frankl learned that they were getting a divorce—and, worse, they refused to reimburse him for the purchases.

He was able to return some, but not all, of the furniture and other decorative objects. The remainder he put on sale at the loft, which he hastily converted into a showroom. "For the second time," he wrote, "I was stuck in decorating."[18]

Frankl's new showroom was located in Midtown, at 4 East Forty-eighth Street, just around the corner from Fifth Avenue. It was a prestigious address, but Frankl's small space occupied the second floor and, without a street-level show window, was ill suited to retail trade. Yet, with the funds he had managed to bring with him from Vienna almost depleted, he was forced to try to make the showroom a success. In his first years in New York, he had done his best business with textiles, and so, in August 1921, he launched his new Frankl Galleries, specializing in "decorative fabrics" from Europe and the United States (fig. 30).

Frankl featured contemporary designs, especially linens from France and Austria, as well as traditional brocades and chintzes. Like Rosenthal, he also offered small decorative objects—boxes, vases, flowerpots, and figurines— mostly imports from Austria, as well as wallpapers and lighting fixtures. He was wary of attempting to sell modern furniture, convinced that there was not yet a market for it. The experience of his friend Urban the following year only confirmed that his instincts were correct.

In the summer of 1919, Urban had made the first of several return trips to Vienna. Alarmed by the plight of his fellow designers there, many of whom had become destitute in the wake of the Austrian economy's collapse, he decided to establish a branch of the Wiener Werkstätte in New York. (The company had, in fact, discussed the possibility in 1914, but the outbreak of the war forestalled the plan.)[19] Rather than forcing the artists and craftspeople to wait for their commissions until the objects were sold, Urban purchased as many as he could afford with cash, providing them with immediate financial relief. In June 1922, he opened a showroom of the Wiener Werkstätte of America on the second floor of 581 Fifth Avenue—just around the corner from Frankl's gallery.[20]

Urban's was not the only retail outlet in New York that offered contemporary European furnishings. In 1917, the Scandinavian Art Shop, which imported the newest designs from Sweden, had opened at 738 Madison Avenue.[21] But the elegant spaces Urban created to serve as the backdrop for the Werkstätte's products were far more extensive and advanced, revealing for the first time to the American public the full impact of the new, postwar aesthetic (fig. 31).[22] The showroom, consisting of a suite of six rooms, displayed not only recent works by the Werkstätte's designers and artisans (including Josef Hoffmann, Dagobert Peche, and

Fig. 31. Joseph Urban, showroom of the Wiener Werkstätte of America, New York, 1922

Fig. 32. Paul T. Frankl,
flyer announcing the
expansion of the Frankl
Galleries, 1923. Collection
Paulette Frankl

Michael Powolny) but also paintings by Gustav Klimt, Egon
Schiele, and other Austrian modernists.

The opening of the showroom—and several exhibitions Urban arranged in other major cities—aroused considerable interest in both the popular and professional
press.[23] A reviewer for the *Christian Science Monitor*
expressed hope that the displays might encourage
Americans to accept modernism: "Something of . . . the
Puritan strain persists in the United States and even
American artists are inclined to look with suspicion on
gayety [*sic*] in art. But here in the Viennese exhibit are lots
of things done just almost in the spirit of fun and yet no
less beautiful."[24] Other observers, however, asked
whether homeowners would ever embrace the new look.[25]
The question turned out to be prophetic: in the end, the
Wiener Werkstätte furnishings and other objects were too

severe and foreign for American tastes. Wartime preju-
dices still lingered; few Americans were willing to accept
such radical new designs. After a little more than a year,
Urban had to close his showroom. The entire venture cost
$150,000, nearly bankrupting him.[26]

Frankl was quick to grasp the lessons of the Werkstätte's demise. The time was not yet ripe, he conclud-
ed—at least for the effusive modernism of the Viennese:
"The American public, I realized, had first to be made
to understand and to like what we were doing before it
could be sold. I, therefore, embarked on an educational
campaign, pure and simple. A slow way, to be sure,
but without limitless funds for publicity and advertising
it was the only approach open."[27]

For the next several years, Frankl took every opportunity
to present his ideas to the public. Progress, he found, was
agonizingly slow. He gave frequent talks before the Art-
in-Trades Club, an organization of manufacturers,
designers, decorators, buyers, advertisers, and others
involved in the "industrial arts." But the group remained
"deeply entrenched in the traditional styles of the past
and deathly afraid of modern."[28]

Undismayed, Frankl found other avenues to spread the
word. When an acquaintance of his, Sherrill Whiton, director of the New York School of Interior Decoration, asked
him to join the faculty, he promptly accepted.[29] Frankl
turned out to be a natural teacher. He was enthusiastic,
engaging, and, as ever, charming. Part of his success was
due to the relaxed atmosphere he created. "I never lec-
tured," he wrote later. "I always tried to talk common sense,
explaining whatever subject was before us in simple
terms—realizing that we had to see problems in their
utmost simplicity before even attempting to solve them."
Frankl's approach was novel in other ways as well: "I always
thought it best to visualize decorating in its three-dimen-
sional aspect, and therefore started my sketches in perspective rather than in two-dimensional floor plans and
equally flat elevations. The floor surface I divided into traffic lanes and parking spaces—the latter set aside for the

placement of furniture—furniture always to be used with
restraint, never in abundance, never over-furnish. Those
talks I illustrated with broad strokes of colorful chalks, held
on edge, quickly thrown on newsprint paper. The students,
uncertain at first, came around and sided with me." [30]

Teaching proved to be one of Frankl's few rewards.
Business was dismal. The gallery, in spite of his best
efforts, remained barely profitable. [31]

Rather than sit by idly, he decided in 1922 to take his
crusade on the road. He hired a booking agent to arrange a
lecture tour of the East and Midwest. He gave the first talk
in New Jersey, at the Newark Museum. He followed it with
a series of "one-night stands" in cities up and down the
East Coast and in the Midwest. "I talked to crowds of star-
tled people," he would recall years afterward, "discussed
problems that puzzle and confuse anyone who undertakes
to furnish a home. I talked to them about the houses they
lived in, explaining my job, delivered my message in simple words anybody could understand. As free Americans I
told them not to be befuddled and confused into believing
that they had to please some French Louis or Elizabethian
[*sic*] Queen with the furnishings they had in their homes.
They were 'king' and modern decoration bowed to no one,
but was intended for the comfort and pleasure of the men
and women for whom it was designed." [32]

When Frankl returned to New York in early 1923, he
learned that the art gallery that occupied the ground floor
below his loft was preparing to vacate. The building's
owner offered him the space. Frankl lacked the capital to
expand, and at first he hesitated. Lotte Stoehr, his former
client, convinced him that adding the ground floor made
sense, and she offered to underwrite the venture as a
silent partner. Assured by her financial backing, he signed
the lease and took over the downstairs rooms (fig. 32).

The move to prime ground-floor retail space, with a
show window just off Fifth Avenue, greatly increased the
gallery's visibility. To attract the throngs of midtown shop-
pers, Frankl paid careful attention to the show window. He
changed the displays daily, featuring colorful decorative

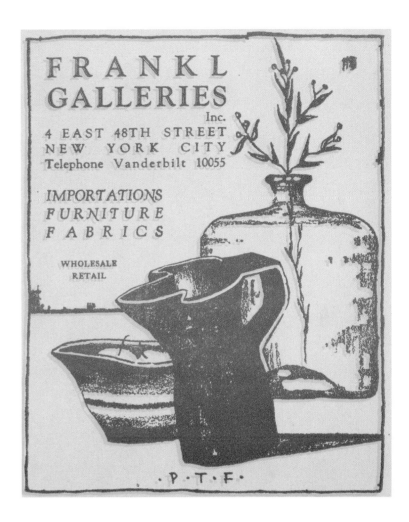

accessories "of the unusual and distinctive"—as one of his
advertisements proclaimed. [33] The enlarged sales area
allowed him to expand the gallery's offerings. Still unable
to find the sort of modern and handmade objects he wanted in the United States, he turned to Europe. He hired
Thérèse Bonney, an American expatriate living in Paris, to
serve as his purchasing agent and to keep him abreast of
the latest developments in France.

Bonney, who had studied French theater at the
Sorbonne, established a press service in the early 1920s,
specializing in photographs and written accounts of
modern French design and architecture. Her vivid photographs of shop fronts, window displays, graphic art, cafés,
restaurants, theaters, nightclubs, and bars captured the
latest in chic design. She regularly dispatched prints to

Fig. 33. Paul T. Frankl,
advertisement for the
Frankl Galleries, c. 1923.
Collection Paulette Frankl

Fig. 34. Postcard from Frankl to his son, Peter, 1925, featuring a print by Georg Grosz. Private collection

Frankl and made the rounds of the shops and ateliers for him, acquiring a broad assortment of objects, textiles, and small furnishings.[34]

In an effort to keep up the flow of decorative articles, he and Isa also began to make annual trips across the Atlantic in the late summer to search for new merchandise.[35] Their usual itinerary took them first to Paris, and from there to Austria, Germany, and Italy. In addition to recent Parisian designs, Frankl, by 1923, was importing rustic pottery from Florence, Murano and Bohemian glass, Daum crystal, linens made by the Lyon manufacturer Bianchini and Ferrier (with motifs by the painter Raoul Dufy), pottery by H. A. Kahler from Denmark, and other "objets d'art."[36] He also acquired modern Viennese ceramics by Susi Singer and Vally Wieselthier.[37] To recoup the costs of maintaining his Paris buying office, he began purchasing ever-larger quantities of goods. When he discovered that the shop's retail trade alone was insufficient to sell all of his acquisitions, he launched a wholesale business, shipping to department stores and gift shops across the country (fig. 33).[38]

Frankl also used his frequent stays in Europe to research the latest trends in architecture and design. He was especially drawn to the works of Parisian architects Robert Mallet-Stevens and André Lurçat, Dutch architect J. J. P. Oud, French furniture designers Georges Djo-

Bourgeois and Louis Sognot, Swedish designer Carl Malmsten, and German designers Bruno Paul and Heinrich Tessenow. Much of what attracted his interest might now be characterized as "conservative modernism." But Frankl's dogged pursuit of the new also led him to look farther afield. By 1924, he had more than a passing familiarity with the avant-garde. He read Le Corbusier's texts and the writings of other prominent modernists; he collected books and prints of Paul Klee, Georg Grosz, and other artists; and, while on one of his trips to Germany, he visited the Bauhaus in Weimar (fig. 34).

Frankl found his trips to Europe instructive and stimulating, yet they were also frustrating. The rapid advance of modernism across the Atlantic caused him to question anew its slow progress in the United States. He saw that there were hints of the future all around him in New York, and he took it upon himself to be the messenger of that news. During his travels abroad, he began to lecture on contemporary developments in architecture in the United States. In 1924, while in Paris, he presented a talk to the Société des Architectes Française on the new skyscrapers, showing photographs of the buildings taken by his friend Ralph Steiner. He repeated the lecture a week later in Vienna before the Österreichischer Architekten-Verein (Austrian Association of Architects). "These lectures on modern architecture, or rather the slides illustrating them," he reported, "created a furor amongst architects, both in Paris and Vienna, and the discussions that followed made me realize the impact they had on the audience. Seeing the first stepback structures in New York had aroused deep excitement in me—that was the reason I took the pictures abroad, surmising that they would be of interest to others—never expecting the spontaneous, unreserved, implicit acceptance." Frankl understood immediately the significance of the response: "Then and there I came to realize that America had come of age. The skyscraper, at first but an overgrown architectural freak, at last had found its legitimate place in architecture—its new setback form void of meaningless trimmings, an appropriate solution for its function—setting a style expressive of our time."[39]

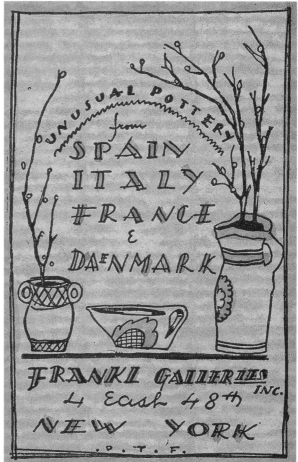

But in 1924, what the skyscraper form might mean in terms of a new design aesthetic, he was not yet prepared to see.

With the enlargement of the gallery space and the inclusion of an expanding array of decorative articles, Frankl established the foundation of the shop for the next decade. Even in its heyday in the late 1920s, his commercial fortunes relied less on his custom furniture than on import sales and the fees he earned as an interior design consultant. It was Frankl's ability to find alluring objects—and to display them beautifully in the shop's window and showroom—that allowed him to appeal to a clientele still unconvinced by modernism. Isa, who discovered her own skill for arranging the displays, became his very able assistant.

Frankl's promise to offer "the unusual and distinctive," however, was not entirely dependent on imports. Undaunted by the tepid reception to modern design, he gradually

Far left:
Fig. 35. Paul T. Frankl, flyer advertising Christmas cards and gifts at the Frankl Galleries, c. 1923. Collection Paulette Frankl

Above:
Fig. 36. Paul T. Frankl, package seals, Frankl Galleries, 1923–24. Collection Paulette Frankl

Left:
Fig. 37. Paul T. Frankl, flyer advertising the Frankl Galleries, 1924. Collection Paulette Frankl

Fig. 38. Paul T. Frankl,
Peasant Furniture,
on display at the Frankl
Galleries in the late
summer of 1925

introduced his own and others' examples of the new aesthetic. His first attempt was a line of Christmas cards. Frankl devised a simple, outwardly naive rendering style featuring crudely drawn symbols of the holidays—wreaths, candles, and Christmas trees—to adorn the hand-printed cards (fig. 35). In spite of their evident allegiance to modernist austerity, the cards became surprisingly popular, and they accounted for one of the gallery's first breakthroughs.⁴⁰ Several newspapers and magazines carried articles about them, prompting a flurry of sales. Frankl also designed almost all of the company's advertisements, sales flyers, and packaging (figs. 36, 37); his spare, ebullient style

became a hallmark of the gallery and a visible testament to his commitment to the new aesthetic culture.

But Frankl's greatest early commercial success sprang from an unexpected source. Lotte Stoehr, who remained an enthusiastic supporter of Frankl's mission to introduce modern design, turned out to be more than a silent partner. While Frankl was away on a buying trip to Europe, she happened upon a German company that produced matches with sparkling, multihued heads. The so-called chintz matches were packaged in colorful boxes, and Stoehr, unable to resist, placed a large order with the manufacturer. When Frankl returned a few months later, he found the basement of the gallery jammed with crates of the matches. He "was taken aback and failed to see why anyone would import matches to a country where they were given away free." Fearing financial disaster, he hesitantly put the matches on display in the shop only to discover, to his astonishment, that they were hugely popular. Frankl sold the matches for thirty-five cents a box—a hefty amount at the time. He also wholesaled them to gift stores around the country and marketed them directly through national magazine advertisements; within a few months, the gallery was selling five hundred dollars in matches a day. [41] The income Frankl generated from the chintz matches and other imports was more than enough to keep the gallery afloat. With a steady base of income established, he finally felt secure enough to experiment with more ambitious design ideas.

His first effort was a group of "Peasant Furniture" (fig. 38) based on earlier English and, especially, American colonial models. The vogue for American colonial furniture went back to the 1890s, part of the neoclassical revival that followed the World's Columbian Exposition. Both antiques and period reproductions of the colonial era remained popular in the 1920s; they were among the best-selling furniture style for the middle-class market. Frankl's interest in the colonial revival style was fired by his belief in the importance of asserting American values. But the designs also reflected his continuing devotion to the ideals of the Arts and Crafts movement: in their spare forms, he found a means for enunciating the qualities of simplicity and craft first announced by John Ruskin, William Morris, and their followers years before.

The impact of the English Arts and Crafts movement had been deeply felt in Austria and Germany before the war. Frankl, like many of the designers of his generation, saw in the continuation of the Arts and Crafts vision one still-viable route to modernism: the recourse to earlier "peasant" forms suggested a new basis for design, one freed of the artifice of historicism. That most of his Peasant pieces bore the clear mark of the past was less important to him than the implication of a new truthfulness. The

Fig. 39. Frankl at his desk in Woodstock, mid-1920s

expression of integrity was not merely formal; Frankl drew from the Arts and Crafts ideal of the honest presentation of natural materials: "The greatest Art of the Cabinet maker is to preserve the life and beauty in a Tree and to give it new expression through his work. ART IS LIFE," proclaimed one of his brochures for the Peasant Furniture. [42]

Although Frankl acknowledged his debt to the English reform movement, his more immediate inspiration for the Peasant Furniture came from his experiences in Woodstock, New York, where he bought a small cabin in the early 1920s. The little community in the Catskill Mountains had, by the time he arrived, been an artists' colony for more than two decades. Founded just after the turn of the century by Ralph Radcliffe Whitehead, a devotee of Ruskin and Morris, and novelist Hervey White, Woodstock gained renown for its free-spirited, bohemian atmosphere. Because of its close proximity to Manhattan, it offered a ready place for artists to escape from the city—and to work and exhibit. In 1919, the local artists, both traditional and modern, united to found the Woodstock Artists Association, which organized exhibitions during the summer when most of the New York galleries were dormant. [43]

Frankl often drove up to Woodstock on the weekends, and he spent part of each summer there. He used his time to paint and write, and to socialize (fig. 39). Ever affable

Fig. 40. Paul T. Frankl, announcement for an exhibition of peasant costumes in Woodstock mounted by the Frankl Galleries, 1925. Collection Paulette Frankl

and open, he was most happy in groups of artists and intellectuals, and he formed friendships with many of the Woodstock regulars. Painters George Bellows, John Carroll, Leon Kroll, Yasuo Kuniyoshi, and Eugene Speicher; sculptor Alexander Archipenko; potter Carl Walters; photographer Margaret Bourke-White; writers Manuel Komroff, Frank Scully, and J. P. McEvoy; and publisher Alfred A. Knopf all belonged to Frankl's regular circle. His small cabin, perched on a steep wooded hillside near Bearsville, had a large back porch that became, as he would remember, a center of "animated, at times bristling conversation."[44]

Frankl loved the informality of Woodstock. The entrance to the cabin was through the kitchen, and his many friends often stopped in unannounced. He decorated the two-room space simply, making use of some basic, rustic furnishings he found in secondhand shops around the area. What he was unable to scavenge he fashioned himself out of materials from the local hardware store. His own living space thus became a field for experimentation, a place to try out new ideas and materials. In the casual and unaffected surroundings of Woodstock, Frankl found a domestic ideal of plainness. He translated that idea into the Peasant Furniture.

The rustic furniture fit perfectly into the gallery's program. Much of what he and Isa had been importing from Europe was founded on older ideas of handicraft; the new furniture was merely an extension of the same appreciation of plainness and artistry. But Frankl's growing interest in folk design extended beyond furniture: beginning in 1923, he started to acquire peasant costumes during his European buying trips, and in the summer of 1925, he mounted an exhibition of traditional clothing at the Jack Horner Shop in Woodstock (fig. 40). The success of the show, which drew the attention and praise of the Woodstock culturati, offered further encouragement to introduce his new furniture line that fall.

The Peasant Furniture was well received by the shop's clientele and the critics alike. In spite of their somewhat unconventional look, the designs were regarded — in

$90, the "Welsh Dresser" at $160—far more than comparable pieces in most stores (fig. 42).

The effect of the ensemble was one of deluxe austerity, an image of country simplicity intended for a wealthy elite. It was a potent, and in many ways original, expression. But it was not yet a truly modern one.

· P R I C E   L I S T ·
PAUL T. FRANKL PEASANT FURNITURE

All prices F.O.B. New York City.   Crating and shipping at cost.

W   O   O   D   S   T   O   C   K   S   E   T

P T F	2601 /6'	Large Table, 6 ft. long, 32 in. wide, 30 in. high	$75.00
P T F	2601 /7'	Large Table, 7 ft. long, 32 in. wide, 30 in. high	80.00
P T F	2601 /8'	Large Table, 8 ft. long, 36 in. wide, 30 in. high	90.00
P T F	2602	Bench to match Tables	30—35
P T F	2605	Welsh Dresser, White Pine	160.00
P T F	2608	Cottage Bed—single, White Pine	90.00
P T F	2609	Cottage Bed—double, White Pine	110.00
P T F	1659	Windsor Armchair, Maple	48.00

F R A N K L   G A L L E R I E S, INC.
4 East 48th Street, New York City
Sole distributors of Paul T. Frankl Furniture.

Above left:
Fig. 41. Paul T. Frankl, dining room hutch from the Peasant Furniture collection, c. 1925

Above right:
Fig. 42. Peasant Furniture price list, c. 1925. Collection Paulette Frankl

contrast to the Wiener Werkstätte objects Urban had introduced three years before—as reasonable and acceptable.[45] Some of the pieces, like the Windsor chair and the trestle table, were modeled directly on older examples; others, such as Frankl's dining room hutch (fig. 41), betrayed the unmistakable imprint of his distinctive aesthetic sensibility. They were at once, as he intended them, manifestly old *and* new.

The rustic cast of the furniture belied its costliness. Frankl had the individual pieces made by local cabinetmakers, who fashioned them from relatively inexpensive woods; nonetheless, their prices greatly exceeded what many Americans were able to afford—even in the very prosperous 1920s. The double "Cottage Bed" was listed at

CHAPTER SIX

Experiments in Form

Frankl's Peasant Furniture expressed a nascent version of modernism. But by the end of 1925, he was at work on a series of designs that would demonstrate more fully than any of his previous works his commitment to the new aesthetic.

Opposite:
Paul T. Frankl, Puzzle
Desk, c. 1925 (detail of
fig. 46)

The story of the sudden emergence of Frankl's new manner is today clouded, and will likely remain so. He may have already begun to sell his own modern furniture in his shop as early as the spring of 1925. If he did, the press paid no attention; the earliest published evidence of his modern designs does not appear until 1926. [1] Frankl later wrote little about his specific activities in this time. In his autobiography, he makes a few passing references to his belief in the need to create a "contemporary American" furniture style, but he is otherwise silent on his early activities as a furniture designer. [2] What is clear from the few published images and the small handful of surviving examples is that the period between the fall of 1925 and the end of 1926 was for Frankl one of intense experimentation. It was to be his annus mirabilis. In the brief span of little more than a year, he laid the foundation for a novel and personal design idiom.

Fig. 43. Paul T. Frankl, table with canted supports, c. 1925

Early on, Frankl, like most of his fellow American modernists, drew insistently from contemporary European designs. A large table with canted supports, which probably dates to the middle of 1925, borrowed from the early postwar designs of Josef Hoffmann and Dagobert Peche (fig. 43). Not only is the dark, ebonized finish redolent of the Austrian modernists, but Frankl's addition of fluting along the base is an almost literal quotation of Hoffmann's neoclassicism.[3] Frankl also borrowed from other sources. A veneered cabinet published in Edwin Avery Park's book *New Backgrounds for a New Age* (1927), an important early review of modern American design, reveals the influence of contemporary Parisian designers, in particular, Jacques-Emile Ruhlmann, Georges Djo-Bourgeois, Edgar Brandt, and Paul Follot (fig. 44).[4]

Modern French design had attracted interest from Americans already in the early 1920s. In the aftermath of the war, the American cultural elite continued to look to France for ideas, and the latest accomplishments of the French were discussed and debated in the leading art and trade publications.[5] But the new French mode found little acceptance in the United States until the 1925 Paris Exposition Internationale des Arts Décoratifs et Industriels Modernes.

The exhibition, the first of its kind mounted after the war, offered a glimpse at the full spectrum of contemporary European design currents, from the elegant gestures of the French designers to the more extreme offerings of Le Corbusier and Konstantin Melnikov. It was originally conceived in 1912 as a reaction to the success of the show of German crafts at the 1910 Salon d'Automne. The French, fearing the loss of their prestige and the commercial advantage they had long held over the Germans in the design field, planned the show for 1915. With the outbreak of World War I, however, it had to be postponed, and it was not until 1922 that planning for the exhibition resumed. A large number of countries eventually participated, but conspicuously absent were Germany, which was not invited because of persistent anti-German feelings in France, and the United States, which declined to take part.

The account of the United States' refusal to send a national display has been much repeated. Although the French organizers of the exhibition extended an invitation to the United States in 1922 and offered a prime site for the American pavilion, the call stipulated that all of the works "represent the modern decorative and industrial arts."[6] Any imitation of historical styles was "strictly prohibited." In almost every later version, the decision for the United States' refusal rests with Herbert Hoover, then U.S. Secretary of Commerce, who sent inquiries to prominent educators, manufacturers, and leaders in the arts establishment about whether there was anything to exhibit and was informed that the United States had made scant or no progress in modern design. The later Hoover Commission report on the Paris exposition, which states that the invitation "was declined on the ground that American manufacturers and craftsmen had almost nothing to exhibit conceived in the modern spirit," bolstered this explanation.[7]

In truth, there were other reasons for the U.S. decision. Government authorities, and indeed many within the design world, were unclear about what exactly constituted modern design. Frankl and the small number of other designers working in modern styles—mostly in New York and on the West Coast—were outsiders, almost invisible to U.S. trade and business organizations. Also, the Commerce Department conducted its survey during the Christmas season—undoubtedly why many of those queried failed to respond. Moreover, Hoover was reluctant to expend a large amount of money on the exhibition, especially because he feared that the U.S. display would be vastly inferior to that of the French.[8]

Though the United States was not represented, Hoover did appoint a commission to visit Paris and prepare a report for the benefit of American manufacturers. Thousands of other Americans crossed the Atlantic to see the exhibition, including representatives of the various U.S. trade associations. The wide-ranging displays presented a clear view of the new design in all its varied guises. But American critics, artists, and tourists alike focused their gaze on the French section, which covered nearly two-thirds of the fifty-seven-acre site. Preoccupied with a perceived German superiority in both design production and education, the French authorities sought to overwhelm their visitors with an impression of French excellence, originality, and artisanship.[9]

What the French designers presented was a pared-down classicism, with borrowings from Cubism, Futurism, and Expressionism. Most American visitors recognized the attempt to fashion a new aesthetic without jettisoning past traditions and forms. Yet the reaction of many, notwithstanding their admiration of French culture, was outspokenly negative. One New York decorator wrote afterward that the furniture was "entirely freakish…extreme in its tendencies and not adaptable to the ordinary lives of our people."[10] Ellow H. Hostache, another American designer who visited the exhibition, described the offerings as the "bastard offspring of anemic artisanship and efficient salesmanship…the dictatorship of ornament."[11]

But a few prominent voices extolled the French Art Moderne. Henry W. Frohne, editor of *Good Furniture Magazine*, wrote on his return to New York that he believed that "the new art will undoubtedly influence American designers."[12] From the tiny cast of modernists in the United States also came praise. Kem Weber, who visited the Paris exposition that summer, became even more determined to pursue the new design, and he urged Americans to look to Europe for inspiration.[13]

One of those who heeded the call was Eugene Schoen. Born in 1880, Schoen studied at Columbia University and subsequently made a pilgrimage to Vienna, where he met Hoffmann, Otto Wagner, and several of the other leading Secessionists. When he returned to New York in 1905, he established his own architectural practice. After seeing the Paris exposition, Schoen converted his practice to interiors and furnishings in the Art Moderne style. He purchased a building on East Sixtieth Street to house his new office and opened a retail gallery space on the ground floor to display his own and others' designs of furniture, lighting, textiles, and objects.[14] Schoen's designs merged the pure geometries and material sumptuousness he had

Fig. 44. Paul T. Frankl, veneered cabinet, c. 1925

Fig. 45. Eugene Schoen, living room ensemble, c. 1926

taken from the Viennese with the elegance and softened contours of the French (fig. 45). His innovative mixture was animated and urbane; its evident refinement immediately won over a number of clients.

The heavy press coverage of the Paris exposition and Schoen's provocative furnishings aided in sounding the alarm of impending change. But the loudest indications came from a series of exhibitions in the United States. The first was a traveling exhibition of furniture and other objects from the Paris exposition that took place in 1926.[15] The show's organizer was Charles R. Richards, whom Hoover had appointed to head the commission to report on the Paris show. After the exhibit closed, Richards selected a representative group of objects to tour the United States. The exhibition opened in Boston and stopped next at The Metropolitan Museum of Art in New

York, before traveling on to Cleveland, Chicago, Detroit, St. Louis, Minneapolis, and Philadelphia, attracting impressive crowds at every venue.[16]

Across the country, American department stores, eager to introduce the new aesthetic to their customers, put on their own exhibitions of the leading French designers.[17] Lord and Taylor exhibited a modernist room at its store in the fall of 1925, featuring objects from France, Germany, Austria, and Italy, and employed two French artists, Drian and Boutet de Monvel, to design its Fifth Avenue windows.[18] Several other stores, including Macy's and Wanamaker's, followed suit. The impact of these shows was almost immediate. Within a year of the Paris exposition, a number of designers and firms in New York were producing works in the "modern manner": Arthur Crisp, Walter Kantack, Max Kuehne, the Arden Studios, F. Schumacher and Company, and W. and J. Sloan all began offering objects in the Art Moderne style. And Parisian designer Jules Bouy, who moved to New York to oversee the American branch of Ferrobrandt, Edgar Brandt's metalwork company, brought a direct French interpretation of the new mode.[19]

The Paris exhibition may have been a revelation for Schoen and others, but for Frankl, who regularly read French design and architecture magazines and had been traveling to Paris annually, it was merely confirmation of what he already knew well. In the Exposition des Arts Décoratifs et Industriels Modernes, he found not aesthetic epiphany but opportunity: the burgeoning interest in modern design offered the first hints of its acceptance in the United States. Frankl perceived the changed mood, and he sought to exploit his advantage.

But how to do so? Frankl's veneered cabinet, which probably dates to the fall of 1925, reproduced the smooth lines and classical sensibility of the French designers. It was a summons to the public to witness firsthand the new design—and to buy it. Equally for Frankl, the cabinet was an experiment in form making, one of his many attempts to work out a new manner. The problem, as he discovered, lay in part in translating the French style to New York. Like Schoen, whose first designs mimicked the prominent

Parisian designers, Frankl had the piece crafted by local cabinetmakers, whose skills often fell below their French counterparts. At first glance, the cabinet bore the look of Ruhlmann and Djo-Bourgeois, but it lacked the fine execution of the French originals. Although Frankl's design posed a challenge to period revivalism, it could in no way have been mistaken for its Parisian models.

Frankl, who for the moment was less concerned with quality than with form, also looked beyond France for creative stimulus. He continued to observe the scene in Germany. He remained especially interested in the works of Bruno Paul.[20] And Frankl was not the only designer in New York promoting contemporary German ideas in 1925. The graphic artist Lucian Bernhard, a close friend of Frankl's who had arrived from Berlin two years before, brought with him the latest concepts of the German Werkbund; within a short time, he was producing not only innovative posters but also trademarks, packaging, type, textiles, and furniture.[21]

Frankl, though, remained committed to finding an idiom that conveyed not only modern realities but also the spirit of America—without cadging it from the Europeans. Throughout the fall of 1925 and the early winter of 1926, he continued his pursuit of an appropriate design language. His "Puzzle Desk" (fig. 46), which likely dates from the end of 1925, presented a tentative answer. Its contours and overall form hinted at the influence of French design, but its elemental forms and the random placement of its silver-leafed drawers revealed a decidedly different attitude. Even with its "suggestion of the oriental," as Edwin Park put it, the desk was inarguably new, a ringing statement of modernity.[22] With it, Frankl announced a shift in his work, away from European models and toward a novel and personal design vision.

By the middle of 1926, the Frankl Galleries sported numerous examples of his new manner, including various chairs, étagères, cabinets, a "telephone desk," and several lamps. Frankl's contribution was almost immediately recognized. His works were highlighted in two articles published in the fall of that year celebrating the breakthrough of the Art Moderne, and Eugene Clute, former

editor of *Architectural Review* and *Pencil Points*, devoted several full pages of plates to Frankl's designs in his book *The Treatment of Interiors*.[23]

Despite his success, Frankl realized that the Puzzle Desk and his other new furniture still lacked what Clute called a "distinct national character."[24] But already in the summer of 1925, he had begun to work out the basis for a design vocabulary that would offer an unmistakably American interpretation of modernism and thrust him into the forefront of the new design movement in the United States.

Fig. 46. Paul T. Frankl, Puzzle Desk, c. 1925

SKY
SCRAPER
FURNITURE
FRANKL GALLERIES
4 EAST 48th ST. NEW YORK

CHAPTER SEVEN

Skyscraper Style

Frankl spent the summer of 1925 in Woodstock. Isa, who never shared his fondness for the Catskills, took their son, Peter, and went to Vienna for the season. Many of his friends and acquaintances set off for Paris to see the Exposition Internationale. But Frankl, "realizing that we had to work on our own solution and in order not to be influenced by the French exhibit," decided to stay home.[1]

He spent his time painting and sketching out ideas for new furniture designs. He also did some work for Lotte Stoehr, who had moved several old barns and other outbuildings to her nearby farm and asked Frankl to convert them into studios. He enjoyed the challenge. He had long been convinced that old barns fit better into the rolling landscape than new houses, and the task gave him a rare opportunity to hone his architectural skills. To furnish the spaces, he fashioned a few trestle tables and benches of local chestnut, which he had sandblasted to highlight the grain. Rather than finishing the pieces, he sealed the surfaces with boiled linseed oil and then waxed them. These first, robust furnishings became the basis of the "Woodstock Set" of his Peasant Furniture, which he introduced that fall.[2]

Frankl also spent time that summer renovating and rearranging the interiors of his cabin. One of his projects was to transform his work—and, ultimately, the direction of modern American design.

Opposite:
Paul T. Frankl, cover of Skyscraper Furniture brochure, c. 1927 (see fig. 62)

Fig. 47. Frankl's son, Peter, with the first Skyscraper bookcase in Woodstock, mid-1920s

The idea came to him while trying to reduce the clutter in the small cabin. "I had an assemblage of books littered all over the house," he would remember years afterward, "amongst them profusely illustrated architectural tomes, large in format, some coverless, awkward to handle, impossible to fit in any existing space. To straighten things out and bring order out of chaos, I went after some boards and with a saw set to work fitting the case to the books, since the books would not fit a case. . . . The result was a corner bookcase with a rather large, bulky lower section and a slender, shallow upper part going straight to the ceiling. It was a natural—the top of the lower part formed a table to hold a lamp, flowers, magazines and the like. It had a new look; the neighbors came and said, 'It looks just like the new skyscrapers'" (fig. 47).[3]

Frankl was soon making other versions of the new "Skyscraper" bookcases for friends in Woodstock, each time improving on his first, rudimentary design. What attracted him was not only their practicality. It also struck him that their form had arisen directly from experience: "The design—not even put on pencil and paper—was developed solely from the need it fulfilled—call it functional if you must—its appeal, its utilitarian purpose, like water flowing into crevices and crannies to find its own level." Frankl realized that the skyscraper form offered a first, tentative answer to the problem of finding an unabashedly American expression. "Unknowingly, almost effortlessly," he would write, "I had accomplished what I was striving for, expressing the creative spirit of the time that prompted it." Late that summer, he began drawing "all kinds of space-saving" furniture, "all of it plain in design, void of decoration, rising from the floor, clinging to the wall, often to ceiling height" (fig. 48).[4]

His discovery came precisely at the right moment. In the wake of the Paris exposition, Frankl sensed that the time might finally be right to introduce modern furniture in America. That summer, he had traveled into the city from time to time to attend to the shop. While there, he received reports from Thérèse Bonney about the progress of the Paris exposition. From her descriptions and the accounts he heard from people returning from France, he became convinced that a change in the public opinion about modernism was in the offing.[5]

To take advantage of what he believed would be a new demand for modern furniture, Frankl rented the fifth floor of one of the buildings adjacent to the shop and rearranged it into a showroom, using his new Skyscraper designs as the centerpiece of the space. The effect was dramatic. One entered the new showroom directly from the elevator. Toward the north, he described, the room

had a solid expanse of glass. . . . The cold light was mellowed by flimsy curtains of chartreuse chiffon hanging from ceiling to floor. The rays filtering through their ample fullness gave a subdued elegance to that room. Silhouetted against the curtains was a long, low modern step-table, lacquered black, Chinese in feeling; on either side, resting on elaborately carved teakwood stands, stood two huge glass jars. They were filled with water, and black and gold Japanese fantails floated amongst rocks, lush with water ferns. Opposite the entrance was a combination bookcase desk of skyscraper design that reached to the ceiling. That large piece was made of redwood, which I used extensively to underscore the American origin of that furniture—other pieces made of plywood were finished with two-tone opaque lacquer, sprayed with a gun—spraying then a new technique. The room adjacent, a dining room, had walls covered in large squares of light beige-colored Japanese grass-cloth, put up in checkerboard fashion. The dining table, mirror-topped like a pool, reflected the sparkling silver, crystal and china adorning it. The rooms opened into each other through the square-topped arches, cut into partitions were narrow niches, allowing the eye to wander on, adding interest to the wall, also providing attractive frames for the organ cacti placed in them—their simple lines relating them to the modern home.[6]

The expense of setting up the new showroom consumed nearly all of Frankl's available capital. But the gamble paid off. Edwin Park observed a year and a half

Fig. 48. Paul T. Frankl, Skyscraper bookcase, c. 1927

*"Don't you just love my
skyscraper furniture?"*

Fig. 49. Cartoon from
the *New Yorker*,
10 March 1928

later that Frankl's decision to seize the opportunity had
thrust him into the forefront of the movement: "After
long years of trying to show the public that modern art was
less dangerous than beautiful, courageous years of scant
success, Mr. Frankl is at length, and partly due to his own
efforts, in a most advantageous situation, for as the taste
for things modern permeates our society, the field is
almost all his."[7]

The exploding popularity of his designs brought Frankl a
different problem. Suddenly, he was selling modern
pieces, but he lacked the production facilities to make
them. In addition to the Skyscraper bookcases and
Peasant Furniture, the Frankl Galleries now featured an
array of modern cabinets, tables, and chairs, as well as
upholstered sofas. To meet the rising demand, Frankl
contracted with artisans and workshops across the city.
He made carefully rendered, measured drawings of his
designs and discussed the details with the various cabinetmakers and upholsterers. But as was customary in
Europe, where respect for master craftspeople dictated

a hands-off approach, he left it up to them to interpret
his ideas. They were thus free to fashion the pieces as they
wanted as long as they did not alter his designs.[8] The
result was great variation in the quality and execution of
the pieces. Some of the Skyscraper bookcases and other
furnishings were well made, but many were not. Frankl
sometimes resorted to sprayed lacquer finishes to cloak
some of the worst deficiencies. Still, some of the pieces
he sold in the mid-1920s fell far below the quality of the
European modernists'—or even his own—best works.

A solution to Frankl's production problem presented
itself in the fall of 1925. An old acquaintance, T. Jefferson
Penn, owner of the American Tobacco Company (which
made Lucky Strike cigarettes), offered to build a furniture
factory near his two-thousand-acre plantation outside
Reidville, North Carolina. Penn had recently returned
from seeing the Paris exhibition and was "most enthused";
he told Frankl he would put up a million dollars to construct an up-to-date plant if Frankl would supply the
designs and oversee production. The offer was tempting,
but Frankl worried that he lacked the necessary experience
in manufacturing and that overseeing the plant would con-
sume too much of his time. Also, he was unwilling to leave
New York just at the moment he was beginning to enjoy his
first real success. After long and anguished reflection, he
declined the offer. It was a fateful decision, one he much
regretted later when it became burdensome for him to
make and market his designs.[9] Frankl did not know it at
the time, but his resolution to remain in New York and
continue to rely on handicraft would determine the course
of his career for many years. It would be more than two
decades before he would find the right opportunity to
mass-produce his designs.

His production problems notwithstanding, by the last
months of 1926, Frankl's Skyscraper bookcases had
become, as *Good Furniture Magazine* reported, "the fad of
the moment . . . as American and as New Yorkish as Fifth
Avenue itself. Anyone in New York who feels sufficiently
sophisticated to long for modern interiors, rushes forth-

with to the galleries where Mr. Frankl has on display what is the most astounding collection of modern furniture in America today." [10]

The immediate appeal of Frankl's Skyscraper line rested, of course, in its associations with the city's tall buildings. But it was not just that the skyscraper offered, as one contemporary writer put it, an expression of "America's commercial triumph," borne of "dignity, purpose, practicality, and rare imagination." [11] Artists, architects, and intellectuals on both sides of the Atlantic recognized that the great buildings constituted a distinctly American contribution. Already in the 1890s, the skyscraper had become the very trademark of American modernity, lauded by a diverse cast of artists and writers, from William Merritt Chase and Alfred Stieglitz to William James and John Dewey. [12] And it was not only New York that felt the impact of the new towers. The building boom of the 1920s, which fueled the erection of scores of tall buildings in midtown Manhattan and beyond, propelled the skyscraper into the nation's psyche. At the end of the decade, almost every American urban skyline was punctuated with high-rise, steel-framed buildings. [13] The impact of the skyscraper resonated through American art, music, and literature of the 1920s. Novels of the decade, like John Dos Passos's *Manhattan Transfer* (1925) and Janet Flanner's *The Cubical City* (1926), were set against the backdrop of the new high-rises. Critics related the syncopated beat of jazz to the zigzags of skyscraper form. And artists as varied as Walker Evans, Louis Lozowick, John Marin, Georgia O'Keeffe, Edward Steichen, Alfred Stieglitz, and Max Weber all made Manhattan's jagged profile a subject for their work.

Frankl's Skyscraper Furniture promoted the look of the new buildings and affirmed the ideals of American progress and commercial prowess. Yet more than that, Frankl knew that the skyscraper offered a clear and understandable way to "put [modern] across with the great American public." In contrast to the French Art Moderne, which most Americans found puzzling and foreign, "the name 'Skyscraper Furniture' told the story. It

Fig. 50. Paul T. Frankl, library in the apartment of Manuel Komroff, New York, c. 1928, featuring an array of Frankl's Skyscraper bookcases

was tied up with the big city and its tall buildings ... an expression of our day and age." [14]

Both name and image soon permeated American culture. Frankl's Skyscraper Furniture found its way into innumerable newspaper articles and advertisements—and even several *New Yorker* cartoons (fig. 49). [15] It served, too, as an elegant set piece for Samuel Spewack's popular whodunit of 1928, *The Skyscraper Murder*. The detective of the story, upon finding the inhabitant of a posh New York penthouse murdered, is astonished by the apartment's up-to-date decor:

"What is this?" he asked.
Marx pointed to an unusual piece of furniture, built in blocks of mahogany, and in the form of a modern skyscraper.

"That," explained the doctor, "is a futurist secretary. Mr. Sewell apparently was a true New Yorker. He swallowed up the fashions in furniture to the minute. All the best people have now adopted futurism for the home."[16]

Frankl lost no opportunity to champion his belief that the "skyscraper style" was both a logical expression of the new age and quintessentially American. In an article in the February 1927 issue of *House and Garden*, he explained that unlike the "Louis Seize chair, the massive Tudor chest and the gilded Medici bed," which were "designed for a public that had leisure," the new furniture "evolved as an ideal of speed, based on the fact that a straight line is the shortest distance between two points.... Surely, we can create a furniture expressive of the modern scheme of life just as we have evolved a modern music." Americans, Frankl declared, also had a proprietary claim to modernism: "If possession is nine-tenths of the law, then everything is in our favor; it was an American who created the entire current of modern architecture and decorative art: Frank Lloyd Wright. Secondly—we as a younger nation *possess* the right because we have the spirit to adapt ourselves more readily to the New. We've proven it repeatedly."[17]

Frankl's swelling optimism in the motive force and rightness of American modernism was matched by the increasing exuberance of his designs. His first Skyscraper bookcases were squat compositions—not unlike the earliest of New York's tall buildings. By the end of 1926, his pieces had begun to mimic the slim, soaring profiles of the mature skyscraper form. Frankl sometimes massed a series of Skyscraper bookcases together to suggest the appearance of the New York skyline (fig. 50), and he began incorporating similar imagery into other furniture types, including various desks (figs. 51, 52, 53), a vanity (fig. 54), a chair (fig. 55), and several occasional tables (figs. 56, 57, 58).[18]

His designs gradually took on a look of refinement. By 1927, some of his Skyscraper bookcases were sporting silver leaf detailing and simple, elegant handles, emphasizing further their attenuated and blocky forms (fig. 59). The luxurious appearance of his pieces allowed Frankl to entice the very well-to-do, who formed much of his client base. The new Skyscraper bookcases and other designs were not only expensive (the large desk was priced at $450, the vanity at $550), but they required large rooms. "The people who are interested in Mr. Frankl's not inexpensive art," *Good Furniture Magazine* noted, "are those who have the floor space they require at their command ... [though] they find in the set-back, towering structures something vastly intriguing and suggestive of New York's Babylonian sky-line."[19]

If the clean, pure lines of his mature Skyscraper pieces became, almost overnight, one of the most recognizable images of 1920s design, unfortunately for Frankl they also proved very easy to copy. By 1927, pieces bearing his distinctive stair-stepped profile were being marketed by numerous imitators, among them the Almco Galleries, on Park Avenue, and the Bristol Company, on Sixty-second Street. The largest producers of furnishings bearing the Skyscraper look, though, were Modernage, in New York, and the Johnson Furniture Company, in Grand Rapids, Michigan, which introduced its stair-stepped "Dynamique Creations" line in 1928. Both companies promoted their lines as "authentic modernist" design and—just as important for enticing the broad public—as "practical and comfortable" furniture for everyday use.[20]

The mass-produced versions put Frankl's design ideas within reach of middle-class consumers—something he was still unable to do given his shop's high overhead and the cost of making his pieces by hand. But Frankl's problems were not limited to his competitors. His practice of engaging multiple cabinetmakers to produce his furniture led to a flooding of the market of supposedly "authentic" pieces. Unscrupulous workers made "extras" after hours, passing them on directly to customers or through dealers. Early on, Frankl tried affixing small paper labels to some of his furniture to identify his work (fig. 60).[21] The paper labels were easy to copy, however, and did little to stem the rising number of imitations. Finally, in 1927, the problem became so acute he began using metal labels, based on the

Opposite, top:
Fig. 51. Paul T. Frankl, Skyscraper desk, c. 1927

Opposite, bottom:
Fig. 52. Paul T. Frankl, Skyscraper desk, c. 1927. Wood and formica, 44 7/8 x 55 3/8 x 31 1/4 in. (114 x 140.7 x 79.4 cm). The Metropolitan Museum of Art, New York, Collection of John C. Waddell

Left:
Fig. 53. Paul T. Frankl, Skyscraper bookcase and desk, c. 1928. Walnut, paint, and brass handles, 83 x 48 3/4 x 21 1/4 in. (210.8 x 123.8 x 54 cm). Museum of Fine Arts, Boston, Collection of John P. Axelrod

Fig. 54. Paul T. Frankl, dressing table and mirror, c. 1927. Lacquered wood with silver leaf detailing

Opposite, top left:
Fig. 55. Paul T. Frankl, Skyscraper chair, c. 1927. Red lacquered wood with silver leaf detailing (restored), 26 x 20 x 18 in. (66 x 50.8 x 45.7 cm). The Minneapolis Institute of Arts, The Modernism Collection. Gift of Norwest Bank, Minn. [98.276.57]

Opposite, top right:
Fig. 56. Paul T. Frankl, end table, c. 1927. Wood with black lacquered detailing, 25 1/2 x 19 1/2 x 19 1/2 in. (64.8 x 49.5 x 49.5 cm). Courtesy of Richard Wright, Chicago

Opposite, bottom left:
Fig. 57. Paul T. Frankl, Skyscraper occasional table, c. 1930. Lacquered wood, 18.8 x 36 x 12 in. (47.8 x 91.4 x 30.5 cm). Courtesy of Richard Wright, Chicago

Opposite, bottom right:
Fig. 58. Paul T. Frankl, occasional table, c. 1930. Lacquered wood with silver leaf detailing, height 18 in. (45.7 cm), diameter 24 in. (61 cm). Courtesy of Richard Wright, Chicago

store's new logo, to authenticate his designs (figs. 61, 62). Nonetheless, in spite of all precautions, his designs continued to be pirated and sold without his permission.[22]

The plethora of copies cut into Frankl's business, but they did much to spread his fame and influence. The distinctive look of the Skyscraper line was adopted by a host of other American designers, who appropriated both the name and its imagery. Silversmith Louis W. Rice, for example, created a series of Skyscraper tableware designs in 1928, and, around the same time, Walter von Nessen designed several lamps with similar stair-stepped forms.[23]

Frankl's own modernist program was not restricted to his Skyscraper furniture. Throughout the later 1920s, he continued to import new designs from Europe. His most successful line was a group of textiles from France with patterns by Pierre Dariel, Raoul Dufy, François Jourdain, and Paul Poiret. Hand printed on linen and cotton, the fabrics featured bold color contrasts and plain, figurative forms—resembling, as one reporter described, "the naïve drawings of children."[24] Frankl promoted the patterns for use as wall hangings and upholstery, and he wholesaled several of the fabrics to the garment trade for women's apparel.[25] Beginning in late 1927, he also introduced a collection of patterns by Paul Rodier, who at Frankl's request had designed them exclusively for the Frankl Galleries (figs. 63, 64). Despite being priced at a hefty $12.50 to $15 per yard, they sold well, and Frankl opened a new department on a separate floor of the gallery's annex devoted to the Rodier fabrics, modern wallpapers, and his own lighting fixtures.[26]

Over the course of the next year, Frankl designed and produced an array of furnishings intended to complement his Skyscraper furniture collection. Among the pieces he offered was a wood-frame, upholstered chair (with a Dufy-designed fabric covering) and a metal, mirror-topped end table (fig. 65). Frankl also hired the young Donald Deskey, recently returned from Paris, to paint a series of decorative screens for the gallery (fig. 66). (Frankl paid Deskey thir-

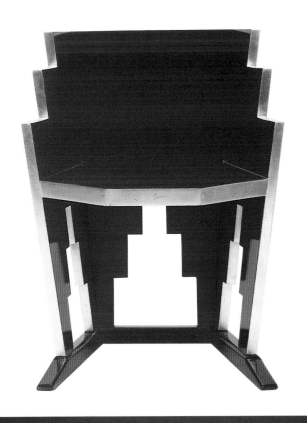

Fig. 59. Paul T. Frankl, Skyscraper bookcase, c. 1927. Lacquered wood with silver leaf detailing, 84 x 33 x 15 ³/₄ in. (213.4 x 83.8 x 40 cm). Restricted gift of the Antiquarian Society through Mr. and Mrs. Thomas B. Hunter III and Mr. and Mrs. Morris S. Weeden, 1998.567, The Art Institute of Chicago

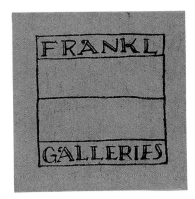

Fig. 60. Paul T. Frankl, Frankl Galleries paper label, c. 1926. Collection Paulette Frankl

Fig. 61. Paul T. Frankl, Frankl Galleries metal label, c. 1928. Courtesy Sotheby's, New York

Fig. 62. Paul T. Frankl, cover of Skyscraper Furniture brochure, c. 1927. Collection Paulette Frankl

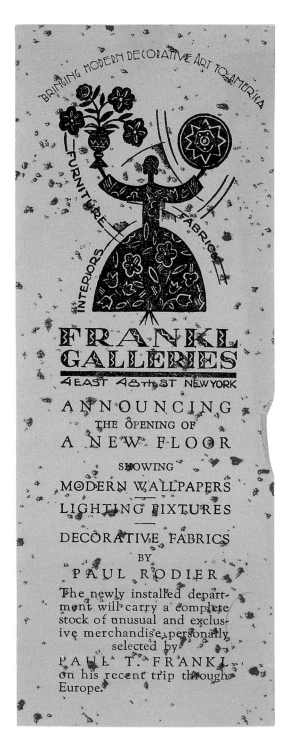

Fig 63. Ilonka Karasz, advertisement for the Frankl Galleries on East Forty-eighth Street, c. 1927. Collection Paulette Frankl

Fig. 64. Paul T. Frankl, model living room in the Frankl Galleries, with textiles by Paul Rodier, c. 1927

Below:
Fig. 65. Paul T. Frankl, chair and end table, c. 1928

ty-five dollars each plus the cost of materials to make the three-paneled screens, while selling them for four hundred dollars, turning a tidy profit.) [27]

All of the pieces Frankl offered made an insistent and clarified modernist statement. Not only were their forms novel, but their materials and finishes posed a conspicuous move away from tradition. In his pursuit of modernist form, Frankl continued to mine the contemporary European design world for ideas. A writing desk with zebrawood veneers he designed around 1928 echoed the stark geometries of Dutch De Stijl and international Constructivism—and perhaps, also, of Frank Lloyd Wright's earlier Prairie Style (fig. 67). On the other hand, Frankl's lighting fixtures, like his designs for chairs, cabinets, and bathrooms, appropriated—more or less explicitly—the forms of French Art Moderne. [28]

Frankl also drew on other, older sources. In contrast to his more radical counterparts in Germany and the

Fig. 66. Donald Deskey, screen for the Frankl Galleries, c. 1928. Oil paint and metal leaf on canvas, 77 ³/₄ x 58 ³/₄ x 1 ¹/₄ in. (197.5 x 149.2 x 2.9 cm). Virginia Museum of Fine Arts, Richmond, Va. Gift of Sydney and Frances Lewis Foundation

Fig. 67. Paul T. Frankl, writing desk, c. 1928. Lacquered zebrawood

Fig. 68. Paul T. Frankl, dressing mirror and chair, c. 1927

Opposite:
Fig. 69. Paul T. Frankl, vanity seat, 1928. Lacquered wood and cloth upholstery, 23 1/4 x 35 x 14 1/2 in. (59 x 88.9 x 36.8 cm). Courtesy of Richard Wright, Chicago

Netherlands, he was unwilling to make a wholesale break with the past. A large silvered dressing mirror, which dates to the middle of 1927, was based on ancient Egyptian models, though Frankl altered both their scale and arrangement to communicate the modern mood (fig. 68). This same strategy of formal transformation is even more pronounced in a vanity seat he designed in 1928 (fig. 69). Here Frankl blended together the language of classicism with the free and jagged lines of the Jazz Age. The result was one of his most lyrical and arresting works.

Frankl's ability to find compelling and acceptable forms for his works did much to further the cause of the new aesthetic. Nonetheless, many observers continued to wonder aloud whether modernism was nothing more than a "passing fancy." In an opinion piece in *Good Furniture Magazine*, editor Henry W. Frohne wrote that he thought that "the modernistic movement in home furnishing" was "gaining momentum" and would "go far and deep." Yet Frohne conceded what all of the mod-ernists knew very well, that "the great bulk of ambitious American women bent on furnishing their homes in good taste will continue for some time to accept literal tradition as the most desirable note in decorative furnishing." [29]

In spite of his own triumphs, Frankl knew that the battle was far from over. For the next three years, he would work tirelessly to define the look of modern American design and to win over the average consumer.

Apostle of Modern

In October 1926, Frankl turned forty. His previous six years had been filled with promise and even a few small victories in his quest for modernism. The next three years, from the end of 1926 to the onset of the Great Depression, were to be the most fruitful of his career. The new vogue for modern that had commenced at the end of 1925 translated into impressive sales for the Frankl Galleries, and Frankl found himself in ever greater demand as an interior designer. But more than that, the late 1920s saw him thrust into the national spotlight. After years of struggling to promote the cause of modernism, he emerged, suddenly, as its foremost spokesman. For the remainder of the decade, much of Frankl's time and energy were taken up with his effort to persuade Americans of the rightness of modern design. And more than any of his contemporaries, it was Frankl whose views—repeated ceaselessly in the media and summarized in two books he published during those years—would shape American views and tastes (fig. 70).

Opposite:
Fig. 70. Paul T. Frankl, c. 1929

Frankl's efforts to spread the message of modernism after the Paris exposition were aided by a series of exhibitions organized by the leading American department stores. While much of the public remained bewildered by the advent of the new aesthetic, U.S. department stores were, by early 1927, demonstrating a marked willingness to promote it.[1] Department stores had for some time assumed a prominent part in suggesting how Americans should live. As early as the 1880s, American merchants had used model showrooms to sell furniture and related merchandise. After the turn of the century, the stores greatly expanded their offerings. In 1908, Wanamaker's, in New York, launched the "House Palatial," a two-story, twenty-four-room model dwelling in the center of the store's great rotunda, and by the 1910s, the Gimbel brothers had constructed a three-acre display, consuming an entire floor in their New York store.[2] The furniture and interiors on display reflected the dominant historical revival styles, but the large stores did take an early lead in furthering the spread of modern art. While American museums were slow to respond to the revolution in painting and sculpture, the department stores became the leading "educational centers" for the new aesthetic. Inspired by the 1913 Armory Show, the Gimbel brothers began acquiring modern paintings, including the works of Cézanne, Braque, and Picasso, and displaying them in their stores in Cincinnati, Cleveland, New York, and Philadelphia; a few years later, Carson, Pirie, Scott, in Chicago, mounted an exhibition of the works of American painters Robert Henri, George Bellows, William Glackens, and John Sloan.[3]

After the 1925 Paris exposition, the leading American retailers, sensing the changing mood, finally began to promote modern design. In the late spring of 1927, Macy's launched one of the most ambitious exhibitions of modernism to date, the Exposition of Art in Trade. Held at Macy's Thirty-second Street store, it featured the work of many of the New York moderns. In addition to furniture by Frankl (who contributed a "modernistic library" comprised of a suite of Skyscraper pieces), there were works by Aline Bernstein, Jules Bouy, and Paul Zimmermann.[4] The exhibition also proffered an extensive section of decorative arts. On display were fabrics by the Cheney Brothers and F. Schumacher and Company, silverware by Georg Jensen, Wiener Werkstätte designs in brass and ceramic provided by Rena Rosenthal, Orrefors glass from Sweden,

and screens by Barry Faulkner and Ethel Wallace. Lee Simonson, who served as the show's organizer and oversaw the installations, also arranged an impressive selection of recent art, with paintings by Raoul Dufy; sculptures by Paul Manship; photographs by Edward Steichen; theater designs by Norman Bel Geddes; prints by George Bellows, Arthur Davies, Rockwell Kent, Marie Laurencin, and Odilon Redon; and works in various media executed by students from the New York School of Fine and Applied Arts and several other local schools.[5]

Remarkably, the show ran for only a single week, from 2 May to 7 May, but it, along with the landmark Machine-Age Exposition, held just two weeks later in a leased office space on Fifty-seventh Street, confirmed the rising presence—and legitimacy—of modernism in the United States. The latter exhibition, sponsored by the *Little Review*, the New York avant-garde literary journal edited by Jane Heap, focused on the recent trends in European art and design. But it, too, incorporated the work of a number of American-born artists, including Charles Demuth, Hugh Ferriss, and Man Ray.[6]

A series of department store exhibitions followed. In late 1927, Wanamaker's, in New York, emulating the great Parisian department stores, mounted a show highlighting the latest in French design.[7] Publicized under the slogan "Sun, light, air, art," the store created a group of furnished rooms filled with the works of Edgar Brandt, René Lalique, Paul Rodier, Louis Süe and André Mare, and others.[8] In early 1928, Lord and Taylor presented its own exhibition of Modern French Decorative Art.[9] Designed by architect Ely Jacques Kahn, it was the first department store exhibition to rival the earlier museum shows.[10] The exhibition incorporated the works of most of the prominent French designers—Jacques-Emile Ruhlmann, François Jourdain, Jean Dunand, and Pierre Chareau—and it enjoyed immense success, attracting more than one hundred thousand viewers.[11] One reason for the show's popularity had to do with the selection of objects. Dorothy Shaver, the store's director, spent nearly half a year in Europe assembling a broad array of important and well-crafted furnishings. To appeal

to a wider public, however, Shaver shunned the more out-
landish examples of the new style.[12] Her strategy succeeded
brilliantly. An anonymous article in *American Architect*
commended the exhibit for being "modern" while at the
same time avoiding the "freakish and bizarre.... It is the
sanest conception of 'L'Art Moderne' that has been gath-
ered since the movement gained strength, and bids fair to
establish a new period in art."[13]

In the spring, Macy's followed their successful show of
1927 with An International Exposition of Art in Industry.[14]
Once again, Macy's engaged Simonson to serve as exhibition designer. He focused on the leading non-French
European designers (in marked contrast to the
Wanamaker's and Lord and Taylor exhibits), including
Bruno Paul, Gio Ponti, and Josef Hoffmann, but he also
invited Kem Weber, Eugene Schoen, Ralph Walker, and
other American designers to take part.[15] Among the show's
most popular displays were Weber's bathroom, which featured a recessed jade green bathtub and a shower room
with a glass door, and Hoffmann's "all-glass" boudoir. The
latter, with mirrors covering the walls, floor, and ceiling
(offering visitors multiple views of themselves and the
space), became a huge hit; the *New York Times* reported that
"the crowds in front of this room had to be held back."[16]

Department stores in cities across the country followed
New York's lead: Kaufmann's, in Pittsburgh, showed model
apartments "in the modern manner"; Rich Brothers, in
Atlanta, displayed a selection of recent furnishings; and
Marshall Field and Company, in Chicago, presented its
own suite of modern interiors.[17] The impetus for these
shows was not confined to a desire to promote French
modernism: it was also an effort to foster the fledgling
modern American design industry. Most of the stores followed their exhibits with permanent departments of furniture and accessories in the new manner.[18]

Frankl, who seemed to be everywhere in the late 1920s,
assumed a central role in awakening the interest of
department store owners in modern design. He was a close
intimate of Adam Gimbel, owner of Saks and Company,

Fig. 71. Paul T. Frankl,
shoe store for Saks and
Company, Atlantic City,
New Jersey, 1928

and of Edgar J. Kaufmann, the Pittsburgh department
store mogul (and, later, the client for Frank Lloyd Wright's
Fallingwater). Both men were highly influential in retailing circles, and through them, Frankl was able to exert
influence on the retailing industry.[19] His crusade to put
modern design before the public received a special boost
from Gimbel, who commissioned him in 1928 to supply
furniture for Saks's show windows on Fifth Avenue.
Gimbel, pleased with the response, asked Frankl to design
the interiors for the company's upscale shoe store on
Atlantic City's Boardwalk (fig. 71).

The commissions only served to enhance Frankl's reputation in the merchandising world.[20] In the last years of the
decade, he made frequent appearances as both author and
authority in the pages of *Dry Goods Economist*, the leading
organ for the trade, and the top players in the field increasingly consulted him for advice. Frankl's persistent and per-
suasive advocacy paid off, helping to tip the balance for
modernism among the nation's merchants—long before
there was widespread public enthusiasm for the new design.

Frankl's most visible effort to aid the merchandising of
modernism came in a department store exhibit, The
Livable House Transformed, which opened at Abraham
and Straus in Brooklyn in early February 1928. The previ-

ous year, Abraham and Straus had engaged Frankl to update its Livable House exhibit. The original display space, modeled on a Colonial cottage, featured a selection of modestly priced "early American" reproductions. Frankl converted the suite of six rooms into a modernist villa, complete with his signature Skyscraper bookcases, a mirror-topped table, and leather chairs (fig. 72). [21] The space had hints of contemporary European design, especially its textiles and bedroom furnishings, but the overall look fit the emerging American modern style.

Many observers at the time made mention of Frankl's "stark perpendiculars" and "elimination of unnecessary detail." [22] Yet it was his innovative lighting scheme that pro-

Fig. 72. Paul T. Frankl, "Modern Living Room," displayed at the exhibition The Livable House Transformed, sponsored by the Abraham and Straus department store, Brooklyn, 1928

voked the most comment. In place of traditional table lamps, he relied on diffused light to foster a controlled and ambient effect. The living room was illuminated by two vertical rows of bulbs placed behind opaque glass panels on either side of the fireplace and by alabaster ceiling fixtures; in the bedroom, the two glass dressing tables were lighted from within. The soft, glowing spaces imparted an air of sophistication while mitigating the bold and simple lines. [23]

What also stood out to the critics and casual viewers alike was Frankl's effort to offer an acceptable version of the new aesthetic. Nellie Sanford, in *Good Furniture Magazine*, commented that even "those who have felt inclined to quarrel with some of his ideas which they have thought too extreme for American homes, find here a reasonable modification, while still keeping the form true to the modern vogue." The "first requisite" of the livable house was comfort. Frankl had achieved just that: "Now we find [the house] is as livable as ever, but exactly in step with the modern mode." [24]

But the field for modernism in the United States was far from being Frankl's alone. By 1928, a small but growing group of designers, many of them recent arrivals from Europe, had established reputations for their own works in the new manner. In 1925, Wolfgang Hoffmann, son of Josef Hoffmann, immigrated to New York with his wife, Pola. Both had studied at the Vienna Kunstgewerbeschule, where the elder Hoffmann taught, and they brought with them the newest ideas in European design. The following year, they opened their own studio, crafting lighting fixtures, metal furniture, pewter ware, and textiles for private clients. [25] Another recent arrival was Romanian-born Paul Lobel, who studied at the Art Students League in New York and, after seeing the 1925 Paris exposition, began working for Eugene Schoen, making metal fireplaces and other accessories in the modern French manner. [26] Several of the other newcomers already had extensive design experience in Europe before arriving in New York. Peter Müller-Munk had studied with Bruno Paul in Berlin and subsequently apprenticed with silversmith Waldemar Ramisch; he moved to New York in 1926 and worked for Tiffany's before setting up his own studio. [27] And Frederick Kiesler, who arrived in New York the same year, was an internationally acclaimed designer and theater architect, well known in avant-garde circles in Vienna, Berlin, and Paris. [28]

The Europeans were joined by a small number of young, native-born designers. The most important were Gilbert Rohde, the son of a New York cabinetmaker, who, after returning from a visit to France in 1927, set up his own studio to produce custom-made furniture in the French modern mode; and Donald Deskey, who began his career as an artist and, after an extended trip to Europe, started designing show windows for Saks Fifth Avenue and Franklin Simon. [29]

The expansion of the designers' ranks was matched by an increasing number of retail stores devoted to selling modernist objects. By the middle of 1928, several new shops specializing in modern furniture and decorative arts had sprung up in New York: the Danby Company, at 227 East Forty-seventh Street; Hearthstone, at 244 East Fifty-seventh Street; the Mason Art Furniture Company, at 45-51 West Twenty-first Street; and United Arts and Crafts, at 47 West Forty-seventh Street, were only some of the most visible new outlets for "modernistic" designs.

With the burgeoning popularity of the new style came many more decorating commissions for Frankl. Among his executed interiors of the later 1920s were the penthouse of William S. Paley, president of the Columbia Broadcasting System; the mansion of Cathlyn Vanderbilt in Oyster Bay, Long Island; the home of Vadim and Elisabeth Makaroff, half owners of the A&P stores, in Oyster Bay; the estate of railroad heiress Mary Hill in Tarrytown, New York; and the Harlem townhouse of Alelia Walker, daughter of Madame C. J. Walker, the millionaire African American businesswoman who had made her fortune with hair products. [30] Frankl also contributed furnishings for one of the great houses of the era, Mar-a-Lago, the sprawling home of cereal heiress Marjorie Merriweather Post and her second husband, financier E. F. Hutton, in Palm Beach, Florida. Joseph Urban designed the house and much of the furniture, but he asked Frankl to decorate the tower room, which served as a guest space. Frankl responded with one his most exuberant interiors—an extraordinary tour de force of color, form, and pattern that included a number of custom designs, including a large lacquered-wood sofa (fig. 73). [31]

By the late 1920s, Frankl's little gallery on East Forty-

Fig. 73. Paul T. Frankl, sofa from the tower room at Mar-a-Lago, Palm Beach, Florida, 1927. Lacquered wood with silver leaf detailing, with four original throw pillows designed by Frankl and covered in fabric by Paul Rodier, 27 3/8 x 77 3/4 x 37 7/8 in. (69.5 x 197.5 x 96.2 cm). Courtesy Sotheby's, New York

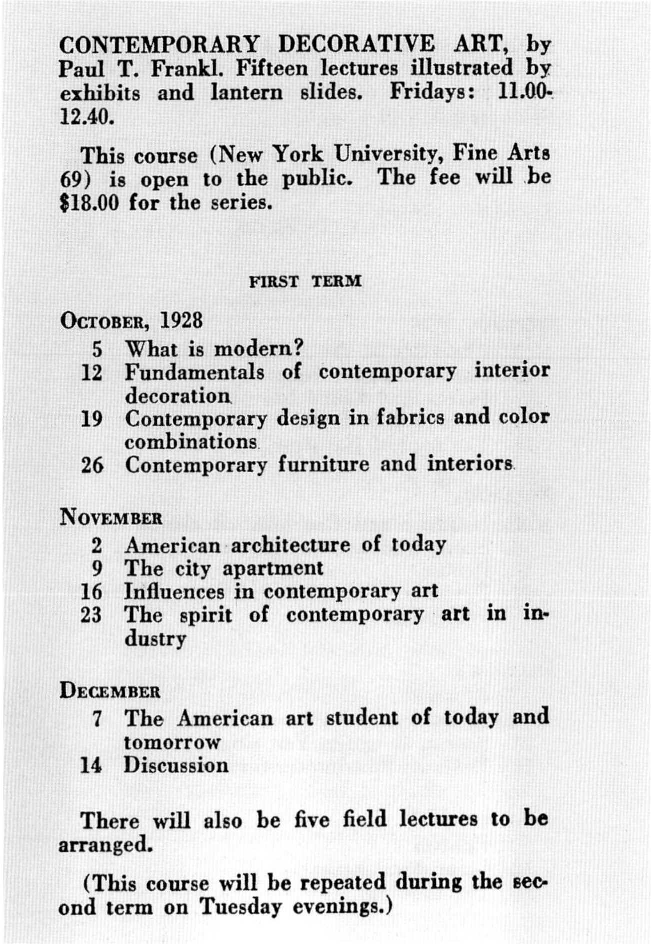

CONTEMPORARY DECORATIVE ART, by
Paul T. Frankl. Fifteen lectures illustrated by
exhibits and lantern slides. Fridays: 11.00-
12.40.

This course (New York University, Fine Arts
69) is open to the public. The fee will be
$18.00 for the series.

FIRST TERM

OCTOBER, 1928
   5 What is modern?
  12 Fundamentals of contemporary interior
      decoration
  19 Contemporary design in fabrics and color
      combinations
  26 Contemporary furniture and interiors

NOVEMBER
   2 American architecture of today
   9 The city apartment
  16 Influences in contemporary art
  23 The spirit of contemporary art in in-
      dustry

DECEMBER
   7 The American art student of today and
      tomorrow
  14 Discussion

There will also be five field lectures to be
arranged.

(This course will be repeated during the second term on Tuesday evenings.)

Fig. 74. Description of Frankl's course, Contemporary Decorative Art, at New York University in the fall of 1928. Collection Paulette Frankl

eighth Street had become a place to see and be seen. Its regular patrons included many of the New York elite: Eleanor Roosevelt regularly dropped in to purchase cards, stationery, and small gifts; and members of the large Vanderbilt and Whitney clans were steady customers.[32] Frankl's mounting reputation also brought commissions and notice from abroad. In the late 1920s, he designed a penthouse for a skyscraper on the Bund, Shanghai's international settlement, and he was called on to create the interior fittings of an oceangoing yacht built by the Krupp Company in Essen, Germany, for Ernst Richard Behrend, founder of the Hammermill Paper Company.[33] Articles about Frankl's work appeared in journals in Germany and France. Hugo Lang, writing in *Innen-Dekoration*, described him as the "leader" and "best known" of the American modernists, and Pierre Migennes, in a piece in *Art et Décoration*, extolled the "singular audacity" of his designs.[34]

Despite his personal and commercial successes, Frankl recognized that his own battle for modernism would have to be fought not only in the design magazines or in the drawing rooms of the wealthy but in the public arena. Beginning in 1927, he expanded his efforts to spread the gospel of modernism through education.

Frankl continued to teach classes at the New York School of Interior Decoration, and, in September 1927, he accepted an offer from the Fine Arts Department of New York University to present a series of lectures at The Metropolitan Museum of Art. The course, Contemporary Decorative Art, was open to the public. In addition to a discussion of the emerging American expression of the new style, it covered techniques of modern design, new materials, and practical tips for recasting the home in modernist guise—all topics essentially aimed at acquiring new converts (fig. 74).[35]

Frankl's educational efforts were not confined to New York. In the early summer of 1928, after a month of prodigious writing and revising, he completed a home study course, based on his Met lectures, for *Arts and Decoration* magazine.[36] Frankl intended for the course to make the principles of "modern decorating" available to anyone in the country, in "six easily mastered lessons."[37] An advertisement in *Arts and Decoration* in July 1928, the month the booklet was published, promised that the course would "not only . . . give you a complete mastery of every phase of this modern movement but you will be expertly qualified to apply your knowledge in your own home or to the decoration of private residences, business offices—and, in fact, wherever the occasion requires decoration in the modern style."[38] Affordably priced, the course sold well, and the magazine continued to promote it well into the 1930s.[39]

In early May 1928, Frankl also embarked on a second national speaking tour. His aim, he told a reporter, was "to build up an appreciative audience and virtually sell the idea of modern art."[40] This time, however, rather than speaking at academic institutions, he targeted department stores in major urban markets. "The stores and their employees," he explained to another reporter, "had to be educated to the new movement first and now their customers must be approached." [41]

The first phase of the tour took him across the Midwest, upper South, and West. Initially, he planned to end the tour in Vancouver, and from there to sail to Japan for a short visit. [42] But an unexpected trip to Havana in midsummer to complete a commission for a wealthy client forced him to cancel his trip to the Far East. He announced instead another round of lectures to begin in September. The fall tour took him to more than thirty cities—mostly in the Midwest and South—with stops in Pittsburgh, Philadelphia, Cincinnati, Indianapolis, Milwaukee, St. Louis, Dallas, Memphis, and Atlanta. [43] Several of his lectures were timed to coincide with displays of the new design, among them exhibits at Schuster's Department Store, in Milwaukee, and at the Herron Art Institute, in Indianapolis. [44]

With his courtly, Old World manner, Frankl proved to be a compelling speaker. Always elegantly attired in tailored suits, he was charming, engaging, and witty; his own apparent sense of confidence helped to calm his listeners' unease with modernism. But his success in reaching audiences stemmed in great part from his evident respect for those he addressed. Throughout his life, Frankl abhorred elitism and pretense. (His son, Peter, remembered that his father once admonished him for not properly greeting the elevator man in the building where he had one of his showrooms.) [45] Rather than talking down to his listeners, he sought to make them understand the message of modernism. With great patience, he explained the tenets of the new style, demonstrating his points with commonplace examples. Often, he drew with pencil or charcoal on large sheets of newsprint as he spoke, illustrating how the new design differed from past styles. He invited his audiences to ask questions, passing out printed slips before each talk to allow his listeners to pose their queries anonymously, without fear of embarrassment. Frankl began each lecture by describing in simple terms how the "contemporary style" offered practical advantages over the "demoded" design of the past: the

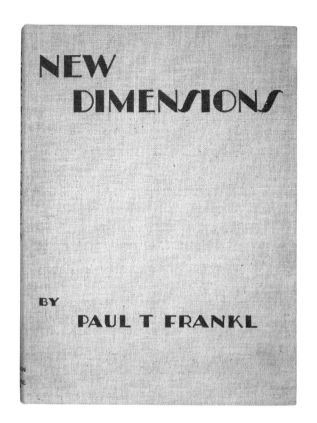

"'modern' idea," he asserted, was "no different from that of the electric washing machine or electric refrigerator." [46]

While on his cross-country tour, Frankl used the opportunity to speak to various women's and business groups. His appeal was founded in part on aesthetic principle: the period revival styles, he told his listeners, no longer corresponded with American tastes and values—or contemporary lifestyles. He stressed, too, his conviction that "modern" made good business sense: there was money to be made in converting to the new aesthetic, and businesses that disregarded the trend did so at their peril. [47]

Frankl summarized his ideas in his book *New Dimensions*, published by Payson and Clarke in the late spring of 1928 (fig. 75). [48] He had begun assembling material for the book more than two years before, waiting for the right moment to release it. *New Dimensions* is a summary of the previous three years of modern design: nearly half of the more than 100 photographs featured his own work and that of his fellow New York modernists; the

Fig. 75. Cover of *New Dimensions* (1928)

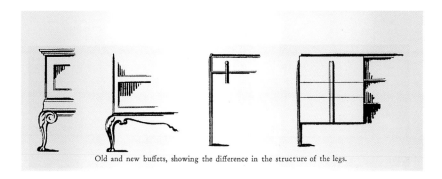

Old and new buffets, showing the difference in the structure of the legs.

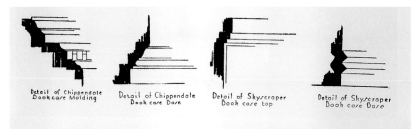

Detail of Chippendale Book case Molding   Detail of Chippendale Book case Base   Detail of Skyscraper Book case top   Detail of Skyscraper Book case Base

Fig. 76. Paul T. Frankl, comparisons of "old" and "new" furniture forms from *New Dimensions* (1928)

remainder showed the work of the leading French, German, and Austrian designers. (Most of the French images came from Thérèse Bonney in Paris; the other photos Frankl either collected from the artists themselves or culled from various European publications.)[49]

The book is a plea for an understanding of modernism in design—and for its broad acceptance—but it also offers a detailed overview of Frankl's somewhat idiosyncratic view of modernism. Its central argument is direct and lucid: the modern age required its own style, one fundamentally different from what had come before. "More and more, we find ourselves out of harmony and completely out of sympathy with period and imitation antique furnishings," Frankl writes. "A Chippendale chair cannot be altered into a modern piece of furniture. . . . [It] expresses the life of the time in which it was created. . . . We must be content to live creatively in our own time."[50] "Simplicity," Frankl argues, is the "keynote" of the new aesthetic—along with "certain other characteristics that help to make a thing modern": "*continuity of line* (as we find in the stream-line body of a car or in the long unbroken lines in fashions), *contrasts in colours* and *sharp contrasts in light and shadow* created through definite and angular moldings and by broken planes." To this list of qualities, Frankl appended several others: "rhythm," "honesty of materials," "informality," and "consistency."[51] He used diagrams to illustrate how these qualities differed from what had come before (fig. 76).

Frankl's checklist of the new aesthetic's attributes is standard modernist fare. Yet there are passages in the book that disclose his distance from the emerging doctrine of the modern movement—at least as it was rising out of the ferment of radical circles in Europe. Frankl believed that "national character" was still a defining mark of the new design ("When we talk to [modern furniture] it will answer in French, German, Czechoslovakian, Dutch, Scandinavian, and perhaps even in English," he writes), which contradicted the radicals' avowal of a new internationalism. Further, his conviction that quality of finish ranked in importance with design ran decidedly counter to their belief in the primacy of form, and it discounted the radicals' increased emphasis on utility and affordability. [52] In seeming defiance of the European avant-garde, he affirms his commitment to comfort: "Only a comfortable chair is beautiful. The first and last test for a chair is to sit in it." [53] And he devotes an entire chapter to a discussion of "The Peasant Influence in Art," charging that the "primitive and crude" look of folk design possessed an authenticity that placed it far "above the conventional, punched-out, two-by-four machine-made product"—an idea that looked back to the Arts and Crafts era but had long since lost its currency. [54]

Most of the critics applauded Frankl's attempt to offer a straightforward introduction to the new art. But there were a few prominent dissenters. C. Adolph Glassgold, perhaps the most perceptive of the American writers on modern design at the time, excoriated the book's "looseness" and "ambiguity." "As a study of the causes, the purpose, logic, and philosophy underlying the development of the new type of decorative arts, as a sociologic study, as a defense of its presence or a plea for its continued employment," he charged, "*New Dimensions* is as naïve in its logic as it is in its style; and it submerges the anxious seeker after truth in deeper currents of confusion." [55]

New Dimensions is indeed a confused book. Frankl's text is rambling, his definition of the new style nebulous. But Glassgold may have missed the point. Frankl's exclusion of the avant-garde and his breezy tone were calculated precisely to appeal to the average reader. The purpose of the book, after all, was to win wide approval for modern design. Still, it is clear that in 1928 Frankl held onto a vision of modernism that did not exclude older notions of aesthetic and material pleasure. For conservative clients, he was willing to wrap designs in the faint cloak of historical revivalism; indeed, much of his work could best be characterized as "moderate"—at least when viewed against the radical designs of the Bauhaus, De Stijl, or Russian Constructivists. [56] The truth, as Frankl realized, was that the position of modernism in America, even in 1928, remained tenuous. To secure large numbers of adherents, it would have to be amended for the U.S. market: "Modernism which ignores the universal demand for comfort, for efficiency, for practi-

cability, usability, and livability," he wrote, would be rejected "by a people which demands the latest and snappiest models in motor cars, insists upon the newest in radio sets, and splashes daily in violet or canary-yellow bathtubs, revels in electrical dishwashers, and buys Stravinsky piano-rolls! . . . A style of today and tomorrow, created by artists who understand our likes and dislikes, who represent our unconscious wishes and desires; such necessarily must be the modernism which can most successfully be developed and exploited in these United States." [57]

Frankl was hardly alone in urging the creation of a more "acceptable" modernist idiom. Most influential writers of the day agreed that designers in the United States would have to fashion a popular and affordable version of the new style. [58] Henry-Russell Hitchcock, who by the later 1920s had become one of the most vocal advocates for modern architecture, believed that a new type of design, adjusted to the American situation, had already begun to manifest itself "with the appearance in America of designers and manufacturers in numbers ready to produce single objects . . . which will make modern decoration no more expensive than retrospective decoration and which will appreciate and incorporate specifically American ideas as the foreign designers can not." [59]

By early 1929, the tide was beginning to turn: there were signs that the broad American public was starting to accept modern design. When Lewis Mumford, design critic for the *New Yorker*, visited the furniture manufacturing center of Grand Rapids, Michigan, in January 1927, he found that only a single suite of modern furniture—based on Parisian models—was in production; two years later, Mumford observed that the New York department stores were now offering a full array of American-designed and American-made modern furnishings. [60]

Leading the charge to "make the modern style American" was the American Union of Decorative Artists and Craftsmen. AUDAC, as it became better known, was founded in 1928 "to give direction to contemporary design in America . . . to do what the Société des Artistes Decorateurs and the Deutscher Werkbund have accomplished in Europe," as a short notice in the *Architectural Record* explained.[61] The organization had its origins, as Frankl would recall years afterward in his autobiography, in the meeting of a few "intimate friends" he had organized after hours at his gallery in November 1925: "Modern art, I felt, was catching on and the time had come when if it expected to make a go of it those few of us keenly interested should get together, talk things over, join and consolidate our efforts.... The contemporary art movement abroad had been successful. There artisans formed guilds comparable to our 'Arts and Crafts' societies, arranging exhibits, having group organs, lectures, employment offices, and other group activities benefiting their members.... We decided to meet again the following Wednesday, same time, same place, and bring along others who might be interested.... From week to week our group grew, attracted newcomers, not only artists but also businessmen, some with new products, especially plastics."[62]

The original circle that met at the Frankl Galleries included Simonson, Witold Gordon, Lucian Bernhard, and graphic designer Robert Leonard. Soon, they were joined by most of the other New York modernists, including Deskey, Kahn, Kiesler, Rohde, Schoen, Steichen, Urban, Zimmermann, Wolfgang and Pola Hoffmann, Raymond Hood, Ilonka Karasz and her sister Mariska, William Lescaze, Winold Reiss, and Walter von Nessen.[63] In addition to the usual Wednesday evening sessions, Frankl organized a series of monthly luncheons, held in the Tulip Room of the Central Park Casino (which had been recently refurbished by Urban), to which he invited "special groups of kindred professions" and members of New York society (among them Mrs. Harry Payne Whitney and Robert Schey). The five-dollars-a-plate events aided in spreading the word and raising money for advertising and operating funds.[64]

Frankl's effort to reach out to the wealthy and influential was more than just a pursuit of support and financial backing: he was all too aware of the outsider status of much of the AUDAC membership. In its early days, so many of the members were fresh arrivals from Central

Europe that it was easier to conduct the meetings in German than in English. And despite the prosperity of the time, many of the less-well-established members were barely scraping by. Frankl also believed in the importance of coupling new forms in the decorative arts with advances in art and architecture; he invited Frank Lloyd Wright, Diego Rivera, and others to present talks at the monthly lunches to enhance AUDAC's prestige and to broaden its reach.[65]

AUDAC's ostensible purpose, as one of its advertisements stated, was "the advancement of the new tendencies in the decorative, industrial and applied arts."[66] But from the outset, the issue of copyright was foremost among Frankl and the other members' concerns. Securing new copyright legislation, in fact, became one of the principal activities of the organization. Copyright laws at the time offered scant protection for designers of furniture or decorative accessories. Like Frankl, almost all of the other designers had seen their ideas appropriated by unscrupulous retailers and manufacturers.[67] The pandemic of design theft became so widespread by the later part of the decade some European modernists refused to show their newest works in New York for fear they would be copied and sold in the United States or in Europe.[68] Calls for new legislation to safeguard designs extended back to the early 1920s, but it was not until the middle of 1927 that the New York modernists launched an effort to get new legislation passed that would prevent design "piracy."[69] The AUDAC leadership engaged prominent attorney Arthur Garfield Hayes. Hayes, a former client of Frankl's, was counsel for the American Civil Liberties Union and had recently served as lead defense attorney in the sensational Sacco-Vanzetti trial. With Hayes's help, Indiana Congressman Albert H. Vestal, then Republican whip, took up their cause and sponsored legislation to extend copyright protection to design. The "Vestal Bill," or Design Copyright Bill (HR 11852) as it was officially known, passed and was signed into law in 1930, though in a somewhat watered-down form. Nevertheless, it offered the first protections for the nascent modern design industry, and it was a major triumph for AUDAC—and for Frankl personally.[70]

Equally important in AUDAC's mission to propagate the new style were several exhibitions held in the late 1920s. Foremost was the American Designers' Gallery, organized in the fall of 1929. Curated by Dutch-born designer Herman Rosse, the show was held at the Chase Bank Building, at 145 West Fifty-seventh Street, and presented works by Deskey, Hoffmann, Ilonka Karasz, Reiss, Urban, and others.[71] Although Frankl and most of the other participants contributed older works, the show was novel in its attempt to demonstrate the "maturing" of American design. As Rosse explained in the foreword to the catalog, the American Designers' Gallery was a response to the "need for a more complete showing of the work" after many previous "isolated exhibitions."[72]

The exhibit, which subsequently traveled to several other major American cities, drew praise from the critics.[73] Still, many questioned whether the work on display was genuinely American. An editorial in *Good Furniture Magazine*, published a few months before the show opened, pointed out the obvious: "When...Joseph Urban, Paul Frankl, Lucian Bernhard, Winold Reiss, and Pola Hoffmann appear in these showings of American designers, it should be remembered that, by years of training, practice and experience, this group is 'American' only in the matter of citizenship. Actually these are European designers. We see in their work a degree of certainty of finish and of technique which it will take most of our designers years to develop."[74]

The editorial's estimate proved, in the end, far too pessimistic. A new American design, made by native-born artists, was already emerging. It would soon alter the course of modernism in the United States—and pose one of Frankl's greatest challenges.

CHAPTER NINE

Domesticating the Machine

Despite his notoriety and punishing schedule, Frankl still managed to find time away from the demands of running the gallery and from the repeated invitations to address or write for popular audiences. Whenever he could, he spent time at the cabin in Woodstock, escaping the city for extended weekends and during the hot summer months. In comparison with his hectic life in Manhattan, his stays in Woodstock were relaxed and carefree. He idled away the hours chatting with friends or hiking in the wooded hills. When in New York, Frankl habitually took prolonged lunch breaks with acquaintances from the art world, discussing for hours the latest trends in ideas and design. In the evenings, he was a regular in the small cafés and bars of Greenwich Village, where he often sat with a few close friends over a bottle of cheap wine until the early morning hours.

Busy as he was, Frankl continued to draw and paint. Throughout the later 1920s, he repeatedly sketched the New York skyline from his penthouse terrace on Riverside Drive (fig. 77). Almost every year, in late winter, he spent a few weeks in Havana drawing and painting at the ocean's edge or in the lush gardens. When time permitted, he read widely. Through subscriptions to the leading European architecture and design journals, he

Opposite:
Paul T. Frankl, Speed lounge chair, c. 1932 (detail of fig. 100)

Fig. 77. Paul T. Frankl, sketch of skyscrapers in New York, c. 1929. Collection Paulette Frankl

kept up with the latest developments across the Atlantic. And he was a regular reader of American trade publications on furniture and retailing, carefully watching the changing directions in marketing.

But Frankl's attempts to promote modernism still held first claim to his attentions. For most of 1929, he was hard at work on his second book, *Form and Re-Form: A Practical Handbook of Modern Interiors*. Like *New Dimensions*, *Form and Re-Form*, published in February 1930, was an attempt to confirm the legitimacy of the new design and to spell out its defining features. It repeats many of Frankl's earlier ideas: his belief in the importance of comfort, his devotion to material richness, his plea for formal simplicity. At the book's heart, though, is Frankl's contention that a novel style, at once modern *and* American, had at last made its appearance.[1]

The shift away from European dominance is immediately apparent in the illustrations. More than half of the photographs in *New Dimensions* documented the work of European designers, particularly the French; in *Form and*

Re-Form, the Americans (albeit overwhelmingly from European backgrounds) predominate. But it was not only the provenance of the objects and interiors that had changed: their look was indeed different. They exhibited a new refinement—a flatness, plainness, and precision that had been absent in the first, tentative experiments of the New York modernists. This boldness of gesture is echoed by the book's layout, which relies on striking photographs and geometric graphics (fig. 78).

The response to *Form and Re-Form* was, on the whole, more positive than it had been for Frankl's first book. Henry-Russell Hitchcock praised it despite finding its design "clumsy and pretentious." C. Adolph Glassgold commended Frankl for providing "one with a good picture of modern decorative arts." And an unsigned review in *Arts and Decoration* called the book "the most remarkable single collection of illustrations of new American work to appear."[2]

Surprisingly, none of the contemporary reviews noted what, in retrospect, are the most conspicuous new trends manifest in the illustrations: the increasing evidence of machine-age imagery and, even more striking, the advent of streamlined forms. Both currents were already visible in 1929, when Frankl was at work on the manuscript. In the late winter of that year, The Metropolitan Museum of Art in New York organized its eleventh Exhibition of Contemporary American Design. The show was devoted to "The Architect and the Industrial Arts" and featured thirteen rooms designed by nine architects.[3] The decision to engage architects rather than designers, as Henry Kent, the assistant secretary of the museum, explained, was due to the fact that designers had yet to exert much influence on industry. Yet, Kent continued, "the architect, with his strong position in relation to the manufacturing world and his strategic position with regard to the dictation of styles to be used, has been able to give illuminating exposition of what might result in the realm of design if the designer himself were to occupy a position of authority."[4]

The objects and spaces created by the architects—among them, such notables as Raymond Hood and John

Wellborn Root—incorporated most of the hallmarks of contemporary American modernism, though with greater restraint. In comparison with the department store shows of the previous year, one can detect a newfound reliance on metal furnishings and clean, simple geometries. The appearance of metal chairs, sofas, and tables was in large part a result of their proliferation in Europe, especially in Germany, France, and the Netherlands. Americans, as usual, were about two years behind the trend: metal furnishings, aside from lamps, did not begin to enter the U.S. marketplace until the middle of 1929. The first examples of mass-produced pieces began reaching the stores in 1930, when Ficks Reed, the Simmons Company, Ypsilanti, and other firms introduced their own metal furniture.[5]

But it was not only the use of metal in American furnishings that stood out. Far more, it was the streamlining of their surfaces—the accentuation of their fluid, unbroken lines—that signaled the emergence of a novel aesthetic direction. The idea of streamlining grew out of the fascination with speed and dynamism that captured the public imagination at the end of the 1920s. When applied to locomotives and airplanes, teardrop- or bullet-shaped designs reduced air resistance and enhanced ease of movement. But streamlining came to mean much more: it was a condensed and direct avowal of mobility, speed, efficiency, hygiene, and—in its purest expression—modernity. It was the power of this language to articulate a brave new world of modernism that hastened streamlining's popularity. The appeal of the streamlined aesthetic was so great that, although it made little sense in terms of aerodynamics, American designers were soon applying it to household objects, such as furniture, radios, vacuum cleaners—even toasters.

The streamlined style was the creative product of a group of younger designers, most of them native born, who were committed to the ideas of modern mass production. The great visionary of the group was Norman Bel

Fig. 78. Pages from *Form and Re-Form* (1930)

Opposite, top left:
Fig. 79. Paul T. Frankl,
end table, c. 1927.
Cadmium-plated steel and
glass, 24 3/8 x 17 x 17 in.
(61.9 x 43.2 x 43.2 cm).
Indianapolis Museum of
Art. Gift of Mr. and Mrs.
Robert Hosmer Morse,
Jr., 71.214.2

Opposite, top right:
Fig. 80. Paul T. Frankl,
coffee table, c. 1930.
Nickel-plated steel and
silvered glass, height
16 1/2 in. (41.9 cm),
diameter 25 in. (63.5 cm).
Courtesy of Richard
Wright, Chicago

Geddes. Only a few years younger than Frankl, Bel Geddes belonged to a different generation—those who had come of age during and after World War I, when the experience of the Arts and Crafts movement and Art Nouveau was a fading memory; their intellectual world was molded by the specter of mechanized killing in the war and of the great industrial surge in postwar America. And it was in the machine, not in the application of the traditional applied arts, that Bel Geddes and the other younger modernists would find their aesthetic premise.

Born in a small town in Michigan, Bel Geddes worked for a time in the 1920s as a stage designer for the Metropolitan Opera. In 1925, he traveled to Paris to design a production of the play *Jeanne d'Arc*. While there, he visited the Exposition Internationale des Arts Décoratifs et Industriels Modernes. He was little impressed with the stylistic experiments of Ruhlmann and the other French designers—or, even, the cutting-edge work of Le Corbusier and Melnikov. Rather, he saw that, despite the outpouring of consummate artisanship, handicraft itself was giving way to the machine—industry was becoming the driving engine of the new age. Not long after returning to New York, he opened his own industrial design office; by the late 1920s, he was making his first designs for corporate patrons.[6]

Bel Geddes's book *Horizons* (1932), with its dramatic images of speeding motorcars, ships, trains, and airliners, did much to popularize the new aesthetic. But even before then, he was joined by a number of other, mostly younger designers working in a kindred spirit. Several, including Walter Dorwin Teague and Raymond Loewy, were commercial artists who had previously been in advertising; others, such as Henry Dreyfuss, came from the theater, as Bel Geddes had. What united all of the new industrial designers was a belief in the necessity of spurning older notions of handicraft: they sought to fashion not individual art objects but prototypes that could be serially reproduced. This meant more than just the abandonment of older ideas of art: their method implied a wholly different way of expressing the realities of the industrial age. Rather than concocting allusions to the machine, their designs

were machined—they were the outcome of a stylistic logic rooted in the manufacturing process itself.[7]

Very quickly, industrial design evolved into a profession. By 1934, the Metropolitan Museum was turning to the industrial designers for the latest ideas to showcase in its annual exhibitions. Their ascendancy was driven by the workings of American industry: in the fiercely competitive atmosphere of the Great Depression, manufacturers were keen to give their products a modern look, and they relied increasingly on the advice of Bel Geddes, Loewy, Teague, and the others. But more than that, the triumph of the industrial designers derived from the stylistic language they had developed, one that was compelling, distinctive, and identifiably American. Far more than the first wave of American modernism in the 1920s, the imagery of streamlining and of the machine became the visual counterpart of American exceptionalism.

Frankl was slow to confront the challenge of industrial design. He was not unaware of the trend: in the early 1930s, he, too, collaborated from time to time with manufacturers. He found it difficult, however, to compete with Bel Geddes and the others. He had neither the staff nor the resources to make the transition to a very different mode of design.

Yet the issue was not solely one of economics. Frankl, whose aesthetic vision had been shaped in the age of Arts and Crafts, held on to a very different design philosophy. He readily incorporated new materials and processes in his works. But he still drew a clear distinction between art and engineering. And he continued to regard art and purpose as separate categories. Design, for Frankl, was fundamentally about the expression of an aesthetic ideal; the issue of how an object was made was secondary. But the persistence of older notions of art did not preclude Frankl's investigation of new concepts or materials. In that sense, he was closer to his fellow designers at the Bauhaus, most of whom carried on the prewar Arts and Crafts ethos even while experimenting with radical new forms.

Frankl had, in fact, long been a leader in the use of metal for furniture. As early as 1927, he had produced a

three-tiered end table of cadmium-plated steel and glass (fig. 79). (Later, he designed a related small coffee table in nickel-plated steel; fig. 80.) By the end of the 1920s, Frankl was also experimenting with brass fittings for his mirrors (fig. 81), and he began using steel for his chair designs (fig. 82) and spun aluminum for torchères (fig. 83). Around the same time, he began to make his own tubular steel furnishings. An upholstered sofa (fig. 84) he added to the Frankl Galleries catalog in 1929 was among the earliest examples of such furniture produced in the United States.[8] Yet all of these designs were still indebted to established notions of furniture assembly and form—and the conventions of handicraft.

Despite Frankl's slow embrace of the new manufacturing processes, his work from this period evinces a clear interest in new aesthetic ideas. By the later 1920s, he was investigating the possibilities of strict and pure geometry. In 1929, he took part in the Modern American Design in Metal exhibit at the Newark Museum, one of a series of shows organized by John Cotton Dana, the museum's

Fig. 81. Paul T. Frankl, dressing table, c. 1929. Lacquer, brass, and mirrored glass, 68 x 86 ¹/₂ x 18 ¹/₂ in. (172.7 x 219.7 x 47 cm). Collection of John P. Axelrod, Boston

director, to publicize the latest developments in the "industrial arts."[9] Frankl exhibited several of his recent metal designs, including two small nickel-plated occasional tables. Other works also attest to his efforts to come to terms with the latest European currents. A 1929 advertisement for his new furniture line hints at the influence of contemporary German and Dutch graphic work (fig. 85), and a red-lacquered desk with chromium-plated steel supports that probably dates from 1930 almost certainly drew from the latest German furnishings (fig. 86).[10]

Frankl was not the only American designer whose work demonstrated this shift in sensibility. By the beginning of 1930, most of the New York modernists and some of those on the West Coast had come to embrace the new look of formal clarity and simplicity. The change is recorded in the pages of the *Annual of American Design*, which appeared toward the end of the year. Published under the auspices of the American Union of Decorative Artists and Craftsmen (AUDAC) and edited by Robert Leonard and Adolph Glassgold, the book offered examples by almost every American modernist designer of note. There are interiors and furnishings by Frankl, Winold Reiss, Eugene Schoen, Joseph Urban, Kem Weber, Paul Zimmermann, and other members of the "older" generation of American moderns, as well as many of the emerging industrial designers. (The

book also reproduces buildings and projects by Raymond Hood, Albert Kahn, Ely Jacques Kahn, Frank Lloyd Wright, and his son Lloyd Wright, as well as Bel Geddes, George Howe and William Lescaze, and Frederick Kiesler.) The majority of the works illustrated fall more or less into the broad category of a new purified modernism. But one can discern two distinct and different approaches: Frankl and the other older designers often merely implied the appearance of the machine age—that is, its visual language; the younger "industrial designers," by contrast, were intent upon forging an aesthetic that was the direct outcome of machine production. The works of the traditional designers were still handmade in many cases, regardless of their polished finishes and industrial-age materials, and generally expensive; those of the new industrial designers were serially reproducible—and they were intended, at least, to be more affordable.[11]

These differences in approach were restated in two exhibitions in the early 1930s. The first, the Home Show, held from 31 March to 4 April 1930 at the Grand Central

Right:
Fig. 82. Paul T. Frankl, armchair, c. 1929. Nickel-plated steel and leather upholstery, height 31 3/8 in. (79.7 cm). Courtesy Sotheby's, New York

Left:
Fig. 83. Paul T. Frankl, torchère, c. 1929. Spun aluminum, height 66 in. (167.7 cm), diameter (shade) 11 in. (27.9 cm). Collection of John P. Axelrod, Boston

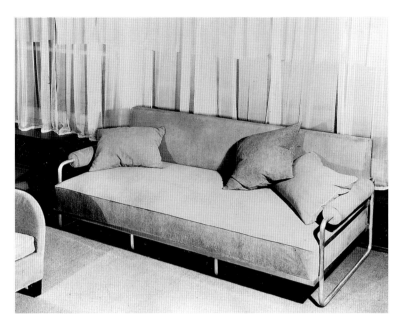

Fig. 84. Paul T. Frankl, sofa, c. 1929. Tubular brushed-chromium frame and cloth upholstery

Fig. 85. Paul T. Frankl, advertisement for the Frankl Galleries, 1929

Palace in New York, presented a series of room installations and a large display of rugs, textiles, and other objects for the home.[12] AUDAC was prominently represented (fig. 87). From the start, one of the organization's stated aims had been to encourage cooperation between industry and designers; the items on exhibit, it was hoped, would attract new interest on the part of manufacturers for modern design. Nonetheless, the AUDAC contributions to the show, which included five complete room installations (among them, an office with Kiesler's remarkable "flying desk"; fig. 88), were almost evenly divided between "decorative" and "industrial" art—yielding something of a mixed message, but accurately depicting the divided nature of the organization's membership.

The split between the two design cultures was even more apparent at another AUDAC exhibit, Modern Industrial and Decorative Art, held at the Brooklyn Museum from June to September 1931. Almost all of the top designers were represented. Donald Deskey, Walter von Nessen, Hugo Gnam, Jr., Wolfgang and Pola Hoffmann, Gilbert Rohde, Kem Weber, and Alexander Kachinsky created individual rooms. Frankl contributed a living room with a swirl-patterned

Fig. 86. Paul T. Frankl, desk, c. 1930. Red-lacquered hardwood (restored) and chromium-plated steel supports, 31 x 27 1/2 x 20 1/2 in. (78.7 x 69.8 x 52.1 cm). The Minneapolis Institute of Arts, The Modernism Collection. Gift of Norwest Bank, Minn. [98.276.116]

Fig. 87. The AUDAC Home Show at the Grand Central Palace in New York,
31 March – 4 April 1930

Fig. 88. Frederick Kiesler, flying desk, exhibited at the AUDAC
Home Show, 1930

wallpaper in vermilion and gold, a metal lamp and table,
and twin armchairs covered in faux zebra skin. Many of the
other AUDAC designers exhibited individual objects.[13]

Donald McGregor, writing in *Good Furniture and
Decoration*, praised the show, calling it "one of the most
interesting and descriptive exhibitions of contemporary
arts and crafts since the wave of so-called Modernism
broke over a surprised and rather bewildered world of aes-
thetics."[14] Adolph Glassgold, who reviewed the exhibit for
Creative Art, also had words of praise for the "essential good
taste and high quality material displayed." Nonetheless,
Glassgold asked whether the American modernists of
either camp had fully grasped the meanings of "industrial
designing": the advent of designing for manufacturers "led
to a definitely stated revolt against . . . 'the self-expression
of easel painting.'" Design, he charged, should no longer
be about "the esthetic problem per se," but rather "reproduce itself on a mass production scale; inexpensively,
durably, with both eyes on function and an ear to the
ground of the wide public need."[15]

In a short essay in the *Annual of American Design*, Frankl
acknowledged the need for changing how household articles were developed and fabricated: "Machines have swept
away any pretense as well as the old-time sentimentality
concerning the home." In the future, he continued, "furniture and furnishing will be manufactured as scientifically
and as efficiently and . . . with as great variety as motor cars
or airplanes are today. . . . Good design must be as much a

commonplace in the American home of tomorrow as perfect plumbing and heating are today." [16]

If Frankl recognized industrial design as the wave of the future, his own success at selling costly, handmade articles made it difficult for him to embrace the new trend. Nonetheless, he did accept offers from several manufacturers to design products. [17] In 1927, the Warren Telechron Company, a leading maker of electric clocks, commissioned him to create a "modern" clock. Frankl responded with a scaled-down version of his Skyscraper furnishings (fig. 89). The "Modernique," as the company christened it, made use of the newest materials: Bakelite, chrome, and steel. With its bold massing and refined materials, the design was an elegant and complete statement of the new style. But it proved to be a hard sell. At nearly eight inches tall, it was larger than any of the company's other clocks—and, because it was so elaborate, it required more assembly time. It was also more expensive, retailing for fifty dollars—considerably more than most of Telechron's other clocks. Only a small number were sold, and the company discontinued the model after a few years.

Nor did Frankl find much success with two toilet sets he designed for the Celluloid Corporation of America in 1929. Unlike Bakelite, which was a recent discovery, celluloid had a long history. Its American inventor, John Wesley Hyatt, had come up with a process for making the early plastic in 1866; by the 1920s, it was in widespread use as photographic film for still and motion pictures. The Celluloid Corporation's managers were eager to find new uses for their product and were convinced that Frankl's name would improve their sales. They engaged him to "style" the two toilet sets in the hope of appealing to the modernist trend. Borrowing from his own design vocabulary, Frankl based one version on variations of squares and rectangles, the other on circles (fig. 90). [18] Both offered convincing illustrations of how celluloid could be cast to make practical objects for daily use. Once more, though, production costs for the two sets exceeded that of comparable products, and the company soon abandoned the experiment.

Fig. 89. Paul T. Frankl, clock, manufactured by the Warren Telechron Company, Ashland, Massachusetts (model no. 431), c. 1928. Bakelite, brush-burnished silver, chrome, and enamel, 7 3/4 x 5 3/4 x 3 3/4 in. (19.7 x 14.6 x 9.5 cm). The Art Institute of Chicago. Gift of Susan and Jerome Kahn [2000.19]

Fig. 90. Paul T. Frankl, pieces from two toilet sets, manufactured by the Celluloid Corporation of America, 1929. Celluloid with natural bristles, length of comb 7 1/4 in. (18.4 cm). Courtesy Sotheby's, New York

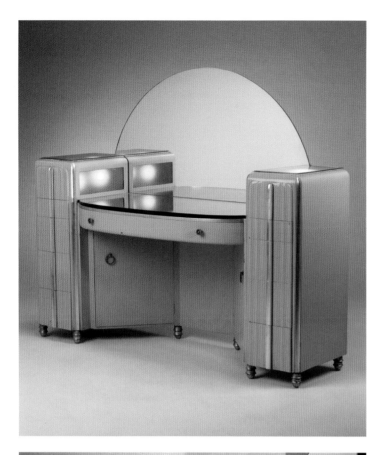

Below, top:
Fig. 92. Paul T. Frankl, drawing for a dressing table and stool, c. 1930

Below, bottom:
Fig. 94. Paul T. Frankl, drawing for a conference table and chairs, c. 1930

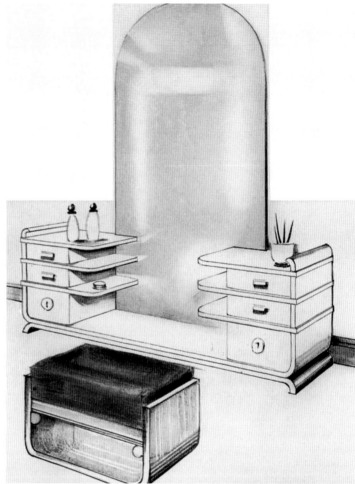

Above, top:
Fig. 91. Paul T. Frankl, vanity, c. 1928. Lacquered wood, mirrored glass, frosted glass, and steel, 54 1/4 x 66 x 19 1/2 in. (137.8 x 167.6 x 49.5 cm). Courtesy of Richard Wright, Chicago

Above, bottom:
Fig. 93. Paul T. Frankl, bedroom, c. 1931. Black-lacquered hardwood with metal banding

Frankl received several other commissions from manufacturers, including an appeal from automobile magnate Walter Chrysler in 1934 to redesign the front grill for his new De Soto model. He also produced railroad car interiors for the Great Northern Railway.[19] But the truth was that Frankl had only nominal experience with product design and no support staff. Almost all of the work went to Dreyfuss, Teague, Russel Wright, and the other industrial designers, who already had established practices and far greater resources.[20]

Frankl may have taken a backseat to the industrial designers in the burgeoning field of product design, but he continued to hold the lead in other areas. By 1928, ahead of most of the other American furniture designers, he was introducing streamlined elements into his furniture (fig. 91). Two years later, in the *Annual of American Design*, he published a complete version of the idea in the form of a vanity and matching seat (fig. 92). The rounded shape, repeated in the mirror, the base of the table and seat, and the shelves, yielded a look of smooth refinement.

What was lacking was any overt indication of speed. Frankl solved the problem—as Loewy, Bel Geddes, Teague, and others also did—by emphasizing the horizontal elements of his pieces with banding along the edges. A streamlined bed he designed in 1931 had metal striping that wrapped around its curving contours (fig. 93). To further the impression of continuity, Frankl integrated the twin nightstands, extending the same sweeping lines along their surfaces.

The suggestion of "uninterrupted flow" soon became one of the leitmotifs of Frankl's design.[21] He discovered that rounding the corners of his furnishings was unnecessary: the extended horizontal "speed lines" themselves sufficed to imply accelerated motion. By the beginning of the 1930s, a number of his works incorporated this imagery of extended lines accenting boxy forms. The most imposing was a design for a massive conference table he published in the *Annual of American Design* (fig. 94), but the same arrangement shows up in his suite of wooden outdoor furniture

Fig. 95. Paul T. Frankl, outdoor seating group, 1929. Wood, red leather upholstery, and printed German fabric

(fig. 95) and in his facade for a Manhattan candy shop, the Confiserie Vienna (fig. 96). Frankl was experimenting, too, with a more reduced streamlined vocabulary. A number of his designs from the early 1930s display a plain, elemental version of the style (figs. 97, 98), and within a short time he was sometimes dispensing with rounded forms altogether, producing works based on pure, straight lines (fig. 99).

If the precise forms of these works were original, the overall concept was not. Many of the other New York modernists were making use of identical motifs. But toward the end of 1931, Frankl had an idea for a new design that would become one of his most recognizable works. For some time, he had been thinking about making a large, upholstered lounge chair that could replace the older club chairs on the market. Rather than resorting to applied lines, he began investigating how to adjust the form of the chair itself to evoke the impression of speed. After some experimentation, he found that he could lengthen the seat and bevel the front and rear surfaces of the arms so that they inclined sharply downward and inward. The long, low profile of the chair—in combination with its angular lines—engendered an immediate impression of movement.[22] The earliest of his so-called Speed chairs were upholstered with monk's cloth over a wooden frame (fig. 100). Eventually, he produced them with a variety of coverings, including contrasting leathers, fleece, and pony skin. Many, especially those

Fig. 96. Paul T. Frankl, facade for the Confiserie Vienna, New York, c. 1930

Above, top:
Fig. 97. Paul T. Frankl, coffee table, c. 1930. Crackle-lacquered wood, glass, mirror, and nickel-plated steel, height 19 1/2 in. (49.5 cm), diameter 32.5 in. (82.6 cm). Courtesy of Richard Wright, Chicago

Above, bottom:
Fig. 99. Paul T. Frankl, side table, early 1930s. Crackle-lacquered wood and glass. Courtesy of Richard Wright, Chicago

Above, top:
Fig. 98. Paul T. Frankl, coffee table, c. 1930. Lacquered mahogany, height 15 1/2 in. (39.4 cm), diameter 45 in. (114.3 cm). Courtesy of Richard Wright, Chicago

Above, bottom:
Fig. 100. Paul T. Frankl, Speed lounge chair, c. 1932. Wood, cork, and monk's cloth upholstery, 24 1/2 x 36 x 41 in. (61.5 x 91.4 x 104.1 cm). The Metropolitan Museum of Art, New York, Collection of John C. Waddell

with cloth upholstery, had sheets of cork on the arms to protect them against wear. The model became one of his best-selling designs, and Frankl continued to make and sell them through the early 1950s.

Though still busy with his own design work, Frankl continued his efforts to promote AUDAC. The two AUDAC exhibitions and the publication of the *Annual of American Design* marked the high point in the organization's fortunes. With the deepening of the Depression, however, AUDAC started to falter. As business declined, many of the designers, Frankl wrote, "went back into hibernation. No more fancy parties at the Casino—not even the Wednesday outings with the dollar dinner—everything had to be dropped. The artists could no longer afford the luxury of an evening out. . . . It became impossible to keep secretary and office."[23] The membership declined markedly. Annual dues for AUDAC were twenty-five dollars, a business membership one hundred dollars.[24] Many of the rank and file simply could not afford the cost.

Frankl did all he could to keep AUDAC afloat. He revived the Wednesday evening soirees at the gallery, offering drinks and dinner to all comers for fifty cents. In the midst of Prohibition, he hoped the appeal of cheap alcohol would be a strong incentive for the designers to attend. To guard against losing money on the venture, he planned to serve hot dogs from a wagon and "bathtub martinis."

After a long search, he found a dilapidated hotdog cart from a secondhand shop on Canal Street and asked Witold Gordon to repaint it. The two men then converted part of the top into a bar, and, at the next Wednesday evening party, Frankl had Egmont Ahrens, AUDAC's treasurer, and Deskey serve as bartenders.[25]

The cart became the pièce de résistance of the evening. The following morning, as a joke, Frankl placed it in his show window. What happened next surprised even him: "No sooner was it on display that crowds began to gather; the corner cop, who for two long years never took notice of my existence, came in to ask if he should disperse them. . . . People stood three deep holding their sides

laughing and many came inquiring" about whether it was for sale and how much it cost. Frankl eventually refurbished and sold more than one hundred of the carts. The venture failed to save AUDAC, which withered away after 1932, but it gave Frankl's business a much-needed boost.[26]

Despite his success with the pushcarts and with his streamlined designs, Frankl began to experience increasingly tightened financial circumstances. As the Depression set in during the course of 1930, sales at the shop fell off, and fewer and fewer interior decorating commissions came his way. He had little in the way of savings to fall back on; for some time, he and Isa had been living beyond their means. The rent for the gallery and annex and for their penthouse apartment consumed much of what they were earning from the shop. His custom furnishings fetched high prices, but they were expensive to make and store, so Frankl's profit margin had always been slim. In addition to the costs of running the gallery, the couple was laying out a great deal on entertaining. Several times a week, they invited guests to their apartment or went out on the town. Isa, always immaculately dressed, spent lavishly on clothes. What money they were able to put aside they lost with the onset of the Depression. At Isa's urging, Frankl had invested heavily in the stock market. Most of their savings evaporated in the aftermath of the plunge on Black Thursday.[27]

To compound his woes, he and Isa were having marital problems. Throughout the later 1920s, she had traveled to Europe each spring accompanied only by Peter, leaving Frankl in New York to tend to the business. Her ostensible purpose for the trips was to purchase articles for the gallery. But Frankl discovered that she was having an affair with a wealthy Viennese candy manufacturer. Upon arriving in Austria, she would deposit Peter with Frankl's mother and take off for weeks at a time with her lover.[28] Isa was also seeing other men in New York. Frankl had been having affairs of his own for years, but by the end of 1929 he had had enough of her philandering and ever more frequent outbursts of temper—he demanded a divorce. Although Isa was reluctant at first to grant him one, Frankl held firm, and finally, after several emotional scenes, she went to Reno, Nevada, to obtain the necessary papers. By the time the divorce was finalized, she had moved out, and with money from the settlement she opened an upscale women's clothing boutique on Lexington Avenue.[29]

The divorce aided Frankl's emotional state, but it did nothing to improve his dismal business fortunes. In 1931, in an effort to prop up lagging sales and lower his overhead, he moved the shop from East Forty-eighth Street to a smaller space at 509 Madison Avenue, on the southeast corner of Madison and Fifty-third Street. To finance the move and keep the gallery afloat, he was forced to borrow several thousand dollars from his cousin Max Friedmann.

Friedmann was president of Ed Schuster and Company, a group of department stores in Milwaukee founded by his grandfather. He and Frankl had been close in their youth; during the summers, they had gone hiking together in the Swiss Alps. Later, after Frankl settled in the United States, they saw each other several times a year. Friedmann never failed to visit his cousin during his trips to New York, and Frankl stopped in Milwaukee on each of his lecture tours.[30]

In an effort to further aid his cousin financially, Friedmann engaged him to redesign his home and his office at the store. The office, paneled with imported Honduran mahogany, was dark and ill-suited to modern furniture. Frankl insisted that the room be painted white, an idea Friedmann at first protested vehemently. Frankl eventually won, and he installed a modern suite of furnishings set against a stark white background. For years afterward, Friedmann was fond of telling people that he had the most expensive white walls in the world.[31]

Even with the commissions and loan from Friedmann, Frankl was barely able to make ends meet. By the end of 1931, like many Americans, he was becoming ever more pessimistic. His mounting feelings of resignation and despair are lucidly registered in his book *Machine-Made*

Leisure, which appeared at the beginning of 1932.

Frankl had started work on the book several years earlier, even before he had finished *Form and Re-Form*. In the broadest sense, the book was Frankl's response to the challenges of the new industrial design, especially to the problem of machine production. The first half comprises a lengthy discourse about the rise and impact of the Industrial Revolution. Many of the arguments go back to ideas that Frankl had first expounded during his last years in Berlin. His main thesis is that only through the agency of artists can the machine develop into "a true instrument of creative expression."[32]

But *Machine-Made Leisure* is more than a tacit defense of the role of the designer; it is also an attempt to explore the social meanings of the changes wrought by machine production. "Mechanization of industry," Frankl writes, "has resulted in essential and far-reaching changes in our social structure.... Increased earning power of the workers has provided means to enjoy the better things in life, to acquire more education, to devote more time to social activities, and generally to widen the aesthetic outlook." The problem, as he saw it, was that none of this had resulted in greater leisure; the modern designer's new role was to overcome "the dictatorship of machinery"—to demonstrate to all how to find and fill more free time.[33]

Throughout *Machine-Made Leisure*, Frankl's renunciation of the freewheeling culture and economy of the 1920s is evident. In one memorable passage, he writes: "The skyscraper, considered America's outstanding contribution to the present-day civilization, is but a passing fad. The tallest of them, the Empire State, is but the tombstone on the grave of the era that built it. From a practical and technical viewpoint, skyscrapers are incongruous, as they create traffic problems that we are unable to solve." Frankl also reveals his mounting dissatisfaction with life in the city: "The city, as we know it today, is dying...of hardening of the arteries. It lacks flexibility and creates artificial conditions of life, unhealthy and unendurable. The moment we recognize leisure as an essential of our existence, we turn to the country. The home of the future will

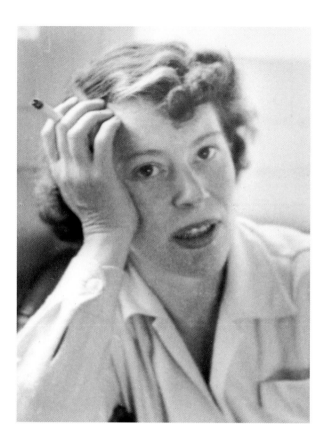

Fig. 101. Mary Ballard Irwin, c. 1935

be built in the country." The book ends, however, on a surprisingly upbeat note: "If the machine can be mobilized toward the creation of a really good life, its tortuous and tragic history will be fully justified and leisure will be once more not a curse but a blessing."[34]

Most of the book's reviewers—perhaps wishing to buoy the spirit of their readers—stressed the positive aspects of Frankl's message. R. L. Duffus, writing in the *New York Times*, found the work "encouraging."[35] But some, including June Barrows Mussey, who reviewed the book for *Creative Art*, found it confusing and difficult to follow.[36] *Machine-Made Leisure* is indeed a difficult text. Frankl's prose is, as ever, mostly straightforward, though his meandering account of the course of industrialization is not easy to follow. But it is not the book's organization that offers the greatest obstacle to the reader's comprehension. What makes it problematic—and, also, somewhat opaque—is Frankl's essential ambivalence about the machine. He seems wary of mechanization and its inherent dangers, yet he also trumpets the machine as the tool for modern man's ultimate salvation. This wavering tone no doubt accurately reflected Frankl's own uncertainty:

he recognized the promise mass production held for the future, but he remained reluctant to fully adopt the new design modus.

The year 1933 was even worse for business than the previous two years. Commissions for custom furniture and interiors virtually dried up, and sales of smaller objects slowed to a trickle. Frankl also missed Isa, who had not only contributed her finely attuned aesthetic sense to the gallery's displays but had served as the office manager, overseeing the day-to-day running of the business. He found her replacement in Mary Ballard Irwin, who quickly assumed a central place in the shop—and in his life (fig. 101).

Born in 1907, Mary Irwin was the youngest of five children in a working-class Atlanta family. In her early twenties, she taught in the public schools in her hometown, but eventually she ran off to New York to escape her hardscrabble existence and to pursue her dream of becoming an actress. Tall and athletic, she won a role as a chorus girl in the Ziegfeld Follies. Her long legs and striking figure served her well as a dancer. They also lured the attention of a number of suitors, including an English aristocrat, with whom she fell madly in love. After the man returned to Britain, she followed him across the Atlantic, only to be curtly dispatched by the family butler at the front door of his London townhouse. It was a humiliation she never forgot. After returning to New York, she resolved never again to be poor. By chance, she happened to sign up for one of Frankl's interior design courses at The Metropolitan Museum of Art. Infatuated from the first moment, she made up her mind that she would marry him.[37]

At the time, Frankl was still married to Isa. To improve her chances of getting close to Frankl, Mary took a sales job at a textile shop across the street from his gallery. She spent as much time as she could at the window watching the goings-on at the Frankl Galleries. When a position finally came open at the gallery, she applied immediately. Frankl, impressed with her eagerness, hired her on the spot. She soon made herself indispensable, and with Isa's departure she gradually assumed the role of business manager. By the end of 1931, she and Frankl were also lovers.[38]

Mary was the opposite of Isa in most respects—dependable, conventional, and focused. She was also, in contrast to Isa, largely without an artistic sensibility. But she made up for her lack of aesthetic abilities with other talents. Above all, she proved more than competent in running the business. Mary turned out to have a flair for accounting—something for which Frankl had neither interest nor aptitude—and she picked up the rudiments of interior design practice, which allowed her to fill in for Frankl whenever he was away.

But with scant demand for expensive custom furnishings, the gallery barely limped along. With abundant time on his hands for the first time in years, Frankl started drawing again, making a series of pencil and charcoal portrait sketches of working-class New Yorkers. He showed the works at the gallery in the late fall of 1931.[39] The exhibit drew positive reviews, and Frankl, encouraged by the response, made arrangements in the spring of 1933 for a larger show of his watercolors and drawings of Cuba and the Manhattan skyline at the venerable Knoedler Galleries in Midtown.[40]

As always when there was little or no work, Frankl used the opportunity to experiment with new ideas. In mid-1933, he undertook an extensive remodeling of his own apartment on Riverside Drive (fig. 102). In place of the jagged forms of his earlier manner, he substituted a softer, cozier look that combined the new streamlined forms with monochrome finishes. Unlike his interiors of the late 1920s, which relied almost exclusively on freestanding pieces, much of the furniture was built in, enhancing the appearance of unity. He also made use of new materials, such as the thin sheets of cork with which he wrapped the fireplace mantel and the sofa and chair frames.

The look contrasted sharply with the purified, machined aesthetic Loewy, Deskey, and the other industrial designers were promoting (fig. 103). For the next several years, until the arrival of the International Style,

Fig. 102. Paul T. Frankl, living room, Frankl Apartment, New York, c. 1933

Fig. 103. Raymond Loewy and Lee Simonson, industrial designer's office, shown at the Contemporary American Industrial Art exhibition, The Metropolitan Museum of Art, New York, 1934

these two approaches—the language of comfort and grace on the one hand, and that of industrial streamlining on the other—would define American modernism.

That fall season Frankl introduced his new style at the gallery. He updated several of the permanent displays, including the model living room (fig. 104), which he did over with a curvilinear fireplace, oversized round mirror, grass cloth–covered wall, and his new Speed chairs and sofas (both now available with either leather or heavily textured cloth upholstery).

He used the same aesthetic and palette of materials—cork, nubby fabrics, and grass matting—for his only two important commissions in the first half of 1934: the penthouse of eccentric jazz-band leader Roger Wolfe Kahn and the apartment of Charles Hubert Winans (fig. 105). Both exemplified, as a write-up in *House and Garden* described, "the new tenets of modernism...the abandonment of grotesque angles" in favor of the curve, which "is beginning to bring an air of grace into our contemporary rooms."[41]

Frankl's commitment to the ideal of comfort did not prevent him from investigating new technologies and artificial materials. In the spring of 1934, he accepted an

invitation to participate in the Newark Museum's Miracles of Chemistry exhibition. The show, which opened in late March, was a demonstration of how the new synthetic materials—such as plastics and nylon—were being adapted for everyday use.[42] Frankl contributed a model living room, complete with a Formica-covered desk, a sofa and chairs upholstered in synthetic fabrics, and several chemical beakers, which served as flower vases. It was his intention, as he explained to one reporter, to show neither "imitations of the past nor projections into the future, but things designed for today's use and made of today's materials by today's methods" that "belong in the truly modern home. Our age is one of invention, machinery, industry, science and commerce."[43]

The Newark exhibition coincided with the Machine Art exhibition, held at the Museum of Modern Art in New York from early March to late April 1934. Curated by Philip Johnson, who was then head of the museum's architecture department, it presented a wide range of manufactured articles, from chairs and household appliances to ball bearings and scientific instruments. Johnson's intention was to demonstrate the broad impact of the machine and how designers were responding to its challenges. The objects, as he wrote in the accompanying catalog, fell into two categories: those that were purely functional, such as watch springs or chemical dishes, and those designed to have "artistic" appeal, such as furnishings.[44] But in either case, as the museum's director, Alfred H. Barr, pointed out in the catalog's foreword, the "refinement of modern materials and the precision of machine manufacture" produced an aesthetic effect.[45]

Coming just two years after the Museum of Modern Art's epochal International Style exhibition, Machine Art represented the museum's attempt to codify the principles of the new design—just as it had for architecture. The small furniture section included tubular steel chairs by Marcel Breuer and Le Corbusier, as well as a set of nesting tables manufactured by the Thonet Company in Vienna. There were also accessories from several of the leading American industrial designers, most notably Russel Wright.

Absent from the exhibit were all of the older, European-born American designers, including Frankl, whose works Johnson apparently believed did not correspond to the new modernism. But the picture presented by the exhibit was far from clear. Johnson, in fact, included in the show a number of manufacturers' products—among them, an electric range from Electromaster, designed by Emil Piron, and a lavatory panel designed by George Sakier—that lacked the purity and refinement of Frankl's best works of the early 1930s. It was evidently Frankl's continued embrace of handicraft that Johnson rejected, rather than his aesthetic vision. But his exclusion from the Machine Art exhibit was a first sign of what would soon become a division between "orthodox" modernism and everything else.

Frankl's Newark installation did receive extensive coverage in the media, including an illustrated article by Walter Rendell Storey in the *New York Times*.[46] The spring of 1934 also marked the twentieth anniversary of Frankl's arrival in the United States, and a spate of articles appeared lauding his achievements.[47]

Frankl, though, was exhausted and dejected. "I was tired of New York," he later wrote, "tired of the Depression, tired of being tired, tired of working like a work horse, tired of paying rent here there and everywhere, and in the end to have nothing but canceled rent receipts to show for my efforts."[48] In the late winter, when an old acquaintance, Nelbert Chouinard, director of the Chouinard Art Institute in Los Angeles, invited him to teach a summer course at the school, he promptly accepted.

In early April, Frankl began making preparations for the trip. To raise money, he sold his expensive, custom-made Auburn Phaeton sedan and purchased a new, less expensive Ford Model A. He also sold off some of his inventory of decorative art objects at bargain prices, and he made arrangements for Mary to run the shop in his absence.

But the question of what to do with his son, Peter, remained. He and Isa had tried sending him to a boarding school in Scarborough-on-the-Hudson, New York, but Peter had done poorly at the school and had trouble fitting in—in no small part because his parents insisted on taking him out of school early in the spring so they could travel, and not returning him until late autumn.[49] Frankl, who had been raised by servants, was convinced that parents were not well equipped to raise their own children, and he began to explore other possibilities.[50] After some thought, he wrote to Frank Lloyd Wright to inquire if Wright might accept Peter for the Taliesin Fellowship, Wright's new private school.[51]

The two men had first met in 1926, when Wright walked unannounced into Frankl's office at the gallery. Almost immediately, they hit it off. "There was a bond between us," Frankl would later recall. "We shared adver-

Fig. 104. Paul T. Frankl, model living room in the Frankl Galleries, c. 1933

Fig. 105. Paul T. Frankl,
Winans Apartment,
New York, 1934

sity. To us both architecture and design were not a mere book of styles to be copied, but the expression of an artist's personality, a message to be put into our own words, a record of the time we live in and the problems confronting us. We were both determined not to trim any Christmas tree but our own."[52]

The two men shared something else: economic woes. In the early 1930s, Wright, too, was experiencing severe financial problems. He had few commissions coming in, and what work he found paid little. In the 1920s, Wright's popularity had plummeted, partly a consequence of the rise of European modernism, partly a result of his own

mercurial personality. Between 1929 and 1932, he failed to complete a single new building; it was not until the mid-1930s, with the commission for Fallingwater, his extraordinary house for Edgar Kaufmann in western Pennsylvania, that his fortunes began to revive.[53]

Frankl and Wright found that they had another bond: their love for Japan. Both had recognized early the importance of Japanese art and architecture for contemporary design. "Many decades before such ideas became accepted here," Frankl wrote, "we had lived [in Japan] in houses with corner windows, sliding doors, cabinets set flush into the walls and walls opening the house toward its garden, and gardens extending into the house. . . . There, at an early date, we got acquainted with the intrinsic beauty that is wood, wood in its many manifestations—always allowed to be itself, never camouflaged." [54] He and Wright often sat for hours recalling their travels to the East. After one visit to New York in 1933, Wright gave Frankl several Hiroshige woodcuts; they remained among his prized possessions. (Frankl reciprocated with a small painting by Gustav Klimt.) [55]

From that first meeting in 1926, the two men saw each other frequently. When Wright came to New York, as he did often in the later 1920s, he and Frankl met regularly, lunching at the Plaza Hotel or visiting mutual friends. Wright's irascibility and demanding personality strained— and often ended—most of his friendships. But Frankl's good-natured disposition and his willingness to overlook Wright's more bellicose moments allowed them to form a deep and lasting relationship. Wright came to respect Frankl for his strong opinions. "We often disagreed," Frankl would say decades later, "and when we did we minced no words." Yet neither man lost sight of what brought them together. In the late 1920s, when Wright was a forgotten figure, Frankl made efforts to bring him back into the modernist mainstream. After founding AUDAC, he convinced Wright to serve as an honorary member and to take part in the alliance's activities; Wright, grateful for the attention and recognition, supplied the foreword to *New Dimensions*. [56]

From the start, the two men recognized that they were fighting the same fight—for a genuinely American modernism: "His [was] a voice in the wilderness of the wild and wooly Middle West," Frankl wrote, "mine, as he put it, on the Fifth Avenue firing line." [57] By the late 1920s, Wright was becoming increasingly alarmed by what he perceived as "European cultural imperialism," especially the growing impact of German, French, and Dutch modernism in the United States. In his 1930 lectures at Princeton University, he called for privately funded "industrial style centers" to develop the country's capacities in craft and design. [58] Nothing came of the idea, but two years later, in the fall of

1932, Wright announced he would open a School of Applied Arts in the expanded and refurbished Hillside Home School in Spring Green, Wisconsin, only a short distance from Taliesin. The Taliesin Fellowship opened in October of the same year. [59]

His close friendship with Frankl notwithstanding, Wright was reluctant to accept Peter as a disciple. He was only twelve at the time—a decade younger than most of the other fellows. It was only after some persistent persuasion from Frankl—and an offer to pay full tuition— that Wright finally agreed to take him on for a year. [60]

In mid-June, after all arrangements had been made, Frankl and Peter set off for Wisconsin. [61] They made a brief stop to visit Max Friedmann in Milwaukee, then continued on to Madison, where they met Wright. Together they drove out to Taliesin, arriving on the afternoon of 17 June. The next evening, Frankl presented a lecture on his work to the fellowship students in the sprawling living room of the main house. [62]

The following morning, alone, he began the long drive west.

CHAPTER TEN

West and East

Frankl arrived in Los Angeles early in the morning on the Fourth of July, 1934 (fig. 106). During his long, solitary drive through Arizona and Nevada, he fell "madly in love with the desert." But he also found the trip dispiriting. Most of the nation was still in the stubborn grip of the Depression, and the roads were filled with impoverished migrants from the Dust Bowl of Oklahoma and Texas seeking a better life in the West. [1]

Opposite:
Paul T. Frankl, patio,
Wilfley House,
Los Angeles, 1936
(detail of fig. 114)

He moved into a small artist's studio (rented for him by Nelbert Chouinard) not far from the school on South Grandview Street. The simple, low-slung house, "tucked away in a lush garden...under large-leaved Japanese rice paper trees," seemed to him the perfect refuge. He was especially taken with the house's open sleeping porch, which allowed him to roll his bed outside at night and sleep under the stars. Even more satisfying, the rent was a mere thirty-five dollars a month, a fraction of what he was accustomed to paying in New York. [2]

Frankl was equally pleased with his first impression of the school. Chouinard had founded her art institute in 1921, shortly after she moved to Los Angeles from Brooklyn. In less than a decade, she had built it into the leading art school on

Fig. 106. Paul T. Frankl, mid-1930s

the West Coast. The school's purpose, she explained in one of its brochures, was to teach students the basics of art technique freed from "fetish style or theories."[3] The faculty, composed mostly of part-time and guest teachers, included many prominent practitioners and educators—among them, Hans Hofmann, Alexander Archipenko, and New Zealand–born designer Joseph Sinel. Chouinard gave them wide latitude to promote their own ideas. Most of the teachers, like Chouinard herself, subscribed to a loosely defined modernism, and students encountered a wide range of styles and approaches.

Chouinard asked Frankl to present a short, three-week-long introductory course on "Modern Interior and Industrial Design." The class schedule required him only to give a single, hour-long lecture each day, leaving him abundant free time to relax and explore the city. After the exhausting whirlwind of New York, his time in Los Angeles, he wrote to Frank Lloyd Wright's wife, Olgivanna, seemed "like heaven." He delighted in the "agreeable" climate, the cool nights, the abundance of flowers.[4] There was none of "the mad rush, the high tension, the relentless drive, the fierce pressure, so constant in New York."[5]

By the time Frankl returned east at the end of the summer, he had resolved to move to Los Angeles and open a branch of the Frankl Galleries. At first, he considered keeping the New York location open, but only two weeks later, fed up with the trials of life in Manhattan, he decided to close the Madison Avenue store and transfer his entire operation to the West Coast.[6] After twenty years in New York, he wrote, "I had made a name and place for myself." But "it was not worth it—what was left of my life I would enjoy. . . . I had no intention to retire, but I was through killing myself."[7]

In early September, Frankl repeated his cross-county trek to California. Mary accompanied him this time; they moved into a two-bedroom house just off Fairfax Avenue. Still deeply in debt, Frankl struggled to scrape together enough money to rent and remodel a large storefront in Hollywood. A portion of the funds came from the sale of the bulk of his New York inventory. But the market for art

and design was still soft, and he was forced to borrow another seven thousand dollars from Max Friedmann. For months, Frankl had so little cash that he fell behind on the tuition he owed to Wright for Peter's stay at Taliesin, a fact that Wright, equally strapped for money, reminded him of in an incessant barrage of letters.[8]

The new shop was located in the 3200 block of Wilshire Boulevard, along the so-called Miracle Mile, the commercial spine of West Los Angeles, which was lined with chic stores and office towers.[9] A few blocks up from Frankl's new gallery was the elegant Bullock's Wilshire Department Store; across the street were the Ambassador Hotel, the grande dame of West Los Angeles, and the famed Cocoanut Grove, Hollywood's premier nightclub and for many years the site of the annual Academy Awards. There was scant pedestrian traffic along Wilshire—at least in comparison with midtown Manhattan. But Frankl knew that most of the Hollywood elite drove by regularly; he hoped that the striking, modernized facade he added to the building, with its large show windows, would beckon passersby to stop and go inside (fig. 107).

The new Frankl Galleries occupied nearly five times the space of his Madison Avenue store and, to Frankl's delight and relief, rented for less than a tenth of what he had paid in New York. He used the large space to assemble an array of different room installations, complete with furniture and accessories, something he had never been able to do in his tiny, cramped New York galleries (fig. 108). He also made use of the ample rear courtyard, which he converted into an outdoor display area with a patio and garden. In the center, he constructed a large goldfish pond; around it, he arranged several interweaving paths of stepping-stones in mock Japanese fashion. During the winter rainy season, Frankl covered the paths with Japanese oilpaper umbrellas, producing a spectacular play of light and shadow.[10]

The shop, however, was not an immediate success. Frankl found fertile ground in Southern California for his distinctive brand of modernism, but the competition was fierce. Hollywood was one of the few places in the nation left largely unscathed by the Depression, and a veritable legion of designers—Annette Frank, Paul Granard, John S. Mason, Benno Simank, among many others—had established practices there. It took Frankl several years to build a client base, and even then, until the end of the 1930s, he continued to rely on commissions from the East Coast to make ends meet.[11]

If the financial advantages initially were small, Frankl's move to the West Coast did aid his effort to spread the message of modernism. The Hollywood scene, depicted in innumerable films, newsreels, and fan magazines, offered an alluring vision of ease and material abundance. Frankl's interiors and furniture, reproduced in *California Arts and Architecture* and other magazines and presented in many films, broadly influenced American design—even if, to his frustration, the publicity more often than not failed to result in sales or commissions.

In a bid to increase their profit margin, he and Mary decided to abandon the Christmas cards, matches, and other small decorative objects that had been the staple of the New York store. They focused instead on furniture, lamps, outdoor seating, and selected antiques, which had a higher markup and were more in accord with the tastes and requirements of their Hollywood clientele.[12] The move also allowed Frankl to concentrate on his own design work—the mid-1930s was one of his most productive periods as a furniture designer—and freed him up to take on an increasing number of interior design commissions as he established his practice.

With the business up and running, Frankl gradually settled into life in Los Angeles. In the fall of 1935, he presented a second course on interior decoration at the Chouinard Art

Fig. 107. Paul T. Frankl, facade for the Frankl Galleries on Wilshire Boulevard, c. 1934

Below:
Fig. 108. Paul T. Frankl, Frankl Galleries showroom, mid-1930s

Opposite:
Fig. 109. Paul T. Frankl, living room, Kuhrts House, Los Angeles, 1935

Institute, and the following year he accepted an offer to teach design at the University of Southern California. He also set about developing a new circle of friends and business associates.

Although Los Angeles seemed a world away from Vienna, Frankl encountered there a small but influential group of Austrian émigré architects and designers. The best known were Rudolph M. Schindler and Richard Neutra.[13] Frankl had met Schindler during his time at the Technische Hochschule in Vienna, where their studies overlapped, and he had become acquainted with Neutra a few years later, during one of his frequent trips home from Berlin.[14] "They were all here," he wrote years later. "Here I saw and

met again all the people that had dropped out of my life since my early school days in Vienna."[15] It might have been logical for Frankl to collaborate with one or more of his compatriots. But he had no desire to revisit his past: Vienna remained for him a disagreeable memory, and seeing his old acquaintances only reminded him of those times. The pull of being American for Frankl was now much stronger than his ties to Austria. Almost all of his close friends—and most of his business colleagues—were native-born. For the next two decades, he labored nearly side by side with Schindler, Neutra, and the other Austrian and German expatriates living in Southern California, but he remained resolutely apart from them, neither seeing them socially nor collaborating with them professionally.[16]

Doubtless, another reason for Frankl's standoffishness—beyond his disdain for most of his fellow Austrians and his wariness about the competition they offered—was his developing allegiance to a different version of modernism. While Neutra and Schindler, each in his own way, pursued an aesthetic of enhanced purity and restraint, Frankl was moving in the opposite direction: his work was becoming more informal and relaxed—and less dependent on standard modernist concepts.

The new style he introduced in his Los Angeles gallery drew on the experiments of his late New York years. But it was now augmented by his experiences in California—and a deepening appreciation for the West Coast lifestyle.

Frankl's new manner first emerged in a house he decorated in the Hollywood Hills only a few months after his return to Los Angeles. The clients, George and Clara Kuhrts, had recently purchased a sprawling 1920s-era Spanish Colonial villa. They wanted to remodel and update the house to reflect the new streamlined style and engaged local architect Milton Black to strip away the house's exterior detailing and reconfigure its outmoded plan. Black recommended Frankl to handle the decoration and to assist with the remodeling of the interior spaces.[17]

Frankl's design for the living room relied mostly on ideas from his New York days, from his now standard

Below:
Fig. 110. Paul T. Frankl,
dining room, Kuhrts
House, Los Angeles, 1935

Opposite:
Fig. 111. Paul T. Frankl,
entry, Wilfley House,
Los Angeles, 1936

Speed chairs to a streamlined fireplace (fig. 109). Yet his overall treatment of the space demonstrated a new loose-ness—expressed in the casual placement of the individual furnishings and objects—and a stronger dependence on monochromatic wall, ceiling, and floor treatments. The dining room showed another developing trend in Frankl's work: his love of contrasting Western and Asian influences (fig. 110). The walls were finished in a pale green Japanese cloth made of grass, and the table base was wrapped in bamboo matting, with the thin strips sown together in regular horizontal rows. The overall cast of the room, however, drew on Central European ideas: the large round dining table and the low, wide chairs mimicked the look of modernist spaces in Vienna in the interwar years.

Around the same time, Frankl was at work on another commission that went even further in his attempt to forge an innovative East-West synthesis. The client, May Wilfley, asked Frankl to furnish her new house in the Hollywood Hills in a way that would show off her large collection of Asian art. He transformed her small, rather ordinary one-story "California modern" cottage into a place of refinement and elegance. The Asian theme was announced right away at the house's entry: Frankl framed the door with several pines, carefully pruned to evoke oversized bonsai trees (fig. 111). Inside, the house constituted a primer on the possibility of mixing together Western and Eastern elements to foster an innovative and affective aesthetic. Frankl covered all of the vertical surfaces in the living room, hall, and rear sitting area with green Japanese grass cloth, laid in large, contrasting squares (fig. 112). To introduce color and heighten the visual impact, he had the ceilings throughout painted a deep Chinese vermilion.

Frankl's treatment of the walls, floors, and ceiling was intended to create an appropriate backdrop for her art collection. The look also suggested an air of antiquity. But Frankl updated the spaces with various "new" furnishings (fig. 113), as well as his own Asian-inspired touches: a low, built-in ash credenza in the living room, sandblasted to highlight the grain (in imitation of Japanese hand-rubbed furniture), and a chaise longue "inspired by the holy bridge of Nikko" in Japan (fig. 114).[18]

By 1936, Frankl was collaborating with a number of Southern California architects. He worked with Lutah Riggs on a sprawling house for Emily von Romberg in Montecito, near Santa Barbara, and he teamed with Sumner Spaulding, Burton Schutt, and Julius Ralph Davidson on other projects.[19] But more important for his developing style was a project on the East Coast. That spring, Frankl received a commission to design the interiors of a new house in Palm Beach, Florida, for Vadim and Elisabeth Harding Makaroff, whose Long Island mansion he had designed years before. He collaborated on the project with Marjory Ulrichs, a well-known New York society decorator.

Fig. 112. Paul T. Frankl,
living room and hall,
Wilfley House, Los Angeles,
1936

Above, right:
Fig. 113. Paul T. Frankl,
chair and table in the
sunroom of the Wilfley
House, Los Angeles, 1936

Right:
Fig. 114. Paul T. Frankl, patio,
Wilfley House, Los Angeles,
1936

The two agreed to divide the responsibilities: Frankl would concentrate on designing the pool area, terraces, and informal interior spaces, and Ulrichs would oversee the furnishing of the remainder of the house.

Inspired by the tropical climate, Frankl wanted to use modern rattan furniture for the house, but he was frustrated to find nothing appropriate on the market. After looking at a wide selection of rattan pieces, he recalled having seen a rattan chair in Los Angeles that had been copied in the Philippines from one of his own wicker models. Impressed with its workmanship and the quality of the materials, he decided to travel to the Philippines and search for a company that could make a full line of his own designs. The trip would give him an excuse to return to Japan, something he had longed to do ever since his hurried departure in 1914. It would also serve as a belated honeymoon: in February 1936, he and Mary had married in Santa Barbara. [20]

In June, the couple, accompanied by an artist friend, Peggy Nichols, set sail from San Pedro Harbor on a Japanese freighter. Twelve days later, they docked in Yokohama. From there, they traveled first to Tokyo, where Frankl once more insisted on staying at a traditional inn—much to the dismay of Mary, whose regular travel diet did not extend much beyond ham sandwiches and Coca-Cola. [21] Deeply uncomfortable with the sleeping arrangements and with the unfamiliar food, she bore up with her usual stoicism, but Frankl relished every moment, eager to try and experience everything he could—and scrutinize even the subtlest details. [22]

While in Tokyo, Frankl purchased a large number of vases, grass cloth, and other decorative objects for the shop, and he made arrangements with an export firm, Morimoto and Company, to buy and ship to Los Angeles a large quantity of bamboo veneers he hoped to use for tables, sideboards, and other furniture. He also used the opportunity to meet with his old friend Tsuguharu Foujita, whom he had not seen since his time in Paris before the war. [23]

After a month-long stay, he left Mary with Nichols in Tokyo and traveled south to Kobe, where he caught an

American President Liner to the Philippines. Upon docking in Manila, Frankl immediately began to make inquiries about rattan manufacturers. From one of the representatives at the American Chamber of Commerce, he learned that an American expatriate, Frank H. Hale, who for many years had operated a shoe factory in the Philippines, had recently built a large modern factory to manufacture rattan furniture. A few days later, Frankl made arrangements to meet Hale at the factory in nearby Santa Ana. The two men quickly came to terms: Hale agreed to produce Frankl's designs according to his precise specifications if Frankl would commit to placing steady orders. [24]

Before departing for Asia, Frankl had made a set of full-scale drawings of the pieces he wanted manufactured. He turned the drawings over to the shop foreman, who supervised production of the prototypes. Frankl himself oversaw the process as well, arriving at the factory early each morning. After several days of intense work, he was satisfied with the models. [25]

The new designs were a stunning departure from the rattan furniture that had been sold in the United States up

Fig. 115. Paul T. Frankl, rattan furniture installation in the Frankl Galleries showroom, mid-1930s

Above, left:
Fig. 116. Paul T. Frankl, rattan furniture installation in the Frankl Galleries showroom, mid-1930s

Above, right:
Fig. 117. Paul T. Frankl, rattan table and chairs, mid-1930s

to that time. Frankl took full advantage of the flexibility and strength of rattan to form it into dramatic shapes. Unlike bamboo, rattan is a member of the palm family (which belongs to the genus *Clamu*) and grows in a long slender stem. Though it often extends for more than one hundred feet, it maintains an almost uniform diameter throughout its length. Frankl found that he could repeat the curving shapes, forming bundles of matched pieces that mimicked the then-popular streamlined look. He stacked individual frames to form the bases of his chairs and sofas, accentuating their horizontal lines; for the arm assemblies, he twisted the rattan into his soon-familiar "square-pretzel" shape (fig. 115).

Frankl also altered the way the pieces were finished. Previously, rattan furniture had been intended solely for exterior use. In most cases, the pieces were brushed with a thick, shiny coat of dark lacquer, intended to preserve them from the elements; little was done to bring out the natural qualities of the material. Taken with the appearance of Philippine rattan in its natural state, Frankl was convinced that the pieces could be used as indoor furniture as well. To protect the rattan, he had the workers hand rub beeswax into the surface, neither altering the rattan's color nor obscuring its fine-grain pattern.[26] The effect was striking, transforming what had been a rather dated type of furniture into something modern and urbane.

Once more, as he had in the mid-1920s, Frankl

became a pioneer, revolutionizing the rattan import business in a single stroke. To cover shipping and manufacturing expenses, he placed substantial orders; he planned to market the furniture through his shop and to wholesale it around the country.[27] With everything set, he began his return trip. He sailed first to Hong Kong, and then to Shanghai, where he made arrangements with another export firm to ship to California an assortment of Chinese screens and other decorative arts objects. He then reunited with Mary in Japan, where the couple spent several days at a small inn in Kyoto while awaiting their ship to Los Angeles.[28]

When Frankl returned to his Wilshire Boulevard gallery, he found his desk piled high with mail. One of the envelopes was from Frank Hale in Manila. It contained a rattan furniture catalog, with one of Frankl's chair designs on the front cover. The catalog, however, was not from Hale's factory but from another Philippine firm. Included with it was an apologetic letter from Hale explaining that the shop foreman, who had supervised the making of the prototypes, had quit the day after Frankl's departure from the Philippines and set up his own rattan factory, and was now pirating Frankl's designs.[29]

The competition cut into Frankl's sales, but his reputation and his connections, especially on the East Coast, enabled him to find orders for a sizable number of pieces. What proved, in fact, to be far more injurious to the launch of his rattan business was a series of longshore-

man strikes, which closed all of the West Coast ports for several months. Frankl was forced to ship the first load of rattan to Vancouver and truck it back to Los Angeles at considerable expense. By the beginning of 1937, however, the strikes were over, and Frankl's business was booming. He was soon selling large numbers of the pieces through the shop, and he began receiving orders from all over the United States as well as from places as far away as Finland, the Cote d'Azur, and the Italian Riviera (fig. 116).[30]

Among Frankl's biggest clients for rattan was the Hollywood film industry. Metro-Goldwyn-Mayer and Paramount placed large orders, using the rattan furnishings in their movies for years afterward.[31] Many Hollywood stars first encountered the pieces on movie sets where they were working, and they, too, bought his designs. Charles Boyer, Charlie Chaplin, Ronald Coleman, Corinne Griffith, Arline Judge, Charles Laughton, and Margaret Sullivan were among his customers. Frankl's clients also included Frank Lloyd Wright and Elsie de Wolfe, who purchased his rattan furniture for her lavish house in Beverly Hills.[32]

Frankl's initial success encouraged him to expand his rattan line. Between the fall of 1936, when he returned

from Asia, and the middle of 1939, he continued to churn out designs, regularly shipping full-scale renderings of new models to Hale in Manila. By the end of the 1930s, his offerings in rattan had grown to more than twenty individual pieces and comprised several dining room sets (fig. 117), chaise longues (fig. 118), and various small tables. He also began to make and sell bamboo furnishings, sometimes adding teak or other tropical woods (fig. 119).

Regardless of material, Frankl made no distinction, either in terms of design or finish, between pieces intended for interior use and those destined for the outdoors. In an article published in 1937, he argued that the dissolution of traditional notions of inside and out marked "the greatest advancement toward a truly modern architecture.... Our Western civilization is beginning to comprehend what the Japanese have practiced for centuries. At last, the modern house has found its *raison d'être*. It is coming to life by opening up and letting life flow from the outside."[33]

The benign Southern California climate was ideally suited for this merging of interior and exterior, and Frankl found numerous clients willing to experiment with his ideas. The most complete illustration of his new manner was a house in Holmby Hills, near Hollywood, for popular

Above, left:
Fig. 118. Paul T. Frankl, rattan chaise longue, mid-1930s

Above, right:
Fig. 119. Paul T. Frankl, bamboo dining table and chairs, late 1930s

Fig. 120. Leland F. Fuller, with Paul T. Frankl, rear view of the Penner House, Holmby Hills, California, 1938

radio comedian Joe Penner and his wife, Eleanor. Frankl collaborated on the project with local architect Leland F. Fuller, best known for a series of modernized classical residences he built throughout Southern California.

Fuller first proposed a hipped-roof structure with abstracted traditional detailing and an open plan. But in spite of its free fenestration, the house was relatively dark inside. At Frankl's urging, Fuller added two large, projecting corner windows upstairs and expanded the Georgian bow window in the living room, greatly opening up the inside (fig. 120).[34] Frankl took full advantage of the resultant spaces. For the rear-facing solarium, he devised an informal sitting area furnished exclusively in rattan

Fig. 121. Paul T. Frankl, solarium, Penner House, Holmby Hills, California, 1938

(fig. 121). He curved the walls and fireplace surround to mimic the flowing lines of the rattan pieces, and he introduced various formal elements—including a mantel niche and valence—to create a subtle tension between 1930s sophistication and his relaxed "tropical modern."

The same contrast is apparent in the adjoining bar (fig. 122). Here Frankl introduced markedly different forms and materials—a woven-wood bar, matchstick blinds, linoleum, and chrome—to make a statement about the possibilities of putting together divergent elements.[35] The private spaces upstairs showed another of Frankl's approaches: his use of dramatic, overscaled objects. The most remarkable was a custom vanity and mirror he installed in Eleanor Penner's bedroom (fig. 123). Lighted with fluorescent bulbs beneath its glass top, the enormous piece, accompanied by a white fur-covered stool, was among Frankl's most singular works. Like the striking leopard-cloth divan in the adjoining boudoir, it underscored the divide between Frankl's work and that of the contemporary European avant-garde (fig. 124).

Still, Frankl's writings of the period stress his continuing allegiance to modernist principles. In an article on the Penner House in *California Arts and Architecture*, Frankl described his interiors as an effort to find "a new conception of building that approaches our present day requirements as closely as possible." The house, he added, "like a tree, must be rooted in the soil it springs from, it must fit its environments and serve its purpose."[36]

Frankl's allusion to a fully integrated approach was no doubt inspired by Wright's concept of "organic architecture." But his notion of organicism differed markedly from Wright's. For Wright, the idea implied a work that was a coherent expression of culture, unified in its materials and construction.[37] For Frankl, however, *organic* had little to do with constructive expression or formal unity: it was bound up instead with purpose and materials, and how these served to foster beauty and fulfill the client's requirements. A "floor plan must be clear, clean-cut, logical, and suited to its needs," he said.[38]

Fig. 122. Paul T. Frankl, bar, Penner House, Holmby Hills, California, 1938

Fig. 123. Paul T. Frankl, vanity, Penner House, Holmby Hills, California, 1938

Pragmatically defined, Frankl's guiding idea was to
shape an interior that fit with the client's lifestyle. He
departed from most of his European contemporaries in
his belief that such considerations extended beyond mere
functionality: a modern house had to express all facets
of modern life, including the requirements of comfort
and nostalgia. And he recognized that modernism was
still too fresh to encapsulate everything that the new age
comprised. It made no sense, he declared, to try to devise
a style: "What we should aim at is to be ourselves, to let
our work express ourselves, and style will well enough
take care of itself."[39]

Fig. 124. Paul T. Frankl, divan, Penner House, Holmby Hills, California, 1938

CHAPTER ELEVEN

Hollywood Designer

By the end of 1938, Frankl had built a flourishing practice in Los Angeles. The gallery was faring well, and profits from the sale of his rattan furnishings—along with Mary's ever-vigilant bookkeeping—allowed them to pay off most of their debt to Max Friedmann. And it was not only Frankl's outward circumstances that had improved: friends who had known him years before in New York were surprised to find him changed, now relaxed, more at ease with himself, his domestic life, and his work. One reason for his more buoyant outlook was the arrival of the couple's first and only child the previous year, a daughter whom they named Paulette after her father. He and Mary immediately hired a nanny to assume most of the responsibility for their daughter's daily care, but Frankl doted on her when he found time and proudly followed her accomplishments as she grew and matured (fig. 125).

Opposite:
Paul T. Frankl, entry hall,
Levine House,
Los Angeles, c. 1938
(see fig. 130)

The late 1930s was a time of renewed exploration for Frankl. He was able to elaborate the relaxed modernism of his first California years and to add to it, discovering new ways to enhance the appearance of lightness and sophistication that defined his best early interiors. He began, too, the investigation of new formal ideas and materials; through blending and amplifying them, he was able to produce some of his most innovative and visually forceful works. Frankl's interiors became at once more elegant and more composite, merging quite disparate forms, colors, and styles. The result was a far-reaching redefinition of the modern interior and a harbinger of the coming transformation of American design.

Fig. 125. Frankl with his
daughter, Paulette, 1937

The look of American modern design was also changing.
By the later 1930s, the impact of European modernism had
become more conspicuous—in large part because of the
continuing influx of architects and designers from
Germany and Austria. There was also a visible move away
from the overtly "machine-age" aesthetic of the previous
years toward a more relaxed and popular idiom. Southern
California became the epicenter of this cultural shift. In the
1930s and early 1940s, the political convulsions in Europe
and the promise of work in the Hollywood film industry
lured legions of émigrés there, among them Bertolt Brecht,
Aldous Huxley, Thomas Mann, Gertrud and Otto Natzler,
Jean Renoir, Arnold Schoenberg, Igor Stravinsky, and
Franz Werfel. They joined the large French, German, and
British "colonies" that had been established in the 1920s.
The Europeans, along with their American counterparts in
the film industry, were drawn to what was fresh and differ-
ent, and they readily embraced the new dwelling culture. [2]

What characterized the Southern California design
scene was its marked diversity. The free mixing of styles,
materials, and forms, and the message of luxury and ease,
became its principal ingredients. But important, too, was
the development of a creative and open atmosphere for
design: far more than in Europe or on the East Coast, a
sense of possibilities reigned among the ranks of Southern
California's architects and decorators; it seemed to many,
including Frankl, the opening of a new era.

With his arrival in California, Frankl had given up his
active attempts to promote modern design. He continued
to teach at the University of Southern California and to
present occasional public lectures. At the request of John
Entenza, the energetic young publisher of *California Arts
and Architecture*, he agreed to serve on the magazine's
board, and from time to time he published short articles
in its pages. [1] Mostly, though, he was content to let his
design work speak for him. He was as active as ever, but
increasingly he shunned the public spotlight.

No doubt, Frankl's lack of personal engagement was a
consequence of the decision he had made after moving to
California to step back and "stop killing himself." But it
grew, too, out of a recognition that modernism had finally
begun to achieve popular acceptance. The leading home
decoration magazines—*House and Garden*, *House Beautiful*,
Ladies' Home Journal, and *Arts and Decoration*—were now
promoting the new style, and manufacturers were coming
increasingly to rely on modern design to sell their products.

Far more than he had in his last years in New York, Frankl
concentrated his attentions on the gallery. Over the years,
he had become a skilled and effective salesman. Peter,
who had moved in with his father after his stay at Taliesin,
often helped out in the Wilshire shop after school, and he
later recalled a lesson in salesmanship his father gave him:
"I started to dust a large coffee table that was part of a
living room grouping. Paul came by just then and told me
not to dust it. When I asked him why, he reached to the
back of a shelf of an end table and brought out a dust rag.
'If a lady is looking at that set and tells me the table is dusty
I hand her the rag. You see, when a woman delivers a baby

it's a total stranger to her, but once she had changed its diaper, it's her baby.'"[3]

Frankl's success stemmed, too, from the flexibility he demonstrated with clients. Otto Lang, a fellow Austrian then just breaking into the film industry as a director and producer, asked Frankl to design his new home in Brentwood:

> I explained to Paul and Mary that our financial resources were limited, unlike the clientele with unlimited funds with whom they were accustomed to doing business. As we strolled through the house looking at various usable pieces, I pointed out an old-fashioned lighting fixture in the dining room ceiling, left by the previous owner, and casually remarked to Paul, "Of course, this unsightly piece will have to go." "Now wait a minute. Don't be so hasty," Paul said. "We can fix it up by painting all its leafy metal branches black with some touches of gold. Then, by adding a few more crystals and replacing the light bulbs, you'll have a charming chandelier at minimum cost." The same thing happened when I pointed out the old-fashioned paneled door of a hallway closet, thinking it would have to be replaced. Again he came up with a simple solution to bring it up to date and give it a contemporary look. . . . When all was finished, the house was comfortable to live in and elegant in an unpretentious way, with a mix of new and old pieces.[4]

Frankl's practical and accommodating manner helped him to secure numerous residential commissions. Nonetheless, a sizable segment of his business, as before, relied on the sales of his rattan furniture, which continued to be robust. To ensure a steady supply of pieces for his retail and wholesale businesses, he increased his orders and stored the extras in a warehouse he installed in the rear of the shop's courtyard. But by 1938, Frankl faced domestic competition: his successful translation of rattan for interior use had persuaded several large furniture manufacturers—most notably Heywood-Wakefield—to enter the field. Other retail shops around the country began offering their own rattan lines. In New York, the Grand Central Wicker Shop imported Philippine rattan,

some of it copied from Frankl's designs. And in Los Angeles, the Rattan Manufacturing Company made and sold its own rattan dining sets and seating.[5] None of the competing furniture equaled Frankl's in either quality or design, and, despite now being in a more crowded arena, he continued to dominate the upper end of the market—so much so that his name became synonymous with the new rattan style. But the competition hurt his attempts to reach a broader market and cut into his wholesale business.

Frankl was now busier than ever with interior design work. In the later 1930s, he found favor with—and received a mounting number of commissions from—the Hollywood film community. Fred Astaire, Fanny Brice, James Cagney, Charlie Chaplin, Claudette Colbert, Julien Duvivier, John Farrow, Cary Grant, Katharine Hepburn, Alfred Hitchcock, John Huston, Paul Ivanoe, Arline Judge, Louis B. Mayer, Walter Pidgeon, and King Vidor were among his many clients. Frankl also designed the residences of Robert E. Gross, president of the Lockheed Corporation; Adolf Spreckels, sugar magnate; and Tom May, head of the May Company department store chain.[6]

The interiors Frankl created were as varied as the personalities of his clientele. Some were formal and serene, others relaxed, even playful. Yet almost all were for the very well-to-do. Though he had long preached the gospel of modernism for all, in the 1930s he found few opportunities to manufacture his designs; he left to others the task of translating the new style for the masses.

Frankl never developed a signature style during his Hollywood years: the diversity of his commissions and his wealthy clientele, who often requested custom work, precluded repetition. But there are qualities—forms, patterns, materials, and strategies—that run through all of his interiors. One of Frankl's trademarks was his ability to achieve a spare look without sacrificing the feelings of warmth or homeyness. While Richard Neutra's interiors of the 1930s were statements of lightness, thinness, and the message of mass production, Frankl sought to preserve the ideal of comfort. He offered places of solace rather than industrial edginess. For Frankl, the home remained a sanctuary from the workaday world, not its simulation. Certain features of the International Style pervade all of his interiors—qualities he described as "plain surfaces simple in color, pleasing in texture; continuous planes melting into each other, uninterrupted in their continuous flow"—but they are combined with older ideas of ease and material richness that place them firmly in a different category of modernism.[7]

Frankl's evolving notions of acceptability, comfort, and propriety matched the broad advance of American modern design in the years just prior to World War II. The same cozy look can be found in the interiors of most of

Fig. 126. Paul T. Frankl, dining room, Levine House, Los Angeles, c. 1938

the leading designers, including Donald Deskey, Paul László, Kem Weber, and Russel Wright. Undoubtedly, the goal of a moderate and popular aesthetic became a defining feature of the American form of the new style, setting it apart from the more radical experiments of the Europeans. But Frankl also offered his own specific contribution to this aesthetic. It can be found, above all, in the ways in which he fused quite diverse sources, not all of them modern, to achieve his own version of the new style.

One of those sources was Asian design. In the last years of the 1930s, Chinese art and furniture occupied a central place in Frankl's interiors. In the dining room of the Levine House, for example, which he designed around 1938, he used a large Chinese painting to provide decorative contrast to an otherwise restrained composition (fig. 126). Frankl was not alone in turning to the Far East for creative stimulus; his reliance on Chinese pieces and motifs was in fact widely shared at the time. (It was fueled in part by American sympathy with China after the Japanese invasion of the country.) But to Frankl, Chinese antiques and decorative articles also offered a suitable and harmonious ingredient to mix with modern elements—both to elaborate the new and to lend a sense of worldliness.[8]

Handcrafted articles and fabrics were another essential component of Frankl's design style. Throughout the later 1930s and early 1940s, he made extensive use of handwoven textiles. He was especially fond of the work of Bavarian-born weaver Maria Kipp. After immigrating to the United States in the 1920s, Kipp had settled in Los Angeles and built a reputation for innovative fabrics, which she custom-produced for interior designers and architects.[9] Frankl was taken with the rich textural quality of her creations; he was convinced that they provided a pleasing visual and haptic contrast to slick, modern materials. For the same reasons, he continued to import handwoven fabrics from France and Austria, and later, in the years just before the war, from Mexico and Guatemala. (For a time, he even experimented with such nontraditional textiles as denim and horse blankets for upholstery or coverlets.) [10] To such artifacts of preindustrial tradition, Frankl added the latest offerings from American manufacturers: sheet glass, modern metal alloys, the first household plastics. He was an early advocate of plywood—then just beginning to come into widespread use—as well as modern veneers and pressboard.

Clues to Frankl's design philosophy of the later 1930s can be found in his fourth book, *Space for Living: Creative Interior Decoration and Design* (1938). In tone and message, the short, 110-page work was a departure from its predecessors. Frankl's previous three books were, to a very great extent, polemics; they were intended to win over a skeptical public to the new design. *Space for Living*, by contrast, is an inherently practical work. It is a basic how-to of modern design, a breviary aimed at those who wanted to achieve the new look, filled with proclamations and admonitions: "The process of elimination of all unnecessary, meaningless decoration is definitely influencing contemporary design. Simplicity and restraint are our aims," he writes. Or, "It is important to avoid overcrowding a room either with too much furniture or with furniture too big and therefore out of proportion to the size of the room." [11] There are chapters on almost every aspect of interior design: color, grouping furniture, appropriate backgrounds, spatial planning, and so on.

Yet there is an odd disjunction between the book's text—most of which was already modernist dogma—and the accompanying illustrations, replete with his very personal ideas. It is evident that Frankl did not wish to reveal all his secrets and, further, that he did not want to elicit imitators. The experience of the 1920s, when so many of his designs had been stolen, was still fresh in his mind. He may have been willing to illustrate the products of his design logic, but not his precise strategies.

It is in those details, however, that Frankl's contribution is most memorably—and most powerfully—preserved. His "Propeller chair," probably designed in late 1937 and illustrated in *Space for Living*, offers a glimpse at Frankl's ability to make an appealing and individual expression (fig. 127). The accompanying caption notes that the chair was "made

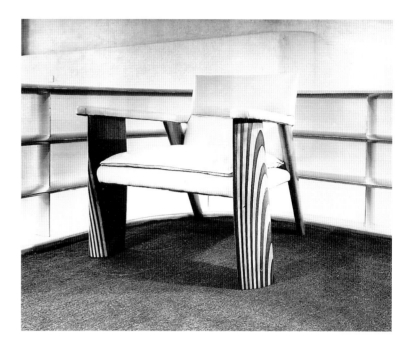

Fig. 127. Paul T. Frankl, Propeller chair, c. 1937. Laminated wood, wood, and leather upholstery

from airplane parts in its entirety" and "was especially designed for the hobby room of one of our outstanding flyers." The front legs were in fact a section of an actual wooden propeller (with alternating layers of light and dark woods laminated together); the hind legs were wing struts. Even the thin upholstered leather seat came from an airplane. [12] The use of such materials is clever and interesting, but it is the formal evocation of flight and movement—achieved by means of its streamlined shape and unusual proportions more than its materials—that makes the chair an exceptional object. The dramatic contrast between thin and thick, plain (the monochrome leather seat) and fancy (the winding lines of the propeller legs), vertical and horizontal planes—all combine to issue a formal declaration of dynamism and grace.

More remarkable still was another chair Frankl designed around the same time (fig. 128). Its side panels, like the accompanying screen shown in a surviving period photograph, were clad with thin slats of birch sewn together, with narrow spaces left between each member. Frankl first introduced the new "woodweave" panels for screens around 1936; soon, he was using the material for dining sets and other furniture (fig. 129). Taken with the

Fig. 128. Paul T. Frankl, woodweave chair, c. 1938. Birch, woven wood panels, and cloth upholstery

ductile quality of the woodweave sheets, which, as he noted, offered the designer "an opportunity to mold them to his fancy," Frankl converted the chair's frame into a flying wedge, inserting into it the upholstered seat.[13] The seat's tilted back and its long, low profile accentuated the illusion of motion. But it was not only the chair's sense of movement that made it exceptional. Its impact, as with the Propeller chair, derived from its oppositions: the juxtaposition between the "static" idea of sitting and the chair's streamlined forms, between the sharp whiteness of the frame and the ebony cotton upholstery, between the vertical slats on the sides and the chair's dominant horizontality.

Frankl's fondness for such oppositions is also evident in many of his interiors of the late 1930s. In the entry hall and living room of the Levine House, he mixed and matched textures, forms, colors, and angles with almost defiant bravado, contriving a scene that was both astringent and voluptuous (figs. 130, 131). The spaces, like most of Frankl's interiors of the period, are at once a declaration of his inventiveness and an apparent challenge to those designers at the time pleading for wholesale purification.[14] And it is within this volatile mix of opposing ideas that the secret of his aesthetic vision resides.

Although Frankl's public success in the late 1930s issued largely from his residential interiors, he was often commissioned to design stores and offices as well. He took pleasure in the challenge of such projects—and in the break from his usual working pattern.

One of these assignments was for the Mosse Linen Shop in New York in 1938. Frankl collaborated with Manhattan-based designer Morris Ketchum, Jr.[15] Although the shop's sleek facade, with its polished granite veneer and bronze-work window frame, was standard for modern retail design by that time, Frankl and Ketchum's slick integration of elements was certainly innovative (fig. 132). As a write-up in *Architectural Forum* described, the design combined "into one unit the display window, door, and awning." The magazine went on to praise the

Above, top:
Fig. 129. Paul T. Frankl, woodweave dining set, c. 1938

Above, bottom:
Fig. 130. Paul T. Frankl, entry hall, Levine House, Los Angeles, c. 1938

Above:
Fig. 131. Paul T. Frankl, living room, Levine House, Los Angeles, c. 1938

Left:
Fig. 132. Paul T. Frankl and Morris Ketchum, Jr., facade for the Mosse Linen Shop, New York, 1938

solution as "one of the most handsome and ingenious designs yet produced in this field." But even more striking was the shop's interior, a restrained, almost minimalist arrangement that repeated the Spartan appearance of the facade—then still a very new idea in the United States for retail spaces (fig. 133).[16]

Frankl also collaborated with architect Gordon B. Kaufmann on an office building in Beverly Hills for talent agent Myron Selznick, brother of producer David O. Selznick. Frankl's design went even further in its avowal of the new aesthetic. The circular building was arranged into two concentric rings of offices, with the inner offices facing onto a round garden court. In accord with Selznick's wishes, Frankl emphasized the impression of privacy and shelter. He introduced indirect lighting throughout, and he had the office walls paneled with unadorned sheets of mahogany. The screening room, too, was clad entirely in mahogany, with the edges set flush to yield a smooth, continuous surface. At the touch of a button, the wall at one end would recede dramatically into the floor, revealing a large projection screen.[17]

The volume of work Frankl received in the later 1930s provided a measure of security he had not known for years. Still, he was not entirely without worries. In early March 1939, his regular shipments of rattan from the Philippines ceased abruptly without explanation. Frankl attempted to uncover the cause, but his repeated letters and telegrams went unanswered. After further inquiries, he learned that Frank Hale was experiencing financial problems. Without waiting to find out the details, Frankl booked passage for himself and Mary on a Norwegian freighter that took them directly from San Pedro Harbor to the Philippines. The day after they docked in Manila, Frankl tried unsuccessfully to telephone Hale. When he arrived at the factory, he found the gates padlocked and the building empty. From a contact at the American Chamber of Commerce, he learned that Hale, who lacked any previous experience in furniture manufacturing, had been forced to rely on a manager to oversee the day-to-

Fig. 133. Paul T. Frankl and Morris Ketchum, Jr., interior of the Mosse Linen Shop, New York, 1938

day operation of the plant. Over the course of three years, he had gone through a series of managers, each successively losing more money; eventually, he had been forced to declare bankruptcy.[18]

Frankl soon found another rattan producer, Gonzalo Puyat, who agreed to take on his designs. But almost immediately he ran into problems: Puyat's men, though remaining faithful to Frankl's designs, were never able to replicate the same quality of work. The later pieces he imported and sold (until the fall of the Philippines to Japan) lacked both the strength and finish of his earlier rattan furnishings.[19]

After several weeks in Manila, Frankl and Mary continued their journey, sailing on to Shanghai. The vast, teeming city was then already under Japanese occupation. While there, Frankl met with Dr. T. G. Ling, who ran his Asian purchasing office (fig. 134). From Ling, he discovered that the Japanese, intent upon crippling Chinese trade, were making it increasingly difficult to export articles, especially antiquities.[20]

Frankl knew that, with war looming, this trip might be his last chance to explore China's interior. Despite ominous signs of the impending conflict, he and Mary decided to risk a hasty trip to Beijing. For years, he had longed

Above, top:
Fig. 134. Frankl with T. G. Ling (*front right*) and his staff, Shanghai, 1939

Above, bottom:
Fig. 135. Edward Durell Stone and Paul T. Frankl, Frankl House, Coldwater Canyon, California, 1940

to see "not the overly carved chests sold to tourists in coastal ports but the age-old furnishings of the better class Chinese . . . simple in design, so void of decoration, so superb in their craftsmanship," as he later recalled. [21] The trip would also allow him to acquire additional objects for import.

After an arduous journey, the couple reached Beijing in late August. Frankl spent as much time as he could exploring the shops and museums, but he bought mostly decorative articles rather than antiques because they represented less risk and would bring a greater return. [22] The couple's stay was cut short when they learned of the German invasion of Poland on 1 September. The following day they were on a train back to the coast; as soon as they were able to book passage, they boarded a freighter bound for Los Angeles. [23]

The risky adventure proved to be highly profitable: Frankl was able to sell everything he purchased in China at a considerable markup. But any attempt to order more objects was out of the question. He immediately set about looking for new sources for decorative objects—not only because he needed accessories for the shop but also because, despite successful sales of his own designs, he and Mary continued to rely on imports to boost profits and entice clients still apprehensive about modernism. With connections to Europe and Asia now severed, Frankl decided that he should investigate Mexico as a possible source.

Early in 1940, he and Mary traveled south. They went first to Mexico City, where they visited Diego Rivera at his studio in San Angel. A few days later, they were invited to the home of Frida Kahlo, Rivera's wife, in nearby Coyoacán. Frankl had met the couple during their time in New York in the early 1930s, when Rivera labored on his ill-fated murals for Rockefeller Center, and they had issued a standing invitation for him to visit them in Mexico.

Together with Rivera, Frankl and Mary drove out to the provincial town of Metepec to shop for clay figurines and earthenware pots. While Mary and Diego climbed the church tower, Frankl scoured the open-air market. "When they returned I was surrounded with the fruits of my labors," Frankl recalled. "Diego was surprised to find that all the pieces I had selected were imperfect, the imperfections typical of the hand of man in contrast to the monotonous perfection of the machine product."[24]

Frankl also found other sources for decorative objects. At Frida's house a few days afterward, he admired a set of carved lava figurines resting on the balustrade of the courtyard. Inquiring about their origin, he learned that they had been made by Mardonio Magaña, a former janitor at the Academy of Fine Arts who, upon being "discovered," had been appointed a professor at the school. Magaña came by the house later and showed them his work; Frankl, impressed, promptly bought several tons of sculptures and had them shipped to Los Angeles.[25]

From the Mexican capital, he and Mary traveled throughout the central and southern regions of the country—to Puebla, Oaxaca, Taxco, and Acapulco—acquiring everything from hand-hammered tin sconces and chandeliers to colonial-era wooden chests.[26] After exploring the Yucatán (with a side trip to the Mayan ruins at Chichén Itzá), the couple returned to Mérida. There they caught a flight to Guatemala, where Frankl intended to purchase handwoven textiles and indigenous plants. Before departing from the United States, he had applied for permission to import exotic plants into California, and during his stay in Guatemala City, he visited the local nurseries, acquiring a large number of rare orchids and bromeliads.[27]

The trip again was a financial success. Frankl's instincts once more proved correct: the Mexican and Guatemalan "primitives" helped to spur robust sales for the shop and to attract an ever-expanding clientele.

With both the gallery and the interior design practice now flourishing, Frankl and Mary, who were living in a rented bungalow on Oakwood Avenue, felt financially secure enough to build their own house. After some searching, Frankl found an undeveloped lot on Coldwater Canyon Drive, just north of Beverly Hills. His choice for the architect was prominent New York modernist Edward Durell Stone, whom Frankl knew from his days in

Manhattan. The two men had become friends after Stone's return from Europe in the late 1920s, and they remained on close terms after Frankl's departure for the West Coast.

Frankl was drawn to Stone's own idiosyncratic interpretation of modernism: his designs were forthright and efficient, but Stone, in seeming defiance of the purists, shunned neither luxurious materials nor decorative detailing. His residential designs, in particular, betrayed the same eclectic tendencies that ran through Frankl's own work.

The long, slender footprint of the house was determined in large measure by the site, a narrow lot framed by a stand of ancient walnut trees on one side and the canyon walls on the other (fig. 135). Its overall appearance bore faint traces of Japanese style, but, as an article in *California Arts and Architecture* described, it was "conceived in the modern spirit and simple and straightforward by the elimination of all things not directly necessary to the mode of life chosen by the owners."[28] The rooms were arrayed in a more or less straight line, stair-stepped in two places to accommodate the sharply sloping terrain. The changes in level corresponded to the functional divisions within: the garage, kitchen, and other service areas were on one level, the dining room and gallery on a second, and the large living room constituting a third. Frankl's design for the interior took advantage of the spatial transitions, lending the house a protean cast that was enhanced through his introduction of various styles, materials, and colors. The interiors were wholly in accord with Frankl's other works of the early 1940s—elegant, comfortable, and tranquil (figs. 136, 137, 138).[29]

Frankl was also at work that summer and early fall on a new gallery space. After six years on Wilshire Boulevard, he wanted to find a location that would be less expensive and more amenable to pedestrians. He set his sights on a lot on nearby Rodeo Drive. At the time, Rodeo was still a jumble of small residential and commercial buildings. The street had been zoned for business several years before, but little new building had yet taken place. Frankl, prescient as always, foresaw that it would become

Above:
Fig. 136. Paul T. Frankl, living room,
Frankl House, Coldwater Canyon, California, 1940

Left:
Fig. 137. Paul T. Frankl, dining room,
Frankl House, Coldwater Canyon, California, 1940

Fig. 138. Paul T. Frankl, stairway, Frankl House, Coldwater Canyon, California, 1940

Fig. 139. Paul T. Frankl, facade for the Frankl Galleries on Rodeo Drive, 1940

Opposite, top:
Fig. 140. Paul T. Frankl, Frankl Galleries showroom on Rodeo Drive, 1940

"Hollywood's new 'high style' street." [30]

He collaborated on the project with local architects Douglas Honnold and George Vernon Russell. (The new shop was one of seven retail spaces the architects constructed on the west side of Rodeo in late 1940.) Frankl allowed Honnold and Russell a free hand with most of the building, but he decided to design the building's front facade himself (fig. 139). Drawing from his established repertoire of formal ideas, he devised a tall, thin show window set into a slate-colored wall of corrugated concrete; two pairs of slender columns supported a narrow portico emblazoned with the gallery's name. In the main show window, he installed a fountain so that a stream of water ran continuously along the surface of the window, setting off the furniture and objects on display. [31]

Inside, the shop was divided into three principal spaces: a main sales floor, a garden room, and a shipping and receiving area. As he had in the Wilshire store, Frankl displayed the furniture and accessories in groups, suggesting how they might be arranged in the home. The new

building was significantly smaller than his old gallery, however, and as a consequence, much of the furniture was available on a custom-order basis only. Because of his recent trip to Guatemala, exotic plants assumed a more prominent role than in his earlier stores. Nearly every corner and surface was covered with pots or trailing vines, transforming the showroom into more "garden" than "machine"—another telling indication of Frankl's distance from high modernism (fig. 140). [32]

The new gallery, located at 339 North Rodeo Drive, opened its doors in December 1940. [33] A short time later, designer Paul László opened his own gallery diagonally across from Frankl's, providing stiff competition. (László later told an interviewer that he and Frankl did not get along. They shared a clientele made up chiefly of Jewish immigrants from Central Europe, many of whom were involved in the film industry, and Frankl, according to László, resented the competition and believed that László had poached some of his designs.) [34]

Nonetheless, Frankl's increased visibility on Rodeo Drive helped to propel his interior design business. The year 1941 was perhaps the most productive of his time in Southern California. In the twelve months between the inaugural of the new gallery and the entry of the United States into World War II, he completed more than a dozen commissions for residences, including some of his most important designs.

Among the largest and most prestigious was the Bel-Air home of Hollywood art director Cedric Gibbons. During his thirty-two years as supervising art director for Metro-Goldwyn-Mayer, Gibbons oversaw some 1,500 films, winning eleven Oscars in the process. He asked Frankl, who was a close friend, to design nearly all of the furniture for his house. Frankl responded with a complete array of seating (much of it long, low sofas and chairs) and occasional tables, a number of them one-of-a-kind designs (fig. 141). He also introduced a new surface cladding: bleached-mahogany wall panels. Together with sliding glass and mahogany doors, they provided a neutral—and sumptuous—backdrop.

Frankl employed the same palette of bleached mahogany and low-slung custom designs for another important commission: the Bel-Air home of Patricia Detring. The hillside house, designed by Burton A. Schutt, featured extended walls of windows facing the rear garden, with one side presenting a breathtaking view of the Pacific Ocean. Frankl's interiors, which had a strongly Japanese flavor, echoed the extensive Japanese-style garden, visible from all of the main rooms. The walls were wrapped throughout with grass cloth or painted a soft gray, offering a subtle contrast to the bleached mahogany bookcases and fireplace surround.[35] The wall treatments and furnishings created a strongly unified effect, giving further prominence to Frankl's distinctive hand.

But sales of Frankl's furniture were not confined to commissions for complete interiors. In the early 1940s, his pieces appeared in a number of spaces designed by other architects or interior designers. Though many of the Los Angeles avant-garde architects—Richard Neutra, Rudolph Schindler, Julius Ralph Davidson, Gregory Ain, and Raphael Soriano—designed their own furniture, pieces by Frankl frequently turned up in their buildings.[36] Clients in some instances purchased suites—or even entire houses—of Frankl furnishings. Well-known illustrator Guy Brown Wiser, for example, though choosing to design the interiors of his new Los Angeles home himself, relied almost exclusively on furnishings and accessories from the Frankl Galleries.[37] In other instances, many of the shop's customers freely combined Frankl's pieces with those of his fellow Los Angeles designers.

The newfound economic prosperity of the early 1940s held out for Frankl the promise of further commissions, but the Japanese bombing of Pearl Harbor in December 1941 brought an abrupt end to peace and to Hollywood's glory days. Though the pace of his practice would be slowed by the war, Frankl continued for another decade to serve the design needs of Hollywood's rich and famous. But already in the late 1930s, he had begun to take the first tentative steps toward the mass production of his designs.

Fig. 141. Paul T. Frankl, extension dining table from the Gibbons House, Bel-Air, California, c. 1941. Lacquered wood with mirrored stand, 28 1/4 x 48 x 48 in. (71.8 x 121.9 x 121.9 cm); fully extended 28 1/4 x 84 x 48 in. (71.8 x 213.4 x 121.9 cm). Courtesy Sotheby's, New York

Combed Wood* – THE ULTIMATE IN MODERN FURNITURE DESIGN!

A Combed-Wood desk and chair which typify the many outstanding pieces to be found in this newest of furniture creations. See this exclusive line of "Designed for Living in the Modern Mode" furniture at leading furniture stores everywhere.

The casual furrowed at random effect . . . the delicate Hawaiian charm . . . the sturdy modern feeling . . . the creative genius of David Saltman and Paul Frankl, all combined . . . have brought into being Combed-Wood Furniture. Here indeed is furniture truly designed for "Living in the Modern Mode."

*Registered Weldtex and made by a patented process.

Brown-Saltman

2570 Tweedy Road, South Gate, Calif.
Telephone LAfayette 2126

CHAPTER TWELVE

Mass Modern

The problems that preoccupied Frankl from the late 1930s on were closely bound up with the mass production of his designs. For most of his working life, he had dreamed of translating his own vision of modernism to the realm of manufacturing. The timing, though, had never seemed right. He had made an initial foray into manufacturing with his rattan furniture, but the plants in the Philippines still relied almost exclusively on manual labor; it was not true mass production. Finally, in 1939, the opportunity he had long awaited presented itself—in the person of David Saltman.

Born in Russia in 1894, Saltman, the son of an itinerant Jewish merchant, immigrated to the United States with his family around the turn of the century. He eventually settled in Los Angeles, where he established a modest furniture manufacturing business, known as Brown-Saltman, with a local partner. At first, Brown-Saltman specialized in reproductions. Saltman soon realized, however, that the increasing acceptance of modern design offered extraordinary opportunities, and in 1939 he resolved to launch a line of contemporary furnishings. In November, he met Frankl at a party thrown by a mutual friend. Overcoming his lifelong shyness, Saltman telephoned the next day and asked Frankl if he would design a line of furniture for him. To Saltman's great surprise, he agreed. (Saltman later confided to Frankl that he had already purchased a number of his pieces and was prepared to copy them—unlicensed—had Frankl declined.)[1]

Opposite:
Fig. 142. Advertisement for Combed-Wood Furniture, manufactured by Brown-Saltman, 1941

Fig. 143. Paul T. Frankl, four-drawer chest, manufactured by Brown-Saltman, c. 1941. Combed wood, with bronze X-shaped handles, 46 x 35 x 20 in. (116.8 x 88.9 x 50.8 cm). Courtesy of Sollo:Rago Modern Auctions, Lambertville, N.J.

The first pieces Brown-Saltman manufactured were based on Frankl's current designs, recast only slightly for mass production. Frankl also modified a dining room suite he had designed for his own house and, to make a full line of furnishings, added several other original prototypes. Saltman marketed the designs nationally, featuring Frankl's name prominently in the advertising (fig. 142).[2] When their initial line proved more successful than either man had dared hope, Frankl began to work on new designs, this time adapting them specifically for manufacturing.

Unlike his earlier handcrafted works, the pieces were intended for the middle-class market. They were simpler than any of his previous designs: the detailing was decidedly pared down—in large part to reduce the costs of assembling and finishing—and they were constructed of less-expensive materials, mostly soft woods, that could be painted or lacquered. To lend "interest of surface," Frankl used "combed wood" for many of the pieces. (Sold under

the name Weldtex, combed wood was a striated, fir-plywood laminate invented by Donald Deskey. Its deeply grooved surface disguised the wood's grain and provided a decorative appearance.) Brown-Saltman's print advertisements, which appeared in most of the country's leading home and design magazines, trumpeted the textured surfaces and their sturdy appearance as ideal designs for "Living in the Modern Mode."[3]

Frankl's designs for Brown-Saltman were also formally innovative. A small four-drawer chest first manufactured at the beginning of 1941 fused combed wood and smooth surfaces; it rested on a base, with short legs canted outward (fig. 143). The angular geometry—repeated in its bronze X-shaped handles—offered a premonitory glimpse at the forms of 1950s modernism and an early indication of Frankl's postwar turn away from orthogonality.

But if their appearance was in some ways novel, the full array of Frankl's first Brown-Saltman furnishings established a summary of forms he had devised over the previous decade—now shorn of their expensive detailing and finishes. Frankl's next round of designs, which appeared in the fall of 1941, marked a decided break with his earlier work. They were harder-edged and more reductivist. They also proved even more popular than his first Brown-Saltman line. The nation's economy had begun to rebound in the early 1940s, and, despite the outbreak of the war, sales exceeded both men's expectations.

In mid-June 1942, Frankl met with Saltman over lunch, and the two men agreed to a long-term contract. "Dave was in high spirits," Frankl later recounted, "and with true Saltman exuberance...said 'now all my worries are over—I have a designer for life—tomorrow I go fishing!'" The next day, Saltman and a friend left for the High Sierras. On a sharp curve a few miles outside the town of Mojave, Saltman, blinded by the late afternoon sun, hit a truck head on. Both men were killed instantly.[4] Brown-Saltman continued to produce Frankl's designs for a short time, but wartime rationing soon put a halt to production; after the war, Frankl, missing his collaboration with Saltman, decided not to continue his partnership with the firm.

With Saltman's death, Frankl's dream of mass-manufacturing his designs stalled once again. The end of their business relationship also left Frankl with renewed financial problems. His interior design business had fallen off precipitously because of the war; he now had only a handful of ongoing commissions, with little new work coming in.[5]

Frankl also had other worries. Having experienced firsthand the impact of aerial bombing in Constantinople during World War I, he was wary of living in a city during wartime. After some deliberation, he and Mary decided to move to the country. They sold the house in Coldwater Canyon and rented a small, two-bedroom house on the Palos Verdes peninsula, twenty miles south of downtown Los Angeles.[6]

At the time, the area was still largely undeveloped. Most of the land belonged to the family of Frank A. Vanderlip, former president of the National Bank of New York, who in 1913 had bought the sixteen-thousand-acre peninsula, sight unseen, with the aim of transforming it into the "most fashionable and exclusive residential colony" in the country. The remote location and the lack of adequate roads thwarted the project, and at the time the United States joined the war, the population was still composed mostly of Japanese farmers.[7]

The house Frankl rented had been the original caretaker's cottage on the Vanderlip estate. The far-off location satisfied his desire for greater security, but the long commute to Beverly Hills each day soon became a trial. Squeezing the family—now consisting of Frankl and Mary, five-year-old Paulette, and a live-in maid, Masako Hammato—into the tiny wood-frame house also proved to be a challenge. (Peter, in the meantime, had moved out and returned to his mother, now married to Henry Boulton, scion of a wealthy Venezuelan family.)[8] To ease the crowdedness, Frankl commenced work in early 1943 on converting the former garage of the house into a separate living unit for himself and Mary. He replaced the original garage doors with large, sliding window walls, opened up the sidewalls with additional windows, and added a pergola and a flagstone patio.[9]

With little work coming in, the house became his design

laboratory. For the dining area, Frankl constructed a long trestle table and matching benches in sandblasted ash, their vertical supports joined and braced by thick dowels extending from end to end (fig. 144). The unalloyed country look of the pieces was an updated version of the Peasant Furniture he had introduced in his early years in New York. But Frankl's treatment of the surfaces and joints exhibited a more refined handling—the result of nearly two decades of experimentation. Still, his interiors throughout the remodeled garage and original house showed how far he had moved from the modernist mainstream: though he had by no means abandoned his faith in the tenets of clarity and simplicity, the interiors proclaimed his newfound love of eclecticism. The rooms brought together elements of his sleek designs of the 1930s with primitive objects—mostly recent imports from Mexico—and Asian-inspired touches and finishes. In the breakfast nook in the original cottage, for example, Frankl combined an old Austrian peasant table with a very modern sideboard and matchstick blinds (fig. 145). The most dramatic fusion of new and old, though, was the massive, low fireplace framed with giant fieldstones in the remodeled garage's living room (fig. 146). It was a spirited summary of his new manner—bold and modern in its sensibilities and forms, while incorporating elements of the past.

Frankl and Mary lived simply during the war years. Because of gas rationing and the long drive into the city— an even longer journey before the construction of the Los Angeles freeways—they rarely went out on the town. Instead, most weekend evenings they entertained at home, having dinner with the Vanderlip family, who lived just up the hill, or with actor Charles Laughton and his wife, actress Elsa Lancaster, who rented a second small cottage on the property.[10]

Elin Vanderlip, who frequently visited the Frankls with her parents, remembered that stepping into the house was like entering another world, "the Paul Frankl world": his "taste extended to EVERYTHING." It was all "chic and beautiful and of absolutely flawless quality."[11]

Fig. 144. Paul T. Frankl, dining room, Frankl House,
Palos Verdes, California, 1943

But Frankl's comfortable lifestyle belied his mounting
financial difficulties. Wartime shortages and rationing
nearly brought his furniture and interior design businesses to a halt.[12] He no longer had his rattan business to
fall back on, and by 1943 he had sold most of the decorative articles he had imported from China and Mexico.
Faced with the prospect of insolvency, Frankl improvised:
he converted much of the showroom space at the gallery
to selling plants and flower arrangements. He had always
been a skilled gardener, and, despite wartime shortages,
he found that plants, pots, and vases were still in ready
supply. He augmented his floral designs with driftwood,
shells, stones, dried branches, and other objects he
picked up on his long walks on the beach or in the Palos

Verdes hills. [13] Frankl hired an experienced gardener to
oversee the day-to-day running of the "plant department" at the gallery, giving him more time to investigate
novel ways to present his plants and flowers.

Over time, his arrangements became spare and
highly controlled, recalling the Japanese examples he so
admired. Often, he selected nontraditional containers for
his plants—old kitchen vessels, dining ware, decorative
pots—to enhance their lines and provide contrasting
textures (figs. 147, 148). His approach, he told a reporter
from *Interiors*, was to emphasize the plants: "Let the plant
be itself—try to bring out its natural intrinsic beauty by
creating the proper setting for it.... Like all artistic
endeavors, restraint has to be exercised if the final result
is to be termed Art. And Art it can well be—a real picture
painted with real plants." [14]

The plant business proved to be Frankl's salvation:
for the next three years, until the end of 1945, he and
Mary were able to earn enough to allow them to make
ends meet. Their profits were small, but their expenses
in Palos Verdes were modest, and the shop's overhead
was much reduced because they greatly scaled back their
production of furniture. [15]

As the war wound down in early 1945, Frankl began to
think about the future of modern design. He was convinced that Southern California offered all of the conditions for fostering a vibrant and distinctive postwar design
culture, and he was now firm in his belief that mass production should be at the core of a new dwelling culture.
Summoning again the arguments in favor of industrial
design he had made in Berlin three decades before, he
admonished the California modernists for not making a
stronger push to appeal to the masses: "Let us understand
that the decorative art movement, as it started here and as
it has existed in Europe for close to forty years, is of but
little interest to the public at large. The reason is that from
the outset it addressed itself to a small minority of the
wealthy, ignoring altogether the one hundred and forty
million customers who today determine the success or

Fig. 145. Paul T. Frankl,
breakfast nook,
Frankl House, Palos
Verdes, California, 1943

Fig. 146. Paul T. Frankl, living room, Frankl House,
Palos Verdes, California, 1943

failure of any enterprise in this country. In California,
as in Europe, the decorative arts and crafts movement
started as a Renaissance of the handicrafts. As such it is
doomed to failure, as the rigid tradition necessary for the
well-being of all crafts is no longer existing."[16]

Frankl himself was hardly blameless of the charge;
aside from his short-lived collaboration with Brown-
Saltman, he too had focused almost exclusively on older
notions of handicraft. Yet it is also true that only a few of
the leading American furniture designers had, by the
time of the war, branched out into mass manufacturing.
The most successful were Gilbert Rohde, who, starting in
1932, designed a wide array of furnishings for the
Herman Miller Company, and Russel Wright, who created

the "Modern Living" furniture line for the Conant Ball Company.[17] Rohde's designs were affordable only to the more well to do, but Wright's works, priced for the lower end of the market, were conspicuously popular. Frankl, late to enter the field, was more convinced than ever that the future of modernism lay in mass production—and he was determined not to fall behind the competition.

In early 1946, he renewed his efforts to make the transition to manufacturing. He closed the Frankl Galleries on Rodeo Drive—and along with it, much of his retail business—and purchased two small bungalows nearby, at 306 North Doheny Drive, to serve as his new industrial design studio.[18] Immediately, he set about modifying the buildings. To provide solace from the busy streets, he walled off the original front doors and erected a high fence around the two lots, forming a single, unified garden. He converted one of the bungalows into a showroom and office; the other he transformed into a studio space, with private living quarters to enable him to stay in town when working late. Inside, Frankl removed several walls, creating open, flowing spaces. Much of the detailing he borrowed from traditional Japanese architecture, yielding, as a write-up in *Interiors* described, "a typical Frankl-ish love of orientalia—of quietness, seclusion, privacy, of smooth matting which absorbs footfalls, of screens which deflect the sun, of uncluttered surfaces punctuated with a few Chinese antiques such as mellow wooden tables and glowing vases" (fig. 149).[19]

Frankl continued to accept occasional decorating jobs, but he focused increasingly on designing for large furniture companies.[20] To reflect the altered direction of his business, he changed the firm's name to Paul Frankl Associates.

His principal "associate" was Peggy Galloway, whom Frankl had first met in 1936 while teaching at the University of Southern California (fig. 150). She was then a student in the architecture program; he recognized her talent, and in late 1937, a year after her graduation, he hired her to be his assistant. Galloway rapidly absorbed

Fig. 147. Paul T. Frankl, plant arrangement, Frankl Galleries, c. 1943

Fig. 148. Paul T. Frankl, plant arrangement, Frankl Galleries, c. 1943

Left:
Fig. 149. Paul T. Frankl, screened storage shelves,
Frankl's studio on North Doheny Drive,
Los Angeles, c. 1946

Above:
Fig. 150. Frankl and Peggy Galloway at their
drafting boards, late 1940s

the rudiments of Frankl's approach, and by the early
1940s she had taken over some of the large volume of
Frankl's projects for interiors. During the later war years,
she left Los Angeles to be with her husband, who was
serving in the army, but she resumed working for Frankl
near the war's end. By the time Frankl launched his new
venture, Galloway, now in her thirties, was a skilled
designer with considerable decorating experience. She
also exhibited a talent for creating furniture to be manufactured, and over time she assumed more and more of
the responsibility for overseeing its production.[21]

But in spite of all preparations, Frankl's first commission was slow in coming. In the summer and fall of 1946,
he made fainthearted overtures to several companies, but

Fig. 151. Paul T. Frankl, living room, May House, Brentwood, California, 1949

he preferred to wait for the right opportunity. Finally, more than a year later, Barry Stuart, sales manager for the Johnson Furniture Company, approached him with an offer to design a complete line of pieces.

The Johnson Company was one of the oldest and most respected furniture manufacturers in Grand Rapids, Michigan, then the center of the American furniture industry.[22] Three brothers from Sweden—Carl, Hjalmar, and Axel Johnson—had founded the company more than fifty years before. They were joined, in 1908, by English cabinetmaker Tom Handley, who had worked for Waring and Gillow in London before immigrating to the United States. Handley assumed the role of the firm's chief designer, helping to establish the company as a leading producer of high-quality period-revival furniture. After his death, his replacement, David Robertson Smith, who had worked for Gustav Stickley devising Arts and Crafts works, introduced the production of modern furniture. Smith's "Dynamique" line, based on the French Art Moderne and Frankl's own Skyscraper designs, became the first complete set of mass-produced modern furniture made in the United States. But, until 1935, the company continued to make and sell a full line of period-revival designs, including sets in the Colonial, Jacobean, Queen Anne, French Provincial, and Chinese Chippendale styles.[23]

The Johnson Company focused on manufacturing

quality pieces for a conservative, middle-class market. Frankl, who had spent most of the previous decade designing for the Hollywood elite, was a perfect fit for the firm: his name carried a certain cachet, and his works avoided the more eccentric or reductive forms that were already defining postwar design.

Stuart, impressed with Frankl's work, negotiated a contract with him to design an exclusive line of furniture. In the spring of 1949, Frankl set to work. He made a sketch of each design and, to test its appearance and suitability for mass production, had it built by artisans in Los Angeles under his personal supervision. He then shipped the finished pieces to the factory in Grand Rapids and met with the foreman to establish how they would be constructed in the factory. (He did not want simply to send plans because, as he told Peter, "If you send them plans they will change the design to fit what will work best with their machines. If they have a model they will figure out a way to copy it.")[24]

Frankl's initial designs for the Johnson Company, like his earliest pieces for Brown-Saltman, were modeled closely on his custom furnishings. The direct inspiration for his designs came from a commission he had undertaken a few years earlier for his friend Cliff May, a noted local architect, who had asked Frankl to design the interiors for his new house in Brentwood.

The house, built in 1939, was a long, low one-story affair, with a broad, sweeping roof and wide, overhanging eaves. It was based on the nineteenth-century California ranch houses that May, a sixth-generation Californian, had known since his youth. In the mid-1930s, May had designed the first of these "rancherias" in the San Diego area.[25] For the Brentwood house, he updated the traditional house form, offering more flexible and open spaces, complete with an attached two-car garage and stable. The sprawling house consisted of two elongated, splayed wings, wrapped around an ample rear patio onto which all of the principal living spaces opened. May retained the long, low rooflines and other features of the historic ranch houses, but updated the plans, materials,

and interior fittings. The result was a house that featured
traditional detailing but that was otherwise inherently
modern. The design, which he would replicate in myriad
forms in the 1940s and 1950s, became the basis of the
ubiquitous ranch house style of the era.[26]

Frankl's interiors for the house represented a modified version of his prewar manner.[27] In the living room, he
combined two large sofas—which borrowed directly from
his Speed chair form—with a coffee table based on one of
his earlier bamboo pieces (fig. 151). For the dining area and
other rooms, he devised a mode that brought together his
relaxed and elegant language of the 1930s with the elemental and angular forms he had created for Brown-Saltman.
In addition to introducing thick elements and broad, canted edges, he treated the surfaces simply, incorporating thin
bleached-cork veneers.

Frankl's first pieces for the Johnson Company developed and extended these basic ideas. The new designs,
which the company premiered in early 1950, were
composed of four principal lines. The centerpiece was
the "Station Wagon Group"—a set, as a feature story for
House Beautiful described, of "relaxed," "natural," and
"unaffected" furnishings intended for the suburban
home. Among the various Station Wagon pieces was a
mahogany-and-maple bed with an accompanying kid-
ney desk and matching end tables (fig. 152). With their
contrasting woods, the designs were intended to evoke
the new station wagon automobiles, which had similar
wooden elements affixed to their exteriors. But the style
was intended, too, as an "attitude" and a "new way of
life"; Frankl's furniture was the latest thing for the well-
heeled suburbanite.[28]

The *House Beautiful* article presented a full portfolio of
Frankl's latest works, all photographed in May's Brentwood
ranch house, which Frankl remodeled in late 1949 for the
occasion. Along with a number of Station Wagon pieces, the
home included a dining area furnished with a selection
from another of his Johnson lines, the "Debonair Group"
(fig. 153). The set featured polished brass X-shaped handles and V-shaped lattices, and combined European pear

Fig. 152. Paul T. Frankl, Station Wagon bedroom set, manufactured
by the Johnson Furniture Company, from a Johnson Company
brochure, c. 1950

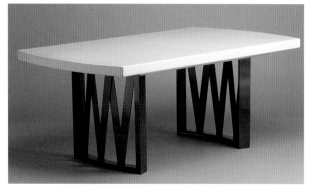

Above:
Fig. 153. Paul T. Frankl, dining area, May House, featuring Debonair furnishings, manufactured by the Johnson Furniture Company, 1950

Right:
Fig. 154. Paul T. Frankl, extension dining table, manufactured by the Johnson Furniture Company (model no. 2253), c. 1950. Bleached-cork top with pear wood and maple legs, 29 x 71 ¹/₂ x 42 in. (73.7 x 181.6 x 106.7 cm); fully extended 29 x 95 ¹/₂ x 42 in. (73.7 x 242.6 x 106.7 cm). Courtesy of Sollo:Rago Auctions, Lambertville, N.J.

wood, mahogany, and bleached cork (and structural parts of maple) with bleached-cork tops (fig. 154). The various pieces were available in several finishes, including chestnut and a white lacquered "Oriental Pearl" surface. The most distinctive designs in the group were the upholstered "plunging neckline" chairs—soon to become a standard feature of Frankl's 1950s interiors (fig. 155).

His designs for the Johnson Company also encompassed a wide array of other bleached-cork tables, bars, consoles, dressers, and vanities (figs. 156, 157). Most were modeled after the long, low, Asian-inspired furniture style he had been using since his move to California, but a few of the designs were entirely new, most notably a biomorphic-shaped cocktail table with a white bleached-cork top (fig. 158). [29]

Between 1949 and 1953, Frankl produced five more lines for the Johnson Company: the Embassy Group, which had large round drawer pulls in burnished gold plate; the Emissary Group, which had rectangular drawer pulls (fig. 159); the Tambour Group, which featured sides and doors composed of narrow vertical wooden slats (similar to a rolltop desk); the Legation Group, which had ribbon motif fitments and molded cabinet fronts; and the Attache Group, which had rectangular pulls, sand-beige finishes, and thin, canted legs. [30]

The popularity of Frankl's designs for the Johnson Company put him once more in the national spotlight. In addition to the *House Beautiful* article in June 1950, his

Fig. 155. Paul T. Frankl, dining table and chairs, manufactured by the Johnson Furniture Company, c. 1950. Table: lacquered cork, enameled steel, and brass, 29.5 x 102 x 40 in. (74.93 x 259 x 101.6 cm). Chairs: mahogany, cloth upholstery, armchairs 32.5 x 24 x 23 in. (82.6 x 61 x 58.4 cm), side chairs 32.5 x 24 x 22 in. (82.6 x 61 x 55.9 cm). Courtesy of Richard Wright, Chicago

Fig. 156. Paul T. Frankl, bar, manufactured by the Johnson Furniture Company, c. 1950. Lacquered cork and bleached mahogany, 27 x 42.5 x 18 in. (68.6 x 107.9 x 45.7 cm). Courtesy of Richard Wright, Chicago

Fig. 157. Paul T. Frankl, console magazine table, manufactured by the Johnson Furniture Company (model no. 5007), c. 1949. Lacquered cork and mahogany, 28 x 72 x 21 in. (71.1 x 182.9 x 58.3 cm). Courtesy of Richard Wright, Chicago

Fig. 158. Paul T. Frankl, cocktail table, manufactured by the Johnson Furniture Company (model no. 5005), c. 1951. Bleached-cork top with mahogany legs, 14 1/4 x 46 3/4 x 36 in. (36.2 x 118.7 x 91.4 cm). Courtesy of Richard Wright, Chicago

Double dresser from the Emissary Group designed by Paul T. Frankl.

Fig. 159. Advertisement for the Johnson Furniture Company showing a double dresser from the Emissary Group, c. 1950. Collection Paulette Frankl

Fig. 160. Paul T. Frankl, living room for a ranch house designed by Cliff May, Borrego Springs, California, c. 1951

work was featured in *House and Garden*, *Interiors*, and the *New York Times Magazine*.[31] But the triumph of Frankl's new furniture could not disguise his slide from the forefront of modern American design. In the years after World War II, a legion of new designers entered the field, among them George Nelson, Charles and Ray Eames, Isamu Noguchi, Eero Saarinen, and Edward Wormley; by the early 1950s, the works of many of the leading European designers—Alvar Aalto, Arne Jacobsen, Carlo Mollino, and Jean Prouvé—were also entering the U.S. market. Together, these designers pushed the boundaries of modernism, establishing a decidedly different look for the new aesthetic. Frankl's interiors of the time presented for many an appealing vision of the modern interior, one that was both comfortable and familiar (fig. 160). But the cozy aesthetic he proffered his clients,

Fig. 161. Charles Eames, interiors for a house, Pacific Palisades, California, c. 1949

for all of its innovative features, was beginning to seem almost dowdy compared with the designs of Noguchi or Charles Eames (fig. 161).

Frankl must have sensed the need to update his work. The interior he created for May's model ranch house in Northern California in 1952 was a strident departure from his early postwar work (fig. 162). May, encouraged by the broad acceptance of his low-cost ranch house design, formed a company with his partner Chris Choate to sell ranch-house plans to various builders.[32] They engaged Frankl to furnish a model of one of the homes. The commission gave Frankl the perfect opportunity to investigate new approaches. His response was to abandon almost entirely his recent style of elegance and luxury in favor of a realistic and utilitarian design language. His turn to metal furniture and plastic-laminated surfaces, which were evident throughout, was undoubtedly an attempt to find less costly alternatives to his more expensive hardwood furniture for the Johnson Company. Yet the rooms also evince a much reduced and clarified handling; they were at once simple, open, versatile, and—as would befit the young families who were the intended purchasers— durable and easy to clean.

Frankl's interiors for the May model home demonstrated that he was still able to devise designs that were as

modern as any of his contemporaries. But his interests were now focused elsewhere. In the early 1950s, he was able to secure lucrative contracts from a number of manufacturers: he produced upholstered pieces for S. H. Campbell in Chicago, a line of rattan furniture for Ficks Reed in Cincinnati, and mirrors for Hart Mirror Plate in Grand Rapids, among others.[33]

Despite his commercial success, Frankl was still not a wealthy man. With only a modest income from retail sales and occasional decorating jobs, he now relied on his contracts with the Johnson Company and other manufacturers to augment his income. But Frankl continued to live well—in large measure because of his ability to foster an illusion of luxury with moderate means. In early 1951, he, Mary, and Paulette moved into a spacious, twenty-six-room Spanish Colonial villa in Palos Verdes. Frankl could not afford to buy the house, which was owned by the adjacent Chadwick School. Instead, the school's board gave the house to Frankl, by then a local celebrity, with the hope that he would renovate it, thereby increasing the stature of the community and, with it, property values. Immediately, Frankl set about modernizing the house, furnishing it with his own designs, most of them his custom pieces from the 1930s and 1940s and antiques he had collected over the years.[34]

In early 1952, Frankl decided to spend a year in Europe. The trip would provide fifteen-year-old Paulette with the opportunity to travel and learn a new language; it would also give Frankl the opportunity to rest and to examine the latest trends in Europe.

In October 1952, the family flew from New York to Madrid, where they installed Paulette in a convent school.[35] They moved into an apartment nearby, within walking distance of the Prado Museum. Frankl used the time to explore the city and to plan his travels throughout the continent. Before they were able to depart, though, Paulette became a concern.[36] She was miserable, in part because instruction at the school, which was run by French nuns, was in French with only occasional transla-

Fig. 162. Paul T. Frankl, interior for a model ranch house, Cupertino, California, 1952

tion into Spanish. Paulette was not fluent in either language and was uncomfortable in the rigid and foreign environment; deeply unhappy, she began suffering a daily rash of nosebleeds. Frankl and Mary decided to remain in Madrid until the end of the term in mid-December. The family then traveled together to Switzerland to spend the Christmas holidays in St. Moritz.

After the holidays, Frankl and Mary decided to enroll their daughter in the Geneva International School. Almost immediately, Paulette showed remarkable improvement. Her turnaround was so dramatic that the couple decided they could now leave her and make an extended trip to Italy.[37]

They spent most of the next several months at a pensione in Portofino, on the Italian Riviera. Frankl found much to praise in the Italian architecture and design studios. As he told an American reporter after his return to the United States, "The Italians are doing the most important job in the decorative arts today. Apartment houses in Rome are more up to date than anything in America. And they're doing a first-class job in modern furniture." But the problem, as Frankl saw it, was that the best designs were not being "produced in quantities, only in special designs for the luxury classes." He added: "Our strength in America is in the machine."[38]

Frankl also undertook several side trips from Portofino, first to Switzerland to research the design scene there, and then to Vienna to see friends and visit his elderly mother. Frankl was impressed with the modern design he saw in Switzerland. "Whatever they do," he told the American reporter, "they do right. The new furniture is somewhat German in feeling—solid, clean, interesting." By contrast, he found Vienna "completely dead." It was the first time he had been back to Austria since the early 1930s, and he was shocked by the pathetic condition of the city after six long and devastating years of war. Though another eight years had passed, Vienna, still under Allied occupation, was experiencing an agonizingly slow recovery. There was little evidence of interesting new design trends, and most of the old design vanguard had dispersed with the rise of the Nazis.

Frankl did receive one pleasant surprise when he paid a courtesy visit to Josef Hoffmann, the grand old man of Viennese design, now in his early eighties, and found him still actively working, churning out new ideas daily.[39] But Frankl found little else in Vienna to admire. Even after the passage of nearly four decades, the city evoked in him feelings of antipathy—and the lingering evidence of anti-Semitism did nothing to warm his view. In the intervening years, his brothers, who had assumed the family real estate concern, had squandered their fortune. His mother, who

had remarried a retired manager from the state railways, continued to live in the old villa on the Auhofstraße, but in much-reduced circumstances.[40] Seeing her and his other relatives only supported his conviction that he had been right to leave. He harbored few feelings of nostalgia for Vienna—or Austria in general. He missed the long hikes in the Alps of his boyhood and his "beloved mother," but little else.

During his sojourn in Vienna, Frankl made a brief, two-day trip to Munich. Once more, he was disappointed with what he saw. "The Germans are not yet doing anything of importance," he told the American reporter.

After Vienna, Frankl returned to Italy, spending April and May in Portofino. When the school term ended for Paulette, he and Mary met her in Geneva and the family traveled together to London, where, in early June, they witnessed the coronation of Queen Elizabeth II. Not long afterward, they returned to Vienna and then went on to Venice for a short vacation (fig. 163). After a stop in Milan to allow Frankl to visit several furniture makers, they departed for New York, sailing from Genoa on the luxury liner *Andrea Doria*. By late summer, they were back in Los Angeles.

In the early fall of 1953, Frankl labored sporadically on several new ideas for the Johnson Company. During his monthlong stay in Vienna, he had collaborated with local draftsmen to produce a group of metal drawer pulls; now he sought to find forms to complement them. Much of his time and attention, though, were focused on the two new books he was writing.

One of the books, *American Textiles*, was a short, general introduction to American textile design, commissioned by an English publisher. Frankl had begun work on it in late 1952, shortly before he departed for Europe, and mostly completed it during his second stay in Portofino. *American Textiles* is a picture book, a straightforward documentation of postwar textile design, emphasizing expensive handwoven and machine-printed examples. It includes works by Florence Knoll,

Laverne Originals, Maria Kipp, Marianne Strengell, and
others, all selected to bolster Frankl's argument that
Americans were now producing their own high-quality
textiles—and that they were the perfect complement to
the new American design.[41]

The more important and meaningful of the books for
Frankl was an autobiography. He hatched the idea of
writing a memoir during his stay in Vienna. Throughout
September and October, he labored assiduously on the
text; by mid-November, as he wrote to his old friend
Manuel Komroff in New York, he had finished about two
hundred typewritten pages. He planned a longer work—
as much as four hundred pages, he told Komroff—without
illustrations. It would tell the story of his travails and successes in promoting modern American design—and allow
"others to judge" what he had accomplished. But most
of the text mirrored Frankl's sober mood. "It may find a
publisher," he wrote to Komroff, "but at the moment I
don't care. I am tired of being pushed around, being used
as doormat, and now leisurely am doing what I want to
do. A publisher at this point would only push me some
more—tell me what he wants and when he wants it. This
is going to be 'my book.'"[42]

Frankl's bitterness and frustration stemmed from
his failure to secure more work and recognition. Sixty-
eight years old, tired and dispirited, he could no longer
summon the energy or optimism of his earlier years. His
working title for the memoir, he revealed to Komroff, was
tinged with acerbity: "I Made Junk Sing! Indiscretions
of America's No. 1 Interior Decorator."[43] It had been
suggested to him by a friend, journalist and author Frank
Scully, who had seen the manuscript and thought the title
an apt fit. But Scully's suggested title, while conjuring
up the gossipy and irreverent tone Frankl aspired to, was
in fact wide of the mark. Most of the manuscript was
written in a breezy tone, and it concentrated on his many
high-profile clients and well-known friends—but the
autobiography was far from a tell-all. There were few
"indiscretions" and only occasional insight into the real
problems and challenges he faced over his career. Frankl

Fig. 163. Frankl with Paulette on the Lido, Venice, 1953

must have sensed that the work wanted for drama and focus. Shortly after he wrote to Komroff, he abandoned the project, without completing the final chapter, which was to cover his return to Vienna.[44] He never sent it to a publisher. The book was, as he had suggested, an exercise in self-reflection.

For much of the next year, Frankl was preoccupied with the search for new manufacturers and showrooms to take his designs. He was mostly absent from his drafting table, leaving the able Peggy Galloway to supervise the office work and execute whatever interior design projects came their way. To secure new commissions, Frankl spent more and more time on the road, traveling to showrooms and factories in various major cities, especially along the West Coast.

His marketing approach was unorthodox. Peter, who had since settled in San Francisco, recalled later that, to his surprise, his father did not customarily bring samples or photographs of his work with him. When they stopped in to see a furniture dealer during one of Frankl's frequent visits to the city, he walked in empty-handed. When the owner inquired whether Frankl could show him any examples of his work, Frankl asked the man if he had any recent copies of *House Beautiful* or *House and Garden*. Because Frankl's designs for the Johnson Company appeared so frequently in the pages of both magazines, he had little problem locating images of his work.[45]

Still, Frankl struggled to expand his line of manufactured furniture. The royalties he received from the Johnson Company, Ficks Reed, and Hart Mirror Plate provided a comfortable income, but finding other opportunities proved laborious and wearying. By the summer of 1955, Frankl had had enough of it all: he resolved to spend the fall traveling abroad.

Foremost among his motives was the chance to spend more time with Paulette. She had finished high school that spring and decided to study art. Frankl, recognizing that his daughter had talent and wary of forcing her into another occupation, as his father had with him, sent her off to the Skowhegan School of Painting and Sculpture, in

Maine, for four weeks in the early summer. Afterward, Paulette enrolled at Stanford University as a trial student. When fall arrived, Frankl, firm in his conviction that experience makes the best teacher, decided to take her out of school and travel. Mary also wanted her daughter to see the world and experience it with her father, so the family booked a thirty-day trip around the world. To provide company for Paulette, the Frankls asked one of her friends from Stanford, Leanne Boccardo, daughter of prominent attorney James Boccardo, to accompany them.

In September, they departed on Pan American Airlines, flying first to Hawaii, then on to Tokyo (staying this time at Frank Lloyd Wright's Imperial Hotel), Kyoto, and Kowloon. After further stops in Bangkok and Calcutta, they reached Delhi, where they visited the Taj Mahal. Frankl thrilled at the purity of Shāh Jāhan's great monument to his beloved wife. But the rigors of so much traveling were beginning to take their toll on him. He was often tired and was forced to take ever more frequent rests. After departing from Delhi, they stopped in Karachi, Tel Aviv, Jerusalem, and Athens, before reaching Rome. Frankl, now completely exhausted, decided to break the journey there; he, Mary, and Paulette spent most of the next two months in Italy.[46]

While there, Frankl arranged for Paulette to have private lessons with Roman artist Peppino Piccolo. He and Mary spent their time surveying the city and taking occasional trips to the countryside. They made one more short trip to Vienna—as it turned out, Frankl's last—to visit his ailing mother. In mid-December, the family departed for home, arriving in Los Angeles just before Christmas 1955.

For the next ten months, Frankl continued to focus on his designs for the Johnson Company. He now worked exclusively at home. After returning from the trip, he closed the office on Doheny Drive and set up a studio in the large basement of the house in Palos Verdes. Peggy Galloway continued to assist him, traveling down from Hollywood several days a week. But Frankl was often fatigued, unable to sit for long periods at his drafting table. For the first time, his prodigious output began to diminish. By fall, it was evident that his health was failing. A doctor's diagnosis confirmed the worst: he had advanced colon cancer.

In the early summer of 1957, Frankl traveled to Stanford Medical Center in Palo Alto to have surgery, but the cancer had now spread throughout his abdomen. There was little his doctors could do; in September, he and Mary returned to Palos Verdes.

Frankl was still working, a little—he made a few drawings of furniture ideas, and he resumed work on his autobiography, though without much progress to show. By the spring of 1958, he was bedridden. He was frequently in pain, and his midriff was distended and filled with fluid, which had to be drained off. Yet he remained alert, seeing a persistent stream of visitors, most of whom sensed it was time to say their final goodbyes. He maintained his wit and charm, but those who came to call found him visibly reduced. Frankl's daughter-in-law, Jane Boulton, last saw him "sitting in his narrow bed, like a small child, his domed head heavy on a thin neck."[47] Finally, on 21 March, he lapsed into a coma; he died later the same day.[48]

The obituaries that appeared over the next few weeks hailed Frankl as a "pioneer in the field of modern decorative art in the United States" and as a leader in the "Southern California school of luxurious, full-blown contemporary design."[49] Many also alluded to Frankl's four books and his recent work for the Johnson Company. But the response to his passing on the whole was subdued. Frankl had outlived his time: the attentions of the design world were focused elsewhere. The experience of the cold war era was changing American culture, and the fading interest in Frankl and the other pioneers from earlier times was only part of a much larger shift in values and ideas.

Epilogue

"**illiam Morris died fighting** against the machine age," Frankl wrote in the conclusion to *New Dimensions* in 1927. "Our progress of the future does not depend on fighting for modernism but on educating ourselves to be part of the world we live in."[1] This simple idea guided Frankl's long quest for modern design (fig. 164). In that sense, he was no different from any of his modernist contemporaries—all saw the essence of their life's labors in the attempt to find a living culture that expressed modern life. But, as Frankl and his cohorts found, the intellectual grounds for their search kept shifting; Frankl strove in his work and his writings to find the mark on a swiftly moving target.

But it was not that mission that made him stand out; rather, Frankl's signal contribution issued from his great ambition, nursed almost from the time he landed in New York Harbor, to forge a distinctively American modern design. That he, a designer with a European eye and intellect, was at the center of this effort is one of the great paradoxes, but also one of the fundamental realities, of the history of American modernism. Frankl, of course, was by no means alone: nearly all of the pioneers of the new design in the United States in the 1920s were born and educated in Europe. And each of these émigré designers, in his or her own way, contributed to the making of the new aesthetic. It was Frankl, though, who discovered, in the work of native architects, the image that would become synonymous with American design of that time: the skyscraper. It was a brilliant gesture—to condense the language of the soaring urban towers into furnishings. The image was bold and arresting but also immediately recognizable. And it was in that legibility that the image's power resided: Frankl's designs were American works and, moreover, symbols of America. If he had contributed nothing else, his Skyscraper furniture would have assured him a place in the modernist index.

But Frankl did much more. With relentless energy, he strove to organize his fellow American modernists, to build a common purpose among them; he launched a one-man campaign to educate the public taste with his books, courses, and lecture tours; and, in the 1930s, he advanced a new design style that brought together older notions of comfort and coziness with an original and compelling form language. After World War II, Frankl's designs for manufacturers aided in the campaign to bring modernism to the homes of the broad public.

Frankl's ability to sum up in his writings the hopes and beliefs of his time contributed to his enduring fame. Quotations from his books appear in almost every account of American design from the 1920s and 1930s. But Frankl was not an original—or even an especially lucid—theoretician of modernism. Rather, his skill lay in assembling and summarizing what others were writing and saying, and in finding ways to popularize and disseminate those ideas. At a time when modern design was still viewed with distrust, he became its most vocal and spirited champion, and his efforts did much to ensure its later popularity.

Even before his death, Frankl's achievements were eclipsed. The pace of modernism was accelerating. But the fact that he was able to remain at the forefront for nearly four decades is in itself remarkable. The purpose of the modernist experiment was always to keep the experiment going. Frankl, more than almost any other designer of his

Opposite:
Fig. 164. Paul T. Frankl, c. 1955

generation, proved to have not only an unusually fecund imagination but also an especially lithe one, allowing him to move readily from one design direction to the next, almost always remaining a few steps ahead of the competition. His tendency to forge ahead took its toll. He expended great energy convincing others of the rightness of his ideas, and he often found his work plagiarized and misrepresented, costing him much personally and financially. But Frankl was not merely productive and visionary. His designs were also beautiful, refined, and memorable. What highlights his long career was his capacity to find distinctive and compelling images: his elegant, cascading bookcases, his graceful Speed chairs, his sweeping rattan designs, his cloud-like cork tables.

The multifarious nature of Frankl's designs points firmly to one other reality of the new design: its insistent variety. Modernism was never a unified "movement." It was instead a broad assault composed of many individual—and sometimes contradictory—battles. The experiences of Frankl, whom Frank Lloyd Wright described as "a soldier...on the Fifth Avenue firing-line of the aesthetic crusade," underscore both the complex course and the splendor of that struggle.[2]

Notes

PROLOGUE

1 Paul T. Frankl, autobiography (unpublished), c. 1954, Collection Paulette Frankl, 68–69. Rudolph Rosenthal and Helena L. Ratzka relate an identical account in *The Story of Modern Applied Art* (New York: Harper and Brothers, 1948), 173. Their source was German-born designer Kem Weber, who apparently heard the story secondhand. According to Weber, Austrian artist Frederick Kiesler was also in the taxicab, but Kiesler did not arrive in the United States from Europe until the following January.

CHAPTER 1. Vienna

1 Paul T. Frankl, autobiography (unpublished), c. 1954, Collection Paulette Frankl, 1–2 (hereafter, FA).

2 Zuckerkandl, quoted in Thomas S. Hines, *Richard Neutra and the Search for Modern Architecture: A Biography and History* (New York: Oxford University Press, 1982), 9.

3 During the first two decades of his life, Paul Frankl used only his first and last names, but in early adulthood he added his middle initial to avoid confusion with the well-known Prague-born art historian Paul Frankl. The other Paul Frankl (1878–1962) trained first to become an architect but in his early thirties turned to the study of art history and, in 1911, submitted his doctoral dissertation at the University of Munich on fifteenth-century stained glass in southern Germany. He was appointed to the chair of art history at Halle University in 1921 but was dismissed from his job by the Nazis in 1934. Four years later, he immigrated to the United States, where he held a research position at Princeton University's Institute of Advanced Study until his death. Among his best known works are *Die Entwicklungsphasen der neueren Baukunst* (Leipzig: B. G. Teubner, 1914), reprinted in English as *Principles of Architectural History: The Four Phases of Architectural Style, 1420–1900*, trans. and ed. James F. O'Gorman (Cambridge, Mass.: MIT Press, 1968); and *Baukunst des Mittelalters: Die frühmittelalterliche und romanische Baukunst* (Wildpark-Potsdam, Germany: Athenaion, 1926).

4 FA, 1.

5 Felix Czeike, "Wiener Wohnbau vom Vormärz bis 1923," in *Kommunaler Wohnbau in Wien: Aufbruch 1923–1934 Ausstrahlung*, ed. Karl Mang (Vienna: Presse- und Informationsdienst der Stadt Wien, 1977).

6 The firm Julius Frankl was officially registered 6 May 1890. Handelsgericht, Handelsregister E, vol. 25, Wiener Stadt- und Landesarchiv. Frankl not only developed his own properties, but he also owned considerable stock in other building companies. See Herbert Matis and Dieter Stiefel, *Mit der vereinigten Kraft des Capitals, des Credits und der Technik: Die Geschichte des österreichischen Bauwesens am Beispiel der Allgemeinen Baugesellschaft A. Porr AG* (Vienna: Böhlau, 1994).

7 Verlassenschaftsabhandlung Julius Frankl, 1908, Wiener Stadt- und Landesarchiv; and letter from Erika Appel to Peter Boulton, 13 October 1991, in possession of the author. My thanks to Frankl's son, Peter Boulton, for sharing this and other documents with me.

8 Verlassenschaftsabhandlung Julius Frankl, 1908.

9 Verlassenschaftsabhandlung Julius Frankl, 1908.

10 Letter from Erika Appel to Peter Boulton, 13 October 1991.

11 Letter from Erika Appel to Peter Boulton, 30 December 1991.

12 Letter from Erika Appel to Peter Boulton, 13 October 1991.

13 Baptismal records, Church of St. Karl, Vienna, 1886; and letter from Erika Appel to Peter Boulton, 19 April 1991.

14 *Lehmanns Allgemeiner Wohnungsanzeiger nebst Handels- und Gewerbe Adreßbuch für die k. u. k. Reichs- Haupt- und Residenzstadt und Umgebung*, Vienna, 1886–1900; and records, Baupolizei, Vienna, MA 37.

15 Letter from Peter Boulton to the author, 13 June 2000.

16 FA, 4–6.

17 Louis La Barbera, "Paul T. Frankl: A Chronological Survey of His Works" (M.A. thesis, University of Southern California, 1951), 23. Julius Frankl also owned a large collection of nine-teenth-century prints depicting scenes of cities and land-scapes from throughout the empire. Part of the collection is now owned by his great-grandson, Nicholas Koenig. Letter from Nicholas Koenig to the author, 10 May 2002.

18 FA, 4–5.

19 Martin Birnbaum, *Introductions: Painters, Sculptors, and Graphic Artists* (New York: Frederic Fairchild Sherman, 1919), 101–5.

20 FA, 7–8.

21 FA, 6–7.

22 Letter from Peter Boulton to Paulette Frankl, 11 August 1998, Collection Paulette Frankl.

23 "Haupt-Kataloge der Oberrealschule, Elbogen, 1902–04," Státní okresní archiv, Fond Réalka Loket, Jindřichovice, Czech Republic.

24 FA, 6.

25 On König's life and work, see Markus Kristan, *Carl König, 1841–1915: Ein neubarocker Großstadtarchitekt in Wien*, exhibition catalog (Vienna: Jüdisches Museum der Stadt Wien, 1999). See also *Bauten und Entwürfe von Carl König herausgegeben von seinen Schülern* (Vienna: Gerlach and Wiedling, [1910]), 5–6; Karl Mayreder, *Zu Karl Königs siebzigstem Geburtstag* (Vienna: Selbstverlag des Karl König-Komitees, 1912); Ulrich Thieme and Felix Becker, eds., "Karl König," in *Allgemeines Lexikon der bildenden Künstler von der Antike bis zur Gegenwart*, vol. 21 (Leipzig: E. A. Seemann, 1935), 157–58; and Renate Wagner-Rieger, "Karl König," in *Österreichisches Biographisches Lexikon, 1815–1950* (Vienna: Böhlau, 1969), 36–37.

26 FA, 9.

27 Marco Pozzetto, "Karl König und die Architektur der Wiener Technischen Hochschule," in *Wien um 1900: Kunst und Kultur*, exhibition catalog, ed. Maria Auböck and Maria Marchetti (Vienna: Christian Brandstetter, 1985), 305; Technische Hochschule Wien, *Lektionskatalog, Studienpläne und Personalstand der Technischen Hochschule in Wien für das Studienjahr 1904-1905* (Vienna, 1904), 32–43; and

Christopher Long, "An Alternative Path to Modernism: Carl König and Architectural Education at the Vienna Technische Hochschule, 1890–1913," *Journal of Architectural Education* 55 (September 2001): 21–30.

28 Frankl, "Acanthus," *California Arts and Architecture* 54 (July 1938): 2.

29 Hauptkatalog, Studienjahr 1904–5, A bis Na. I. Archiv, Technische Universität, Vienna.

30 FA, 9.

31 Frankl's student records, Matrikel-Nummer 18161, Technische Universität, Berlin.

CHAPTER 2. An Expression of Our Age

1 Paul T. Frankl, autobiography (unpublished), c. 1954, Collection Paulette Frankl, 2 (hereafter, FA).

2 Stefan Zweig, *Die Welt von Gestern: Erinnerungen eines Europäers* (Frankfurt am Main: S. Fischer, 1953), 287.

3 Peter Gay, *Weimar Culture: The Insider as Outsider* (New York: Harper and Row, 1968), 128–29.

4 For contemporary discussion of the differences between Vienna and Berlin and the rise of the new industrial aesthetic, see Julius Bab and Willi Handel, *Wien und Berlin: Vergleichendes zur Kulturgeschichte der beiden Hauptstädte Mitteleuropas* (Berlin: Osterheld, 1918), esp. 258–323; and Joseph August Lux, *Das neue Kunstgewerbe in Deutschland* (Leipzig: Klinkhardt and Biermann, 1908).

5 Charles-Édouard Jeanneret [Le Corbusier], *Étude sur le mouvement d'Art Décoratif en Allemagne* (La Chaux-de-Fonds, Switzerland: Haefeli, 1912), quoted in Tilmann Buddensieg, "Introduction: Aesthetic Opposition and International Style," in *Berlin 1900–1933: Architecture and Design*, exhibition catalog, ed. Tilmann Buddensieg (New York: Cooper-Hewitt Museum/Berlin: Gebr. Mann, 1987), 13.

6 See Laurie A. Stein, "Culture, Style, and the Autonomy of the Object: Applied Arts and Architecture in Germany, from the 1890s to the 1930s," in *New Worlds: German and Austrian Art, 1890–1940*, exhibition catalog, ed. Renée Price, with Pamela Kort and Leslie Topp (New York: Neue Galerie/Cologne: DuMont, 2001), 518–20.

7 Joseph August Lux, *Ingenieur-Ästhetik* (Munich: G. Lammers, 1910), 8.

[8] Robert Suckale, "Die Bauakademie nach Schinkel und die sogenannte 'Berliner Schule,'" in *Von der Bauakademie zur Technischen Universität Berlin: Geschichte und Zukunft, 1799–1999*, exhibition catalog, ed. Karl Schwarz (Berlin: Ernst and Sohn, 2000), 76–77. On the history of the school, see Reinhard Rürup, ed., *Wissenschaft und Gesellschaft: Beiträge zur Geschichte der Technischen Universität Berlin, 1879–1979* (Berlin: Springer, 1979); and Karl Schwarz, ed., *Von der Bauakademie zur Technischen Universität: 200 Jahre Forschung und Lehre* (Berlin, 1999).

[9] Königliche Technische Hochschule zu Berlin, *Program für das Studienjahr 1905–1906* (Berlin, 1905).

[10] FA, 9–10.

[11] Frankl's military service records: Hauptgrundbuchblatt, Grundbuchsevidenz, Wien, Karton 1025; and Qualifikationsliste, Qualifikationslisten, Karton 688, both from Österreichisches Staatsarchiv, Kriegsarchiv, Vienna.

[12] FA, 10.

[13] Frankl's military service records, Hauptgrundbuchblatt, Grundbuchsevidenz, Wien, Karton 1025.

[14] Letter from Peter Boulton to the author, 8 March 2000.

[15] The grave is located in the Hietzinger Friedhof, Group 17, Grave 17.

[16] Hauptkatalog, Studienjahr 1908–9, Archiv, Technische Universität, Vienna.

[17] Frankl's student records, Matrikel-Nummer 20016, Technische Universität, Berlin.

[18] Paula was born on 26 February 1885. She and Frankl married in Berlin-Charlottenburg on 9 October 1911. Registration records (Heimatrollen), Magistratsamt 61, Vienna.

[19] FA, 11.

[20] See Helmut Bauer and Elisabeth Tworek, eds., *Schwabing. Kunst und Leben um 1900: Essays* (Munich: Münchner Stadtmuseum, 1998).

[21] Maria Makela, *The Munich Secession: Art and Artists in Turn-of-the-Century Munich* (Princeton, N.J.: Princeton University Press, 1990), 136–37.

[22] Louis La Barbera, "Paul T. Frankl: A Chronological Survey of His Works" (M.A. thesis, University of Southern California, 1951), 25.

[23] FA, 20.

[24] FA, 11.

[25] On Salvisberg's life and work, see Claude Lichtenstein, *O. R. Salvisberg: Die andere Moderne* (Zurich: Institut für Geschichte und Theorie der Architektur, Eidgenössische Technische Hochschule, 1995); "Otto Rudolf Salvisberg, 1882–1940," *Das Werk* 11 (1941): 289–306; "Otto Rudolf Salvisberg, 1882–1940," *Werk-Architese* 10 (1977): 4–54; Paul Westheim, "Architekturen von Otto Salvisberg—Berlin," *Moderne Bauformen* 3 (1914): 113–40; Paul Westheim, *Neuere Arbeiten von O. R. Salvisberg* (Berlin: Hübsch, 1927); and "Zu den Bauten von Otto Rudolf Salvisberg," *Moderne Bauformen* 2 (1925): 33–71.

[26] Critic Paul Westheim described the Lindenhaus as "one of the works that has given us a wholly new knowledge of the properties of concrete." Westheim, "Das Lindenhaus von Otto Salvisberg," *Tonindustrie-Zeitung* 140 (1914): 1.

[27] Ludwig Pietsch, "Das Hohenzollern-Kunstgewerbehaus—Berlin: Aus Anlaß seines 25-jährigen Bestehens," *Deutsche Kunst und Dekoration* 15 (1904–5): 171.

[28] See Max Osborn, "Das Hohenzollern-Kunstgewerbehaus in Berlin," *Innen-Dekoration* 26 (1915): 55–84; and Angela Schönberger, "Es ist eine Lust zu leben, die Geister bewegen sich . . ." in *Berlin 1900–1933: Architecture and Design*, exhibition catalog, ed. Tilmann Buddensieg (New York: Cooper-Hewitt Museum/Berlin: Gebr. Mann, 1987), 87–88.

[29] FA, 12.

[30] FA, 13.

[31] FA, 13-14.

[32] Frankl, "Der Stil unserer Zeit," *Der Baumeister* 12 (November 1913): 15–16.

[33] Frankl, "Die Industrie als Kulturträger," *Der Baumeister* 12 (March 1914): 46–47.

[34] On the rise of the Werkbund and its aims, see Lucius Burckhardt, ed., *The Werkbund: Studies in the History and Ideology of the Deutscher Werkbund, 1907–1933* (London: The Design Council, 1980); Joan Campbell, *The German Werkbund: The Politics of Reform in the Applied Arts* (Princeton, N.J.: Princeton University Press, 1978), esp. chapters 1–3; Kurt Junghanns, *Der Deutsche Werkbund: Sein erstes Jahrzehnt* (Berlin: Henschelverlag Kunst und Gesellschaft, 1982);

and Frederic J. Schwartz, *The Werkbund: Design Theory and Mass Culture Before the First World War* (New Haven: Yale University Press, 1996).

[35] Frankl's name does not appear on the rosters of either the German Werkbund or its sister organization, the Austrian Werkbund, which were published in the two organizations' respective annuals around the time of World War I. See Deutscher Werkbund, *Die Kunst in Industrie und Handel: Jahrbuch des Deutschen Werkbundes 1913* (Jena: Eugen Diederichs, 1914); and Max Eisler, ed., *Österreichische Werkkultur* (Vienna: Anton Schroll, 1916).

[36] Frankl, "Die Industrie als Kulturträger," 48.

[37] See Christopher Long, "'A Symptom of the Werkbund': The Spring 1912 Exhibition at the Austrian Museum for Art and Industry, Vienna," *Studies in the Decorative Arts* 7 (Spring-Summer 2000): 91–121.

[38] Hermann Muthesius, *Die Werkbund-Arbeit der Zukunft und Aussprache darüber* (Jena: Eugen Diederichs, 1914), 33–54. For an excellent discussion of the 1914 Cologne debate, see Stanford Anderson, "Deutscher Werkbund—The 1914 Debate: Hermann Muthesius versus Henry van de Velde," in *Companion to Contemporary Architectural Thought*, ed. Ben Farmer and Hentie Louw (London: Routledge, 1993), 462–67; and Campbell, *The German Werkbund*, 57–81.

[39] FA, 14.

[40] FA, 15.

[41] Ship manifests for 1914, Ellis Island Foundation, New York.

CHAPTER 3. A Gentle Exit

[1] Paul T. Frankl, autobiography (unpublished), c. 1954, Collection Paulette Frankl, 15 (hereafter, FA).

[2] FA, 15.

[3] FA, 13.

[4] FA, 15–16.

[5] Frank Lloyd Wright, *Frank Lloyd Wright, Chicago*, vol. 8, *Sonderheft der Architektur des XX. Jahrhunderts* (Berlin: Ernst Wasmuth, 1911). Noted German architect Bruno Möhring presented Wright's work at a lecture on Berlin to the Union of Berlin Architects in February 1910, but Frankl was not in the audience. Only later, in 1913, did he see

Wright's work in the *Sonderheft*. On Wright's time in Berlin, see Anthony Alofsin, *Frank Lloyd Wright: The Lost Years, 1910–1922* (Chicago: University of Chicago Press, 1993), 30–35.

[6] Cis Zoltowska (Frankl's cousin), interview by author, Los Angeles, 31 May 1999.

[7] On Wright's influence in Europe, see Anthony Alofsin, "Wright, Influence, and the World at Large," in *Frank Lloyd Wright: Europe and Beyond*, ed. Anthony Alofsin (Berkeley: University of California Press, 1999), 1–23.

[8] Cis Zoltowska interview.

[9] Cis Zoltowska interview.

[10] Gray Brechin, "Sailing to Byzantium: The Architecture of the Fair," in *The Anthropology of World's Fairs: San Francisco's Panama Pacific International Exposition of 1915*, exhibition catalog, ed. Burton Benedict (London: The Lowie Museum of Anthropology/Scolar, 1983), 95.

[11] See, for example, William B. Faville, "Phases of Panama-Pacific International Exposition Architecture," *American Architect* 107 (6 January 1915): 5–10, and plates.

[12] FA, 16.

[13] FA, 17.

[14] FA, 17.

[15] Louis La Barbera, "Paul T. Frankl: A Chronological Survey of His Works" (M.A. thesis, University of Southern California, 1951), 30–31.

[16] Frankl, "What Does Modern Art Owe Japan?" *California Arts and Architecture* 51 (March 1937): 17.

[17] Frankl, "What Does Modern Art Owe Japan?" 18.

[18] FA, 14.

[19] Rudolph Rosenthal and Helena L. Ratzka, *The Story of Modern Applied Art* (New York: Harper and Brothers, 1948), 165; *Printing Art* 24 (February 1915): 483–88; and *Trow's New York City Directory* (New York: R. L. Polk, 1916), 868.

[20] Petersham was born Petrezselyem Mikaly in Toeroekszentmiklos, Hungary, in 1888. The Petershams later moved to Woodstock, New York; Frankl remained close friends with them for many years. Maud and Miska Petersham Papers, du Grummond Collection, McCain

Library and Archives, University Libraries, University of Southern Mississippi.

[21] Cis Zoltowska interview.

[22] FA, 18.

[23] Urban had moved to Boston in 1911. He, his wife, Mizzi, and their two daughters were vacationing in Italy when the news of the impending war reached them. Rather than returning to Austria, they made their way to New York. Randolph Carter and Robert Reed Cole, *Joseph Urban: Architecture, Theatre, Opera, Film* (New York: Abbeville Press, 1992), 67–69.

[24] Ship manifests for 1914, Ellis Island Foundation, New York.

[25] FA, 22–25.

[26] Elliot Willensky and Norval White, *AIA Guide to New York City* (San Diego: Harcourt Brace Jovanovich, 1988), 219, 870.

[27] FA, 25.

[28] Frankl placed advertisements in *Arts and Decoration* in March, April, May, June, and July 1915, and in *Vanity Fair* in April and May 1915.

[29] On the decline of the Arts and Crafts movement, see Richard Guy Wilson, "The Arts and Crafts after 1918: Ending and Legacy," in *The Arts and Crafts Movement in California: Living the Good Life*, exhibition catalog, ed. Kenneth R. Trapp et al. (Oakland: The Oakland Museum / New York: Abbeville Press, 1993), 233–46.

[30] Anne Massey, *Interior Design of the Twentieth Century* (London: Thames and Hudson, 1990), 123–26; and Elsie de Wolfe, *The House in Good Taste* (New York: Century, 1913).

[31] Helen Churchill Candee, *Decorative Styles and Periods in the Home* (New York: Frederick A. Stokes, 1906), 3–4.

[32] Wanda M. Corn, *The Great American Thing: Modern Art and National Identity, 1915–1935* (Berkeley: University of California Press, 1999), 16.

[33] On the Austrian pavilion at the St. Louis exhibition, see Imperial Royal Ministry for Public Instruction, *Exhibition of Professional Schools of Arts and Crafts, Universal Exhibition St. Louis 1904*, exhibition catalog (Vienna: Verlag des k. k. Ministeriums, 1904).

[34] Robert Judson Clark and Wendy Kaplan, "Arts and Crafts: Matters of Style," in *"The Art That Is Life": The Arts and Crafts Movement in America, 1875–1920*, exhibition catalog, ed.

Wendy Kaplan (Boston: Museum of Fine Arts / Bulfinch, 1987), 93–94; and C. Matlack Price, "Secessionist Architecture in America: Departures from Academic Traditions of Design," *Arts and Decoration* 3 (December 1912): 51–53.

[35] The show, organized by John Cotton Dana, librarian at the Free Public Library in Newark, New Jersey, in collaboration with the Deutsches Museum für Kunst im Handel und Gewerbe in Hagen, Germany, and the Österreichisches Museum für Kunst und Industrie in Vienna, featured an array of modern German and Austrian designs and objects. Among the designers and artists represented were Peter Behrens, Otto Eckmann, August Endell, Walter Gropius, Josef Hoffmann, Koloman Moser, Emil Nolde, Joseph Maria Olbrich, Emil Orlik, Bruno Paul, Max Pechstein, Michael Powolny, Otto Prutscher, and Richard Riemerschmid. The traveling exhibit was the first such major undertaking to show modern Central European design in the United States since the 1904 Louisiana Purchase Exhibition in St. Louis. It stopped in Newark, Chicago, Indianapolis, Pittsburgh, Cincinnati, and St. Louis before closing at the National Arts Club in New York in March 1913. On the exhibition and its impact, see *Deutsches Kunstgewerbe*, exhibition catalog (St. Louis: City Art Museum of St. Louis, 1912); and Barry Shifman, "Design for Industry: The 'German Applied Arts' Exhibition in the United States, 1912–13," *Journal of the Decorative Arts Society* 22 (1998): 19–31.

[36] For examples of the Aschermans' work, see Louise Brigham, *Box Furniture: How to Make a Hundred Useful Articles for the Home* (New York: Century, 1910); and Edward Stratton Holloway, *The Practical Book of Furnishing the Small House and Apartment* (Philadelphia: J. B. Lippincott, 1922). See also "'Modern' Interior Decoration in American Homes by E. H. and G. G. Aschermann [sic]," *International Studio* 53 (October 1914): 81–85; and "Mr. and Mrs. Aschermann's [sic] Studio Decorations," *New York Times*, 16 April 1914.

[37] Karen Davies, *At Home in Manhattan: Modern Decorative Arts, 1925 to the Depression*, exhibition catalog (New Haven: Yale University Press, 1983), 10–11.

[38] It is worth noting that the chair shown in the photograph, which Frankl apparently had made in New York by local artisans, shows marked similarities with those designed by Hoffmann for the dressing room of the Palais Stoclet in Brussels (1905–11), which Frankl no doubt knew well from contemporary publications. See Eduard F. Sekler, *Josef*

Hoffmann: The Architectural Work (Princeton, N.J.: Princeton University Press, 1985), 97.

[39] See, for example, Robert Judson Clark, "The German Return to Classicism after Jugendstil," *Journal of the Society of Architectural Historians* 29 (October 1970): 273; and Sekler, *Josef Hoffmann*, esp. chapters 5 and 6.

[40] FA, 27.

[41] FA, 20—21.

[42] The Rubinstein salon was located at 15 East Forty-ninth Street. On the contemporary reception of the interiors, see, for example, Grace Hegger, "Beauty Bought and Paid For," *Vogue*, 15 November 1915, 68, 116; and "On Her Dressing Table," *Vogue*, 1 May 1915, 82, 84. See also the full-page advertisement for the salon ("A Famous European House of Beauty") in *Vanity Fair*, March 1915, 75. On Frankl's work for Rubinstein in 1915 and later, see Christopher Long, "The Business of Beauty: Paul T. Frankl," in *Over the Top: Helene Rubinstein: Extraordinary Style, Beauty, Art, Fashion Design*, ed. Suzanne Slesin (New York: Pointed Leaf Press, 2003), 38—39.

[43] FA, 28.

[44] Frankl, "The Modern Art of Interior Decoration," *Arts and Decoration* 5 (May 1915): 270. Frankl was no doubt influenced by Otto Wagner's book *Moderne Architektur*, a work he evidently knew well. A number of his phrases in "The Modern Art of Interior Decoration" are similar to Wagner's. Wagner writes, for example, "All modern creations must correspond to the new materials and demands of the present if they are to suit modern man; they must illustrate our own better, democratic, self-confident, ideal nature and take into account man's colossal technical and scientific achievements, as well as his thoroughly practical tendency—that is surely self-evident." Wagner, *Moderne Architektur*, 3rd. ed. (Vienna: Anton Schroll, 1902), trans. Harry Francis Mallgrave, *Modern Architecture: A Guidebook for His Students to This Field of Art* (Santa Monica, Calif.: The Getty Center for the History of Art and the Humanities, 1988), 78.

[45] Frankl, "The Modern Art of Interior Decoration," 269.

[46] Frankl, "The Modern Art of Interior Decoration," 269.

[47] Frankl, "The Modern Art of Interior Decoration," 270.

[48] Pène du Bois continued: "We read that the Louis XV suite, in Gobelin tapestries, together with sundry other decorative objects of the period, recently constituting one of the Morgan loan exhibits at the Metropolitan Museum of Art, has been acquired by a prominent firm of dealers for a sum quoted as nearly three million dollars." Editor's note in Frankl, "The Modern Art of Interior Decoration," 270.

[49] FA, 30—31. The restaurant, located at 151 East Fifty-fourth Street, remained a popular dining spot for many years.

[50] Lady Duff-Gordon was the designer for Lucille, located at 160 Fifth Avenue, at the time one of the preeminent women's fashion houses in the city. Frankl later remembered how the design concept had developed. Lady Duff-Gordon, he wrote, "was a woman of exquisite taste, and I was flattered to be given that job. When questions of color came up, I tried to consult her, but she never made any suggestions, simply saying, 'It's your job, do as you please! You are the decorator!' We did a beautiful music room for her, built around two old and precious Chinese jewel trees, the whole color scheme built around them. That, I remember, was her suggestion. The only time she expressed any definite preference for color was that chosen for the entrance hall. 'I want it to be green—the color of happiness,' she said, 'I want to be happy when I come home, and being Irish, when I say green, I mean green.' We chose a monotone in sharp, shiny Kelly green—the floor, the walls, the ceiling, all the furniture and furnishings, even to the wall brackets and their shields. Everything was green, and it made [her] happy." FA, 31—32. On Frankl's work for the Austrian ambassador, see FA, 36.

[51] FA, 32—33.

[52] FA, 35.

[53] Linda Hardberger, *The New Stagecraft: Setting an American Style, 1915—1949*, exhibition catalog (San Antonio: Marion Koogler McNay Art Museum, 1997).

[54] Cis Zoltowska interview.

[55] "The Washington Square Players: Its Aims and Organization," quoted in Lawrence Langer, *The Magic Curtain* (New York: E. P. Dutton, 1951), 94. On the formation of the Washington Square Players, see Adele Heller, "The New Theatre," in *1915, The Cultural Moment: The New Politics, the New Woman, the New Psychology, the New Art and the New Theatre in America*, ed. Adele Heller and Lois Rudnick (New Brunswick, N.J.: Rutgers University Press, 1991), 226—28; Oliver M. Sayer, *Our American Theatre* (New York: Brentano's, 1923), 77; and Eugene Miller Wank, "The Washington Square Players: Experiment toward Professionalism" (Ph.D. dissertation, University of Oregon, 1973).

56 The five one-act plays were *Fire and Water*, by Hervey White (first performed 4 October 1915); *Helena's Husband*, by Philip Moeller (first performed 4 October 1915); *Literature*, by Arthur Schnitzler (first performed 8 November 1915); *The Tenor*, by Frank Wedekind (first performed 10 January 1916); and *Bushido*, by Takeda Izumo (first performed 30 August 1916). Frankl's name was inadvertently left off the program for *Bushido*. Wank, "The Washington Square Players," 296—97; and FA, 35. A photograph of Frankl's green room, called the "Fifteen-Minute Room at the Bandbox Theatre," was published in Rebecca van Houghton, "Modern Influences in Interior Decoration," *Town and Country* 70 (November 1915): 27.

57 On the stage designs of the Washington Square Players, see Robert O. Nordvold, "Showcase for the New Stagecraft: The Scenic Designs of the Washington Square Players and the Theatre Guild, 1915—1929" (Ph.D. dissertation, Indiana University, 1973).

58 FA, 35—36; and *Trow's New York City Directory*, 493, 1514.

59 FA, 36.

60 Dagobert Frey, "Arbeiten eines österreichischen Architekten in Amerika (Paul Theodor Frankl)," *Die bildenden Künste/Der Architekt* 1 (1916/1918): 137—48; and Frankl, "Wie wohnt man in Amerika?" *Innen-Dekoration* 29 (1918): 27—43, 76.

61 Joseph Folnesics, ed., *Innenräume und Hausrat der Empire- und Biedermeierzeit in Österreich-Ungarn* (Vienna: Anton Schroll, 1903); Joseph August Lux, "Biedermeier als Erzieher," *Hohe Warte* 1 (1904—5): 145—55; and Paul Mebes, ed., *Um 1800: Architektur und Handwerk im letzten Jahrhundert ihrer traditionellen Entwicklung*, 2 vols. (Munich: F. Bruckmann A.-G., 1908). For an early discussion of the impact of Biedermeier in Germany, see Ernst Wilhelm Bredt, "Bruno Paul—Biedermeier—Empire," *Dekorative Kunst* 8 (March 1905): 217—29.

62 On the influence of Biedermeier at the turn of the century, see Stanford Anderson, "The Legacy of German Neoclassicism and Biedermeier: Behrens, Tessenow, Loos, and Mies," *Assemblage* 15 (August 1991): 63—87; and Paul Asenbaum, Stefan Asenbaum, and Christian Witt-Dörring, eds., *Moderne Vergangenheit: Wien 1800—1900*, exhibition catalog (Vienna: Künstlerhaus, 1981).

63 Frey, "Arbeiten eines österreichischen Architekten in Amerika," 139.

64 Frankl, "Wie wohnt man in Amerika?" *Innen-Dekoration* 29 (1918): 36.

65 Frey, "Arbeiten eines österreichischen Architekten in Amerika," 147.

66 B. Russell Herts, "What Is Modern Decoration?" *House and Garden* 31 (April 1917): 92. Herts insisted that the movement should fully embrace the essence of American life: "The new art is like the new life, buoyant, still too superficial, extravagant, materialistic, quick and confident. Our nation, which has mastered a continent, will certainly be able to control a few academicians . . . for we still have to complete the Americanization of the Modern Art Movement. Thus far its motive power has been European, but there are indications that henceforth the centre of Modern Art, and perhaps of all art, will be on this side of the Atlantic. . . . Thus far our accomplishments on decoration have been in part imitative, and in part crude, tentative and experimental. We have had insufficient opportunity for original expression; there has been but little encouragement, except in the last couple of years, and then more particularly in the designing of interiors for the stage."

CHAPTER 4 . Return to Europe

1 Paul T. Frankl, autobiography (unpublished), c. 1954, Collection Paulette Frankl, 37 (hereafter, FA).

2 FA, 37.

3 FA, 38.

4 Frankl, "Wie wohnt man in Amerika? Vortrag am 27. November 1917 im Österreichischen Ingenieur- und Architektenverein Wien," *Zeitschrift des Österreichischen Ingenieur- und Architektenverein* 70, no. 35 (1918). 387.

5 FA, 38—39.

6 FA, 40. On Count Bernstorff's years in Washington and Constantinople, see Johann Heinrich von Bernstorff, *The Memoirs of Count Bernstorff* (London: William Heinemann, 1936); and Bernstorff, *My Three Years in America* (New York: Charles Scribner's Sons, 1920).

7 FA, 40, 42.

8 Christopher Long, *Josef Frank: Life and Work* (Chicago: University of Chicago Press, 2002), 22—32; and Maria Welzig, *Josef Frank, 1885—1967: Das architektonische Werk* (Vienna: Böhlau, 1998), 31—37.

9 Oskar Wlach, "Oskar Wlach, Bewerbung für die Aufnahme in die Liste der Sachverständigen für Architektur und Hochbaufach," 18 June 1924; and Wlach, "Professional Career of Dr. Oskar Wlach," April 1958. Copies in possession of the author.

10 FA, 42.

11 FA, 42—45.

12 FA, 45—46.

13 Police registration archives, Magistratsamt 8, Wiener Stadt- und Landesarchiv; and Heimatrollen, Magistratsamt 61, Vienna.

14 FA, 46.

15 Peter Gay, *Freud: A Life for Our Time* (New York: W. W. Norton, 1988), 380.

16 Cis Zoltowska (Frankl's cousin), interview by author, Los Angeles, 31 May 1999; and FA, 46.

17 Cis Zoltowska, interview by Paulette Frankl, Los Angeles, 12 July 1987, Collection Paulette Frankl.

18 Letter from Peter Boulton to the author, 13 January 2000.

19 Frankl later wrote that Isa, "never cut out to be married to an artist, could not understand my passionate devotion to a profession that in the end brought so little return." FA, supplement, 11—12.

20 Letter from Peter Boulton to the author, 13 January 2000.

CHAPTER 5. New Beginnings

1 Karen Davies, *At Home in Manhattan: Modern Decorative Arts, 1925 to the Depression*, exhibition catalog (New Haven: Yale University Press, 1983), 10.

2 "Queer Bolshevist Art in Berlin," *Arts and Decoration* 18 (April 1923): 87.

3 W. Frank Purdy, "The Taste of the American People: And the Present Industro-Art Problem in the United States," *Arts and Decoration* 14 (November 1920): 38.

4 Richard F. Bach, "A Note on Producers of Industrial Art and Their Relation to the Public," *Arts and Decoration* 18 (December 1922): 82.

5 Richard F. Bach, "What Is the Matter with Our Industrial Art?" *Arts and Decoration* 18 (January 1923): 14, 15, 46, 49.

On the issue of design education after the war, see Jeffrey L. Meikle, *Twentieth Century Limited: Industrial Design in America, 1925–1939* (Philadelphia: Temple University Press, 1979), 19—21.

6 A few years later, Edwin Avery Park described what he found in Rosenthal's showroom: "Her shop window and the interior behind it are a fairyland of strange and delicate objects, everything from the tiniest brass figures to beautiful pottery bowls and vases of Persian blue. Her objects are small and her choice in buying them wide in its variety. Many of her wares she designs herself and has made for her in Germany and Austria. There is no use trying to get it done in this country, not yet. Her native products indicate this. It is the influence of Dagobert Peche one feels here, of the Wiener Werkstaette, of the Austrian love of color and whimsical form. Things are seen against black backgrounds. She has beautiful silk scarves of cubistic design, and unsuspected laces in modern patterns, in fact a little museum of minor arts today." Edwin Avery Park, *New Backgrounds for a New Age* (New York: Harcourt, Brace, 1927), 169.

7 Ashley Brown, "Ilonka Karasz: Rediscovering a Modernist Pioneer," *Studies in the Decorative Arts* 8 (Fall-Winter 2000—2001): 69—73. Like Helen Speer, another New York designer with close ties to Central Europe, Karasz soon turned her attention to creating furniture and other objects for children—a field for which modern design was more readily accepted. See, for example, the advertisement for the Helen Speer Company ("The Practical Land of Make-Believe") in *Arts and Decoration* 14 (November 1920): 44A.

8 C. Adolph Glassgold, "The Modern Note in Decorative Arts, Part 2," *The Arts* 13 (April 1928): 225.

9 Park, *New Backgrounds for a New Age*, 172.

10 A year after his departure for Boston, the Vienna provincial court issued a warrant for Urban's arrest "for criminal malfeasance" stemming from his alleged mismanagement of the Hagenbund and from financial questions concerning his oversight of the 1908 Imperial Jubilee. On Urban's early years in Vienna, see Markus Kristan, *Joseph Urban: Die Wiener Jahre des Jugendstilarchitekten und Illustrators, 1872–1911* (Vienna: Böhlau, 2000).

11 "Urbanity of 'The Follies,'" *Arts and Decoration* 11 (October 1919): 302.

12 On Urban's theatrical designs, see Arnold Aronson, ed., *Architect of Dreams: The Theatrical Vision of Joseph Urban,*

exhibition catalog (New York: Miriam and Ira D. Wallach Art Gallery, Columbia University, 2000); and Randolph Carter and Robert Reed Cole, *Joseph Urban: Architecture, Theatre, Opera, Film* (New York: Abbeville Press, 1992), 71–97.

[13] J. Stewart Johnson, *American Modern, 1925–1940: Design for a New Age*, exhibition catalog (New York: The Metropolitan Museum of Art / Harry N. Abrams, 2000), 179, 182.

[14] Kem Weber, born Karl Emanuel Martin Weber in Berlin in 1889, first trained as a cabinetmaker under Eduard Schultz. In 1908, he entered the School of Decorative Arts in Berlin, where he studied with Bruno Paul. While still a student, Weber helped oversee the construction of the German Pavilion at the Brussels World's Fair. After graduating in 1912, he continued to work for the German government, assisting on the design for the San Francisco Panama-Pacific International Exposition. On Weber's life and work, see David Gebhard and Harriette Von Breton, *Kem Weber: The Moderne in Southern California, 1920–1941*, exhibition catalog (Santa Barbara: University of California, 1969).

[15] Paul T. Frankl, autobiography (unpublished), c. 1954, Collection Paulette Frankl, 47 (hereafter, FA).

[16] Bobbi Owen, *Scenic Design on Broadway: Designers and Their Credits, 1915–1990* (New York: Greenwood Press, 1991), 67.

[17] Their son, Peter, was born in August 1921. Birth announcement for Peter Frankl, copy in possession of the author.

[18] FA, 47.

[19] Herta Neiß, *100 Jahre Wiener Werkstätte: Mythos und ökonomische Realität* (Vienna: Böhlau, 2004), 68, 70.

[20] Janis Staggs-Flinchum, "A Glimpse into the Showroom of the Wiener Werkstätte of America, 1922–23," in *The International Twentieth Century Arts Fair*, exhibition catalog (New York: Haughton's, 1999), 26–35.

[21] Rawson W. Haddon, "Some Recent Interiors, Art Galleries, and Decorator's Studios," *Architecture* 36 (August 1917): 157–62.

[22] Robert A. M. Stern, Gregory Gilmartin, and Thomas Mellins, *New York 1930: Architecture and Urbanism between the Two World Wars* (New York: Rizzoli, 1987), 322.

[23] "Exhibition Brings Viennese Art Here," *New York Times*, 25 June 1922; William Laurel Harris, "Back to Duncan Phyfe—or Forward to Art Nouveau?" *Good Furniture Magazine* 19

(December 1922): 257–59; David Lloyd, "A Workshop Background by Urban, with Reflections on the Viennese Revolt,"*New York Evening Post*, 17 June 1922; "1,000 Viennese Artists Show Their Work," *New York Times*, 14 June 1922; Mary Fanton Roberts [Giles Edgerton, pseud.], "Curious and Brilliant New Arts and Crafts from Vienna," *Vogue*, 15 October 1922, 81, 104; "Seen in New York: The Modern Art Shop of Joseph Urban," *Good Furniture Magazine* 19 (August 1922): 98–99; "Shall We Succumb to Modern Art," *Decorative Furnisher* 42 (September 1922): 68–69; and Leon V. Solon, "The Viennese Method for Artistic Display: New York Galleries of the Wiener-Werkstaette of America," *Architectural Record* 53 (March 1923): 266–71.

[24] G. S. L., "A Millionaire of Imagination and Refreshing Stream of Art and Craft," *Christian Science Monitor*, 24 July 1922, quoted in Leslie Topp, "Moments in the Reception of Early Twentieth-Century German and Austrian Decorative Arts in the United States," in *New Worlds: German and Austrian Art, 1890–1940*, exhibition catalog, ed. Renée Price, with Pamela Kort and Leslie Topp (New York: Neue Galerie/Cologne: DuMont, 2001), 577.

[25] "The Austrian Exhibition," *Bulletin of the Art Institute of Chicago* 16, no. 6 (November 1922): 84–85.

[26] Carter and Cole, *Joseph Urban*, 108.

[27] FA, 48. See also Frankl, *New Dimensions: The Decorative Arts Today in Words and Pictures* (New York: Payson and Clarke, 1928), 76. Another observer, Kenneth MacGowan, wrote in 1927 that the Wiener Werkstätte of America "was just two years ahead of its time." MacGowan, "Profile: Caprice Viennois," *New Yorker*, 25 June 1927, 21–23.

[28] FA, 48–49.

[29] The school, located at 441 Madison Avenue, had been founded in 1916 to provide "practical training in interior decoration."

[30] FA, 49–50.

[31] FA, 50–51.

[32] FA, 52–53.

[33] Park, *New Backgrounds for a New Age*, 168.

[34] On Bonney's life and work, see Claire Bonney, "Le Service Bonney: Fotojournalismus in 'Paris Moderne,' 1925–1935," *Archithese* 24 (July-August 1994): 54–56; Claire Bonney, *Thérèse Bonney: The Architectural Photographs* (Ph.D. disser-

tation, Universität Zürich, 1995); and Lisa Schlansker Kolosek, *The Invention of Chic: Thérèse Bonney and Paris Moderne* (London: Thames and Hudson, 2002).

[35] Letter from Peter Boulton to Paulette Frankl, 30 June 1998, Collection Paulette Frankl.

[36] FA, 58.

[37] My thanks to Denis Gallion of Historical Design in New York for making me aware of one of Susi Singer's figurines from the early 1920s with a Frankl Galleries label. On Vally Wieselthier's life and work, see Marianne Hörmann, *Vally Wieselthier, 1895–1945: Wien—Paris—New York, Keramik— Skulptur—Design der zwanziger und dreißiger Jahre* (Vienna: Böhlau, 1999).

[38] FA, 54.

[39] FA, 59.

[40] Frankl's were not the first modern Christmas cards sold in New York. The previous year *Arts and Decoration* featured a selection of cards with contemporary designs, including the works of Maude Fuller, Henriette Reiss, and others. "Some Christmas Cards of Artistic Merit," *Arts and Decoration* 18 (December 1922): 29. On Frankl's later Christmas cards, see "Christmas Greetings Take New and Sophisticated Modes of Expression: Sentimentality Gone— Decorative Idea Rules Lovely Paper of Smart Colors," *New York Evening Sun*, 10 December 1927.

[41] FA, 54–55.

[42] Frankl Galleries brochure, c. 1924, Collection Paulette Frankl.

[43] See Alf Evers, *Woodstock: History of an American Town* (Woodstock, N.Y.: Overlook Press, 1988); and Steve Shipp, *American Art Colonies, 1850–1930: A Historical Guide to America's Original Art Colonies and Their Artists* (Westport, Conn.: Greenwood Press, 1996).

[44] FA, 60–63.

[45] "Seen in New York: At the Frankl Galleries," *Good Furniture Magazine* 25 (October 1925): 173–74.

CHAPTER 6. Experiments in Form

[1] See "American Modern Art: Its History and Characteristics," *Good Furniture Magazine* 27 (October 1926): 172–74; and Eugene Clute, *The Treatment of Interiors* (New York: Pencil

Point Press, 1926), esp. 93–96. Frankl's designs are also featured in "Modernist Furniture and Accessories," *House and Garden* 50 (October 1926): 98–99.

[2] Paul T. Frankl, autobiography (unpublished), c. 1954, Collection Paulette Frankl, 60.

[3] A mirror-topped table with similar detailing designed by Frankl around the same time is shown in Clute, *The Treatment of Interiors*, 94.

[4] Nancy J. Troy, *Modernism and the Decorative Arts in France: Art Nouveau to Le Corbusier* (New Haven: Yale University Press, 1991), esp. 159–93.

[5] See, for example, "The 'New Style' Popular in France," *Good Furniture Magazine* 21 (November 1923): 204–5; "Poiret, Interpreter of His Own Age," *Arts and Decoration* 14 (March 1921): 380; and Leo Randole, "The Evolution of Furniture in France: Ruhlmann—Master Furniture Designer," *Arts and Decoration* 15 (August 1921): 226–27.

[6] Charles R. Richards, Henry Creange, and Frank Grant Holmes, *Report of the Commission Appointed by the Secretary of Commerce to Visit and Report upon the International Exposition of Modern Decorative and Industrial Art in Paris, 1925* (Washington, D.C.: Government Printing Office, 1926), 18–19.

[7] Richards, Creange, and Holmes, *Report of the Commission*, 16. An anonymously written piece in *Good Furniture Magazine* in 1923 summed up the American reaction: "In the United States we have never taken the period styles as seriously as was the custom in Europe before the war and consequently our postwar reaction has not been as violent. The United States, however, is in a fair way being left out of the great French exhibition of furnishings scheduled for 1925. The plans are made; the program has been announced, the specific point being accentuated that no furniture or textiles will be exhibited which savor of the period styles. No copies or reproductions can appear; only works of original design and in the modern mode will have the slightest chance of passing the discriminating jury." "Exhibitions of Modern Designs," *Good Furniture Magazine* 21 (November 1923): 204.

[8] Marilyn F. Friedman, "The United States and the 1925 Paris Exposition: Opportunity Lost and Found," *Studies in the Decorative Arts* 13 (Fall-Winter 2005–6): 102–3.

[9] Troy, *Modernism and the Decorative Arts in France*, 62–63.

[10] "While I sympathized with the endeavor to evolve a new style in design or decoration," the unnamed decorator observed, "I cannot see any sense in making strange and exaggerated forms merely for the *sake* of having something new and different from what existed before. I take it that art is an expression of beauty, and the creation of freak forms which are not beautiful can in no sense be classified as art.... None of the stuff shown will make any impression on American taste. It will not be taken up or bought to any extent by our discriminating people, who have not any of the upset mental attitude of the war." "A New York Decorator's Opinion of the Paris Exposition," *Good Furniture Magazine* 25 (November 1925): 260.

[11] Ellow H. Hostache, "Reflections on the Exposition des Arts Décoratifs," *Architectural Forum* 44 (January 1926): 11.

[12] "The International Exposition of Modern Decorative and Industrial Art," *Good Furniture Magazine* 25 (September 1925): 121.

[13] Kem Weber, "Why Should the American Furniture Buyer, Manufacturer and Designer Go to Europe?" *Good Furniture Magazine* 25 (November 1925): 261.

[14] J. Stewart Johnson, *American Modern, 1925–1940: Design for a New Age*, exhibition catalog (New York: The Metropolitan Museum of Art / Harry N. Abrams, 2000), 181.

[15] A room of modernist furniture from the 1925 Paris Exposition Internationale designed by Edgar Brandt, René Lalique, and Paul Follot had also been shown the previous autumn at F. Schumacher and Company in New York. Alastair Duncan, *American Art Deco* (New York: Harry N. Abrams, 1986), 22.

[16] Edwin Avery Park, *New Backgrounds for a New Age* (New York: Harcourt, Brace, 1927), 162–63; and J. Stewart Johnson, *American Modern*, 16. See also the catalog of the exhibition, *A Selected Collection of Objects from the International Exposition of Modern Decorative and Industrial Art, Paris 1925* (New York: American Association of Museums, 1926).

[17] Duncan, *American Art Deco*, 23.

[18] Park, *New Backgrounds for a New Age*, 171, 181–91.

[19] Juliette Broussard, "Art Moderne," *Talk of the Town* 6 (April 1930): 19–22; and Park, *New Backgrounds for a New Age*, 165–67.

[20] On Bruno Paul's work of the postwar period and his influ-

ence, see W. Owen Harrod, *Bruno Paul: The Life and Work of a Pragmatic Modernist* (Stuttgart: Edition Axel Menges, 2005).

[21] Clute, *The Treatment of Interiors*, 90–92.

[22] Park, *New Backgrounds for a New Age*, 168.

[23] "American Modern Art: Its History and Characteristics," *Good Furniture Magazine* 27 (October 1926): 172–74; "Modernist Furniture and Accessories," 98–99; and Clute, *The Treatment of Interiors*, 93–96.

[24] Clute, *The Treatment of Interiors*, 57.

CHAPTER 7 . Skyscraper Style

[1] Paul T. Frankl, autobiography (unpublished), c. 1954, Collection Paulette Frankl, 60 (hereafter, FA).

[2] FA, 60–61.

[3] FA, 64. The story of Frankl's discovery is repeated in one of the early articles on Skyscraper furniture. See Nunnally Johnson, "The New Furniture Gives Every One His Own Skyline," *New York Evening Post*, 19 May 1927.

[4] FA, 64–65.

[5] FA, 66.

[6] FA, 66–67. In 1927, Edwin Avery Park wrote of Frankl's gallery: "His personality invests the place with a sense of audacious quiet, amusing and rich in color. He has designed and made his own ateliers, skyscraper bookcases, strange slender chests of drawers with the most delicious metallic finish, odd chairs and tables, sometimes of metal, all kept very flat and treated in rich all-over colors with different colored edges." Park, *New Backgrounds for a New Age* (New York: Harcourt, Brace, 1927), 168.

[7] Park, *New Backgrounds for a New Age*, 168.

[8] FA, 65.

[9] FA, supplement, 1–2.

[10] "American Modernist Furniture Inspired by Sky-scraper Architecture," *Good Furniture Magazine* 29 (September 1927): 120.

[11] Francis Lorne, "The New Architecture of a Flamboyant Civilization: The Skyscraper as an Expression of America's Commercial Triumph," *Arts and Decoration* 24 (November 1925): 58.

12 On the response of American artists and writers to the sky-scraper, see, for example, Merrill Schleier, *The Skyscraper in American Art, 1890–1931* (New York: Da Capo, 1986), esp. chapters 1–3.

13 On the rise of the skyscraper in New York in the 1920s, see Cervin Robinson and Rosemarie Haag Bletter, *Skyscraper Style: Art Deco New York* (New York: Oxford University Press, 1975).

14 FA, supplement, 2.

15 One print advertisement, for Gotham Photo-Engraving Company of New York, hailed Frankl's design as the epitome of modern: "Skyscraper bookcases by the Frankl Galleries reflect the trend in modern architecture. In the same spirit Gotham service reflects the trend in modern engraving service." *Advertising and Selling* 7 (30 May 1928): 10.

16 Samuel Spewack, *The Skyscraper Murder* (New York: Macauley, 1928), 51.

17 Frankl, "Furniture of the Fourth Dimension: Designed for the New Interior," *House and Garden* 51 (February 1927): 77.

18 Edward Weeks, "Trophy Rooms: Whether Hunter's or Bookman's, These Rooms Bear the Impress of Hobbies Pursued," *House Beautiful* 66 (1929): 580, 622.

19 "American Modernist Furniture Inspired by Sky-scraper Architecture,"120. Frankl's larger pieces sometimes over-whelmed the rooms they were in, as was the case in the offices of Payson and Clarke (publishers of Frankl's first book, *New Dimensions*), which featured one of his imposing Skyscraper desks. See the illustrations in Henry-Russell Hitchcock, Jr., "Some American Interiors in the Modern Style," *Architectural Record* 64 (September 1928): 238, 240.

20 See, for example, the advertisement for Dynamique Creations in *Arts and Decoration* 29 (September 1928): 33.

21 Frankl also attached these paper labels to many of the import items he sold through the shop. The presence of a paper label indicates only that an article was sold by Frankl, not that he was the designer.

22 The large number of "unauthorized" pieces made in the later 1920s may account for some of the disparities in the quality of what is now considered to be Frankl furniture. Some pieces now attributed to Frankl based solely on formal similarities with authenticated pieces undoubtedly represent copies or "extras" produced by the artisans he hired.

23 J. Stewart Johnson, *American Modern, 1925–1940: Design for a New Age*, exhibition catalog (New York: The Metropolitan Museum of Art/Harry N. Abrams, 2000), 27–28, 46–63.

24 "Linen Prints Outstanding in Frankl Collection," *New York Daily News Record*, 16 October 1927. See also M. D. C. Crawford, "Cretonnes and Their Use from the Frankl Galleries," *New York Daily News Record*, 3 November 1927; "Frankl Galleries Displaying Attractive Hand Blocked Linens," *New York Daily News Record*, 26 January 1926; "Two Hand-Blocked Linens Shown by Frankl Galleries," *New York Daily News Record*, 31 December 1927; and "Watch the Modern Vogue in Fabrics!" *Good Furniture Magazine* 30 (May 1928): 237.

25 "Hand-Blocked Decorative Linens of Extreme Design Imported for Apparel," *Women's Wear Daily*, 27 April 1926. Frankl also sold several imported lines of wallpaper. "Walls in Black and White: A New Decorative Scheme," *House and Garden* 53 (April 1928): 94–95.

26 M. D. C. Crawford, "Rodier Fabrics Designed for the Frankl Galleries," *New York Daily News Record*, 1 December 1927; and "Fabrics with a Modern Flavor," *House and Garden* 53 (March 1928): 127.

27 Adam Gimbel, president of Saks and Company, for whom Deskey had been designing display windows after his return from Paris, introduced the two men. Deskey showed Frankl a portfolio of drawings, and Frankl, impressed with the designs, hired him on the spot. David A. Hanks, with Jennifer Toher, *Donald Deskey: Decorative Designs and Interiors* (New York: E. P. Dutton, 1987), 4.

28 Many of the lighting fixtures Frankl sold were imported from France, but he also produced several of his own designs. See "The New Modernist Lights," *House and Garden* 52 (September 1927): 86–87. For examples of Frankl's designs for bathrooms, see Frankl, "Baths and Bath-Dressing Rooms: The Newest Interiors of This Kind Reveal a Pleasing Use of Decorative Wall Treatments," *House and Garden* 52 (August 1927): 51–55, 102.

29 Henry W. Frohne, "Is Modernism a Passing Fancy or a Fact?" *Good Furniture Magazine* 30 (March 1928): 111.

CHAPTER 8. Apostle of Modern

1 Janet Howison Marsh, "Amusing French Furniture in l'Art Moderne," *Arts and Decoration* 27 (May 1927): 74, 76, 91.

[2] William Leach, *Land of Desire: Merchants, Power, and the Rise of a New American Culture* (New York: Pantheon Books, 1993), 80—81.

[3] Leach, *Land of Desire*, 136.

[4] An article in *Good Furniture Magazine* described Frankl's room: "The most impressive [of the model interiors exhibited at Macy's] was perhaps the modernistic library of Paul Theodore Frankl, who demonstrated here most effectively his ideas of the so-called 'skyscraper' furniture of today, of which he is a most enthusiastic sponsor. Here, against a background of California redwood was grouped a most extraordinary arrangement of library fittings, with huge towering bookcases reaching ceiling-ward in a series of set-back terraces, a desk set against the wall, its upper part against a mounting series of compartments, and a large and most modern library table. In contrast to the skyscraping lines of the bookcases and desks, the chairs were strikingly low, and covered with brilliant shades of Morocco leather in bright reds and blues. In this room, as in the entire exposition, the lighting effects were most original, making use of indirect methods, the light units being shaded with a series of planes and angles in various materials." "Decorated Interiors in Retail Stores," *Good Furniture Magazine* 29 (June 1927): 326. See also Nunnally Johnson, "The New Furniture Gives Every One His Own Skyline," *New York Evening Post*, 19 May 1927; and "The Last Word in Interiors: A Modern Library," *New York Times*, 8 May 1927.

[5] *Catalogue of the Exposition of Art in Trade at Macy's, May 2 to May 7, 1927* (New York: R. H. Macy and Company, 1927). See also Marilyn F. Friedman, *Selling Good Design: Promoting the Early Modern Interior* (New York: Rizzoli, 2003), 21—29.

[6] *Machine-Age Exposition*, exhibition catalog (New York: Little Review, 1927).

[7] J. Stewart Johnson, *American Modern, 1925–1940: Design for a New Age*, exhibition catalog (New York: The Metropolitan Museum of Art/Harry N. Abrams, 2000), 22—23; "Modern Art in a Department Store: Wanamaker's Furnished Rooms Arouse Keen Interest," *Good Furniture Magazine* 30 (January 1928): 35; "Modern Art Makes Its Bow in a Commercial Manner," *Decorative Furnisher* 53 (December 1927): 101; and Robert A. M. Stern, Gregory Gilmartin, and Thomas Mellins, *New York 1930: Architecture and Urbanism between the Two World Wars* (New York: Rizzoli, 1987), 336—37.

[8] At the same time, Wanamaker's launched Venturus, a per-

manent collection of modern French designs; it was the first department store in the United States to do so. Friedman, *Selling Good Design*, 31—36; J. Stewart Johnson, *American Modern*, 22—23; and "Modern Art in a Department Store," 35.

[9] *An Exhibition of Modern French Decorative Art*, exhibition catalog (New York: Lord and Taylor, 1928); and Friedman, *Selling Good Design*, 55—73.

[10] Helen Appleton Read, "Modern Decorative Art," *The Arts* 13 (February 1928): 120.

[11] W. E. Skillings, "Is the 'Atmosphere' Window an Economic Waste?" *Advertising and Selling* 11 (May 1928): 34.

[12] Stern, Gilmartin, and Mellins, *New York 1930*, 337.

[13] "Exposition of Modern French Decorative Art," *American Architect* 133 (5 March 1928): 317—22.

[14] *An International Exposition of Art in Industry from May 14 to May 26, 1928 at Macy's* (New York: R. H. Macy and Company, 1928); and Friedman, *Selling Good Design*, 75—111.

[15] Richard F. Bach, "Styles A-Borning: Musings on Contemporary Industrial Art and Decoration," *Creative Art* 2 (June 1928): 36—40; "Modern Art? Without Doubt," *Decorative Furnisher* 54 (June 1928): 97; "R. H. Macy Hold an Exhibition of Modern Art," *Decorative Furnisher* 54 (June 1928): 95, 114; Stern, Gilmartin, and Mellins, *New York 1930*, 337; and "Various Countries Exhibit Modern Art," *American Architect* 133 (June 1928): 823—27.

[16] Leach, *Land of Desire*, 319; and "All Glass Room," *New York Times*, 8 May 1928.

[17] Alastair Duncan, *American Art Deco* (New York: Harry N. Abrams, 1986), 287.

[18] M[ary Byers] S[mith], "What I See in New York," *House Beautiful* 64 (November 1928): 517; and Lee Simonson, "Modern Furniture in the Department Store," *Creative Art* 3 (November 1928): xvi—xxi.

[19] On Frankl's relationship with Kaufmann, see Richard L. Cleary, *Merchant Prince and Master Builder: Edgar J. Kaufmann and Frank Lloyd Wright*, exhibition catalog (Pittsburgh: Heinz Architectural Center, Carnegie Museum of Art, in association with University of Washington Press, 1999), 22—24, 48. Kaufmann's son, Edgar Kaufmann, Jr., later a leading figure in the modern design world, knew Frankl well and regarded him as "an early teacher and important influence." Franklin Toker, *Fallingwater Rising: Frank*

Lloyd Wright, E. J. Kaufmann, and America's Most Extraordinary House (New York: Alfred A. Knopf, 2003), 72.

20 Paul T. Frankl, autobiography (unpublished), c. 1954, Collection Paulette Frankl, 6 (hereafter, FA).

21 "The Art Gallery," *Brooklyn Life*, 11 February 1928; "Boudoir in A. & S. Model House," *Brooklyn Times*, 9 February 1928; Margaret Breuning, "Modern Tendencies in Interior Decoration Shown," *New York Post*, 11 February 1928; Friedman, *Selling Good Design*, 43–52; "'Livable House' Opens to Public View Tomorrow," *Brooklyn Standard Union*, 7 February 1928; "Modern Decorative Art Applied in Brooklyn," *New York Sun*, 11 February 1928; "Modern Furniture Is Shown at A. & S.," *Brooklyn Times*, 7 February 1928; and "Tea Given in Livable House for Art Critics and Museum Directors Yesterday," *Brooklyn Eagle*, 7 February 1928.

22 "New Modern Dress of Livable House Is Shown by A. & S.," *Brooklyn Eagle*, 7 February 1928; and "Modern Decoration," *The Art Digest* (mid-February 1928).

23 "Throngs at A. & S. View Livable House," *Brooklyn Times*, 8 February 1928.

24 Nellie C. Sanford, "The Livable House Transformed: Abraham and Straus Present the Modern Mode," *Good Furniture Magazine* 30 (April 1928): 174, 176.

25 J. Stewart Johnson, *American Modern*, 179.

26 J. Stewart Johnson, *American Modern*, 179.

27 Janet Kardon, ed., *Craft in the Machine Age: 1920–45*, vol. 3 of *The History of Twentieth-Century American Craft*, exhibition catalog (New York: American Craft Museum / Harry N. Abrams, 1995), 240.

28 On Kiesler's early life, see Dieter Bogner, ed., *Friedrich Kiesler: Architekt—Maler—Bildhauer, 1890–1965*, exhibition catalog (Vienna: Museum des 20. Jahrhunderts/Löcker, 1988); and Lisa Phillips, ed., *Frederick Kiesler*, exhibition catalog (New York: Whitney Museum of American Art / W. W. Norton, 1989).

29 On Rohde: J. Stewart Johnson, *American Modern*, 180; and Kardon, *Craft in the Machine Age*, 244. On Deskey: David A. Hanks, with Jennifer Toher, *Donald Deskey: Decorative Designs and Interiors* (New York: E. P. Dutton, 1987), 1–4.

30 FA, 10. Alelia Walker (1885–1931) was the hostess of one of the great salons of the Harlem Renaissance. In her upper Manhattan townhouse, she entertained writers, artists, and musicians from Harlem and Greenwich Village, as well as visiting royalty from Africa and Europe. Walker's glamorous lifestyle, striking looks, and elegant clothing prompted Langston Hughes to call her the "joy goddess of Harlem's 1920s." In his autobiography, Frankl describes the day she first visited the Frankl Galleries: "In the drafting room one day the phone buzzed frantically, summoning me to come downstairs in a hurry. The galleries were crowded with socialites as I walked in, and comfortably seated behind a screen hastily set up were the subjects of the turbulent excitement. Two colored ladies were waiting to see me. Removing the screen, I welcomed them as I would other visitors. My dark hued callers, I was to find out, were Mrs. Alelia Walker and her secretary.... She asked me to do over her town house in Harlem. 'I want to make it into a club where people of all nationalities can meet, discuss their problems, get acquainted and learn to know each other.... I want it to be as new in looks as it is in spirit,' she went on, 'and I trust we can count on you to help us. It is all for charity—mine, not yours.' And with this she turned to her secretary and had her make out a check, high in the four figures, wanting to be sure that we were taking on the job." FA, supplement, 10–11.

31 On the house and its furnishings, see Randolph Carter and Robert Reed Cole, *Joseph Urban: Architecture, Theater, Opera, Film* (New York: Abbeville Press, 1992), 171–75; and *Property from Mar-a-Lago, sold by Donald J. Trump*, auction catalog (New York: Christie's, 1995). The archive at the Hillwood Museum, Washington, D.C., has a small number of photographs showing Frankl's original installation. My thanks to John Waddell for his help in tracking down information on Frankl's tower room.

32 FA, 10.

33 FA, 6–7.

34 H[ugo Lang], "Neue Kunst in Amerika: Arbeiten von Paul T. Frankl—New York," *Innen-Dekoration* 39 (1928): 56; and Pierre Migennes, "Un artiste décorateur américain," *Art et Décoration* 53 (January 1928): 49. See also Hugo Lang, "Luxus-Räume in New York," *Innen-Dekoration* 40 (1929): 358–59; and "Modern Art and Style Dictate in Furniture Field, Declares P. T. Frankl, American Authority Now Here," *New York Herald* (Paris), 7 August 1926.

35 Brochure announcing Frankl's lecture series, Contemporary Decorative Art, at The Metropolitan Museum of Art, New York,

1928, Collection Paulette Frankl; "Frankl's Art Course for N.Y.U. Opens," *Women's Wear Daily*, 6 October 1928; and "Program of Events at Metropolitan Museum," *New York Sun*, 6 October 1928.

[36] Frankl, *The Arts and Decoration Home Study Course Covering the Modern Movement as Applied to Interior Decoration and Kindred Subjects*, six parts (New York: Arts and Decoration, 1928).

[37] The six lessons, in order, were "The Meaning of Modern," "Fundamentals of Modern Interior Decoration," "Colors and Fabrics in Modern Interior Decoration," "Furniture in Modern Interior Decoration," "Modern Art in Modern Business," and "Harmonizing Period Styles with Modern Decoration."

[38] Advertisement for *The Arts and Decoration Home Study Course* in *Arts and Decoration* 29 (July 1928): 91. See also "Home Study Course in Modern Art to Be Given by Publication," *Women's Wear Daily*, 2 May 1928.

[39] "Modern Art Course Finds Favor," *Women's Wear Daily*, 18 August 1928.

[40] "'Modernism' Subject of Frankl's Talk in Store Lecture Tour," *New York Daily News Record*, 3 May 1928.

[41] "Paul Frankl Plans Store Lecture Tour," *Women's Wear Daily*, 20 April 1928.

[42] "Paul Frankl to Sail for Japan July 12," *Women's Wear Daily*, 18 May 1928.

[43] "Frankl Drops Trip to Japan; Resuming Tour," *Women's Wear Daily*, 16 July 1928; and "Frankl to Continue U.S. Lecture Tour," *New York Daily News Record*, 17 July 1928.

[44] "Schuster's Stage Successful Modern Exhibit at Milwaukee 'Home Show,'" *Women's Wear Daily*, 7 April 1928; Lucille E. Morehouse, "Exhibition of Modernistic Furniture Will Be Shown at Herron Art Institute," *Indianapolis Star*, 30 September 1928; and Lucille E. Morehouse, "Herron Institute Displays Exquisite Home Decorations," *Indianapolis Star*, 14 October 1928. See also Lucille E. Morehouse, "Will You Let 'Furniture Moderne' Excite You, Too?" *Indianapolis Star*, 7 October 1928.

[45] Peter Boulton, interview by author, San Diego, 25 August 2001.

[46] Frankl, "Merchandising the Modern Idea in Decoration," *Advertising and Selling* 12 (26 December 1928): 36; and

"The Answer to Modern Art Is 'Be Yourself,'" *Printer's Ink*, 17 May 1928.

[47] Frankl, "Merchandising the Modern Idea in Decoration," 38, 63. On the contemporary discussion of the impact of modern design on business, see "Frankl Sees Style Element in Modernistic Furniture as Means of Increased Turnover," *Women's Wear Daily*, 30 June 1928; and Walter Rendell Storey, "Modernism Enters the Business World," *New York Times*, 18 March 1928.

[48] Frankl also published a three-part series on modern design in *Arts and Decoration*: "Just What Is This Modernistic Movement?" *Arts and Decoration* 29 (May 1928): 56—57, 108, 117—18; "Why We Accept Modernistic Furniture," *Arts and Decoration* 29 (June 1928): 58—59, 90, 99; and "Logic in Modernistic Decoration," *Arts and Decoration* 29 (July 1928): 54—55, 82—83.

[49] Lisa Schlansker Kolosek, *The Invention of Chic: Thérèse Bonney and Paris Moderne* (London: Thames and Hudson, 2002), 163, 165.

[50] Frankl, *New Dimensions: The Decorative Arts of Today in Words and Pictures* (New York: Payson and Clarke, 1928), 16—17.

[51] Frankl, *New Dimensions*, 18—19.

[52] Frankl, *New Dimensions*, 39—40.

[53] Frankl, *New Dimensions*, 43.

[54] Frankl, *New Dimensions*, 71.

[55] C. Adolph Glassgold, review of *New Dimensions*, *The Arts* 14 (September 1928): 168.

[56] "The Dining Room Done in White," *House and Garden* 52 (November 1927): 108—9; and "Modernism in the Library," *House and Garden* 53 (February 1928): 60. See also "Conservative Modernism," *Memphis Evening Appeal*, 7 June 1928. Frankl offered advice for matching the new furniture with older styles. See "How to Blend Modernistic and Period Furniture: Expressions by Lescaze, Paul T. Frankl, Carl Schmieg, Eugene Schoen, and Kem Weber," *Women's Wear Daily*, 26 May 1928. Frankl writes: "I favor furniture from these periods for ensembles with Modernistic pieces: Early American, Empire, Sheraton, Chinese Chippendale, and Early Jacobean. The Early American furniture particularly, I believe, has the same simplicity, the same ideal of beauty, the same feeling, as the present day creations. However, in combining,

I do not think it is so much a matter of periods as materials. In groupings of various periods certain principles have become generally recognized: close grain woods go together; Jacobean oak goes with mission oak; mahogany goes with walnut."

[57] Frankl, "Merchandising the Modern Idea in Decoration," 38, 63.

[58] See Roger Gilman, "Is This Modernistic Furniture More Than a Fad?" *House Beautiful* 65 (February 1929): 162, 198; Homer Eaton Keyes, "Is This Modernistic Furniture More Than a Fad?" *House Beautiful* 65 (February 1929): 163, 198, 200; Charles R. Richards, "Sane and Insane Modernism in Furniture," *Good Furniture Magazine* 32 (January 1929): 8—14; "A Symposium on Modernism in Decoration, by a Group of Well-Known Decorators," *House Beautiful* 65 (March 1929): 306—7, 362, 364—65; and Thomas E. Tallmadge, "Will This Modernism Last?" *House Beautiful* 65 (January 1929): 44—45, 88. See also Wendy Kaplan, "'The Filter of American Taste': Design in the USA in the 1920s," in *Art Deco, 1910—1939*, exhibition catalog, ed. Charlotte Benton, Tim Benton, and Ghislaine Wood (Boston: Bulfinch, 2003), 335—43.

[59] Henry-Russell Hitchcock, Jr., "Some American Interiors in the Modern Style," *Architectural Record* 64 (September 1928): 238—39.

[60] Lewis Mumford, "Modernism for Sale," *American Mercury* 16 (April 1929): 353—55.

[61] "Decorative Artists Form Union," *Architectural Record* 64 (August 1928): 164.

[62] FA, 69—70.

[63] By early 1930, the number of active AUDAC members had grown to more than seventy and also included Egmont H. Arens, Ruth Arens, Norman Bel Geddes, Peter Bitterman, Jr., Jules Bouy, L. V. Carroll, Henry Churchill, Emilie Danielson, Jacques Darcy, Alice Donaldson, Helen Dryden, Lillian Gaertner, C. Adolph Glassgold, Percival Goodman, Kneeland L. Green, Vahan Hagopian, W. K. Harrison, W. S. Harrison, Alfonso Ianelli, A. Drexler Jacobson, Gustav Jensen, Albert Kahn, Walter Kantack, Rockwell Kent, Ellen M. Kern, Teresa Kilham, Jules E. Korchlen, Henry Kreis, Peter Larsen, Robert E. Locher, Erik Magnussen, G. MacCulloch Miller, William Muschenheim, Walter von Nessen, Sara Parsons, Austin Purves, Jr., Ruth Reeves, Henriette Reiss, Louis Rorimer, Herman Rosse, Eliel Saarinen, Walter Salmon, Robert Schey, Elise Seeds, Lee Simonson, Frank Sohn, Walter Dorwin

Teague, Buk Ulreich, H. C. Warner, Kem Weber, Hy Williams, and Frank Lloyd Wright. Advertisement for AUDAC in *Creative Art* 6 (March 1930): supplement, 52—53.

[64] FA, 72.

[65] FA, 72—73.

[66] Advertisement for AUDAC in *Creative Art* 6 (March 1930): supplement, 52—53.

[67] "Manufacturers and Artists Should Combine to Protect Design Rights, Frankl Says," *New York Journal of Commerce*, 12 June 1928.

[68] Advertisement for AUDAC in *Creative Art* 6 (April 1930): supplement, 76—77.

[69] Waldon Fawcett, "Stop Thief! Designs Are Entailed! Why Congress Must Enact a New Law to Prevent the Theft of American Industrial Art Ideas," *Arts and Decoration* 18 (December 1922): 94.

[70] "The Vestal Bill," *Good Furniture and Decoration* 33 (December 1930): 333—34, 337; and "Seen and Heard in the Trade," *Good Furniture and Decoration* 34 (March 1930): 167.

[71] "American Designers' Gallery to Have Their First Modern Art Exhibit," *Dry Goods Economist* (22 September 1928): 223—24.

[72] Herman Rosse, foreword to the American Designers' Gallery catalog, 1928, quoted in C. Adolph Glassgold, "The Decorative Arts," *The Arts* 14 (December 1928): 339.

[73] "Exhibit of American Designers' Gallery: An Ambitious Program in Art Moderne," *Good Furniture Magazine* 32 (January 1929): 40—45; and Mary Fanton Roberts [Giles Edgerton, pseud.], "Beauty Combined with Convenience in Some Modernistic Rooms: In a Recent Exhibition of the American Designers' Gallery, the American Point of View toward This Movement Was Brought Out in Interesting Furniture, Fittings and Room Decoration," *Arts and Decoration* 30 (February 1929): 72—73, 112.

[74] "Designers—European and American," *Good Furniture Magazine* 32 (April 1929): 167, 172. See also "Where Are Our Moderns?" *Good Furniture and Decoration* 34 (March 1930): 115.

CHAPTER 9. Domesticating the Machine

[1] Frankl, *Form and Re-Form: A Practical Handbook of Modern Interiors* (New York: Harper and Brothers, 1930), 1.

[2] Henry-Russell Hitchcock, Jr., review of *Form and Re-Form*, *International Studio* 96 (May 1930): 110; C. Adolph Glassgold, review of *Form and Re-Form*, *Creative Art* 6 (June 1930): supplement, 138; review of *Form and Re-Form*, *Arts and Decoration* 37 (May 1932): 69. See also the contemporary reviews in *American Magazine of Art* 21 (April 1930): 239—40; and *Connoisseur* 85 (May 1930): 321—22.

[3] *The Architect and the Industrial Arts: An Exhibition of Contemporary Design*, exhibition catalog (New York: The Metropolitan Museum of Art, 1929), 24.

[4] Henry W. Kent, "The Motive of the Exhibition of American Industrial Art," *Bulletin of The Metropolitan Museum of Art* 24 (April 1929): 97, quoted in J. Stewart Johnson, *American Modern, 1925—1940: Design for a New Age*, exhibition catalog (New York: The Metropolitan Museum of Art/Harry N. Abrams, 2000), 30. On the 1929 Metropolitan Museum exhibition, see also Kristina Wilson, "Exhibiting Modern Times: American Modernism, Popular Culture, and the Art Exhibit, 1925—1935" (Ph.D. dissertation, Yale University, 2001).

[5] See, for example, the "Krometal by Ficks" advertisement in *Arts and Decoration* 34 (January 1931): 87; and Louise Bonney, "New Metal Furniture for Modern Schemes," *House and Garden* 57 (April 1930): 82—83, 142.

[6] Arthur J. Pulos, "The Restless Genius of Norman Bel Geddes," *Architectural Forum* 133 (January 1970): 46—51.

[7] For a general discussion of the rise of American industrial design, see Sheldon Cheney and Martha Candler Cheney, *Art and the Machine: An Account of Industrial Design in Twentieth-Century America* (New York: Whittlesey House, 1936); Jeffrey L. Meikle, *Twentieth Century Limited: Industrial Design in America, 1925—1939* (Philadelphia: Temple University Press, 1979), esp. chapters 4, 5, and 6; and Arthur J. Pulos, *American Design Ethic: A History of Industrial Design to 1940* (Cambridge, Mass.: MIT Press, 1983), 336—95.

[8] Around the same time, Donald Deskey was designing tubular steel furniture for the Ypsilanti Reed Furniture Company, based in Ionia, Michigan. David A. Hanks, with Jennifer Toher, *Donald Deskey: Decorative Designs and Interiors* (New York: E. P. Dutton, 1987), 177. Frankl was likely inspired by contemporary Austrian designs: the sofa resembles metal pieces made by the Thonet-Mundus Company in Vienna, which he no doubt had seen on his frequent trips to Europe. See the company's 1929 catalog and Gerhard Bott, ed., *Sitz-Gelegenheiten: Bugholz- und Stahlrohrmöbel von Thonet*, exhibition catalog (Nuremberg: Germanisches Nationalmuseum, 1989).

[9] In addition to Frankl, a number of other prominent New York designers displayed their work, among them Donald Deskey, Lee Simonson, Walter von Nessen, and William Zorach. Dean Freiday, "Modern Design at the Newark Museum: A Survey," *The Museum* 4 (Winter-Spring 1952): 17.

[10] For further examples of contemporary furnishings by Frankl and the other American designers, see C. Adolph Glassgold, "Some Modern Furniture Designers," *House Beautiful* 67 (February 1930): 163—66, 214; "New Developments in Modern Furnishing by Eight Leading Designers in America," *House and Garden* 59 (April 1931): 70—72; and "New Models in Fascinating Metal Furniture," *Arts and Decoration* 37 (June 1932): 18—19.

[11] On the split between decorative arts and industrial design, see C. Adolph Glassgold, "Modern American Industrial Design," *Arts and Decoration* 35 (July 1931): 30—31, 87.

[12] "AUDAC News: Protection of Design," *Creative Art* 6 (April 1930): supplement, 77.

[13] C. Adolph Glassgold, "AUDAC Exhibit of Modern Industrial and Decorative Art at the Brooklyn Museum," *Creative Art* 8 (June 1931): 436—40; Elizabeth Hamlin, "The AUDAC Exhibition," *Brooklyn Museum Quarterly* 18 (July 1931): 93; and Donald McGregor, "AUDAC in Brooklyn: A Great Museum Host of Moderns," *Good Furniture and Decoration* 36 (June 1931): 322—25.

[14] McGregor, "AUDAC in Brooklyn," 322.

[15] Glassgold, "AUDAC Exhibit of Modern Industrial and Decorative Art," 437.

[16] Frankl, "The Home of Yesterday, To-day, and To-morrow," in *Annual of American Design*, ed. R. L. Leonard and C. A. Glassgold (New York: Ives Washburn, 1930), 25, 27.

[17] On Frankl's early efforts to collaborate with manufacturers, see Helen Sprackling, "Modern Art and the Artist: The Farseeing Manufacturer Is Proving That He Appreciates the Value of the Artist," *House Beautiful* 65 (February 1929): 151—55.

[18] R. L. Leonard and C. A. Glassgold, eds., *Annual of American Design* (New York: Ives Washburn, 1930), 77.

[19] Letter from Peter Boulton to the author, 27 July 2001.

[20] The problem for designers was having enough staff and expertise not only to carry out commissions but also to market their talents to manufacturers. Because of the pressures of

running his gallery and interior design business, Frankl was neither willing nor able to spend much time looking for commissions. On the effort to sell the new design, see Meikle, *Twentieth Century Limited*, 68–83.

21 Emily Genauer, "The Current Vogue for Streamlining Captures the Modern Interior," *New York World-Telegram*, 3 March 1934.

22 By the mid-1930s, a number of other designers had adopted similar design strategies. See, for example, "Straight Lines and Stream-lines," *Arts and Decoration* 40 (January 1934): 38–41. Frankl emphasized not only the notion of speed, but also comfort—"the most fundamental requirement of any chair," as he explained to one reporter. "On the Theme of Supreme Comfort," *Arts and Decoration* 40 (November 1933): 16–17. See also Frankl's rejoinder to the conservatives in "Furniture for the House of Tomorrow," *Architecture* 69 (April 1934): 189–96.

23 Paul T. Frankl, autobiography (unpublished), c. 1954, Collection Paulette Frankl, 74 (hereafter, FA).

24 *Annual of American Art*, vol. 30 (Washington, D.C.: American Federation of Arts, 1933), 198.

25 FA, 74–75.

26 FA, 75–77.

27 Peter Boulton, interview by Paulette Frankl, San Francisco, 15 September 1987, Collection Paulette Frankl.

28 Letter from Peter Boulton to the author, 13 July 2000.

29 Letter from Peter Boulton to Paulette Frankl, 30 June 1998, Collection Paulette Frankl.

30 FA, 98–99.

31 Letter from Peter Boulton to the author, 13 June 2000.

32 Frankl, *Machine-Made Leisure* (New York: Harper and Brothers, 1932), 5.

33 Frankl, *Machine-Made Leisure*, 43, 44.

34 Frankl, *Machine-Made Leisure*, 140, 183.

35 R. L. Duffus, "The Artist in the Machine Age: Mr. Frankl Discusses Some of the Problems Which Confront the Designer at the Present Time," *New York Times Book Review*, 24 April 1932, 6. See also "Taste in Mass Production: Problem Now Is to Master the Leisure It Creates, Paul T. Frankl Says in

Book," review of *Machine-Made Leisure, New York Times*, 23 April 1932.

36 June Barrows Mussey, review of *Machine-Made Leisure, Creative Art* 10 (June 1932): 490.

37 Paulette Frankl, interview by author, Las Vegas, 28 February 1998.

38 Letter from Peter Boulton to Paulette Frankl, 30 June 1998, Collection Paulette Frankl; and Paulette Frankl, interview by author, Austin, 26 January 2002.

39 K. G. S., "Clever Drawings by Frankl," *New York Times*, 6 December 1931, 8.

40 "In the Galleries," *New York Times*, 9 March 1933; and "In the Market: 'New York, by Paul T. Frankl,'" *Creative Art* 12 (April 1933): 310.

41 "The Apartment of Roger Wolfe Kahn, by Paul T. Frankl," *House and Garden* 66 (July 1934): 55. On the Winans Apartment, see "Retreat for This Modern Man Styled by One of His Fellows," *House and Garden* 67 (March 1935): 65.

42 "Machine Age's Contributions," *New York World-Telegram*, 31 March 1934; and "Modern Room in Newark Industrial Exhibit," *New York Sun*, 3 April 1934.

43 Dorothea Wingert, "Chemistry and Interior Design Mix Well, Exhibit Reveals: Paul T. Frankl, American Decorator Is Responsible for Scientific Room Now on Display at Museum," *Newark Evening News*, 6 April 1934.

44 Philip Johnson, *Machine Art, March 6 to April 30, 1934*, exhibition catalog (New York: Museum of Modern Art, 1934; repr. New York: Arno Press, 1969).

45 Alfred H. Barr, Jr., foreword to Johnson, *Machine Art*.

46 Walter Rendell Storey, "The Chemist Aids the Decorator: Plastic Products and Synthetic Fabrics Lend a New Tone to the Interior," *New York Times*, 8 April 1934.

47 See, for example, the editor's introduction to "The Apartment of Roger Wolfe Kahn, by Paul T. Frankl"; and "A Modernist Celebrates His Twentieth Anniversary," *Retailing* (New York), Home Furnishings Edition, 19 March 1934.

48 FA, 93.

49 Letter from Peter Boulton to the author, 13 July 2000; and letter from Peter Boulton to the author, 8 March 2000.

50 Letter from Peter Boulton to Paulette Frankl, 30 June 1998, Collection Paulette Frankl.

51 Letter from Frankl to Frank Lloyd Wright, 30 March 1934, Collection Paulette Frankl.

52 FA, 79.

53 Franklin Toker, *Fallingwater Rising: Frank Lloyd Wright, E. J. Kaufmann, and America's Most Extraordinary House* (New York: Alfred A. Knopf, 2003), 30.

54 FA, 80.

55 Letter from Frankl to Frank Lloyd Wright, 20 April 1933, Collection Paulette Frankl. Years later, Frankl wrote of their shared enthusiasm for Japanese woodcuts: "We carried away with us a deep appreciation and understanding for Nipponese art, and Mr. Wright brought back one of the finest collections of the Japanese masters of colour prints ever to be permitted to leave that country. Together we spent many an evening in Taliesin admiring his treasures. I still cherish some of the woodcuts he gave me." FA, 80.

56 FA, 79–84.

57 FA, 79.

58 Frank Lloyd Wright, *Modern Architecture: Being the Kahn Lectures for 1930* (Princeton, N.J.: Princeton University Press, 1931).

59 Robert C. Twombly, *Frank Lloyd Wright: An Interpretive Biography* (New York: Harper and Row, 1973), 167–76.

60 Letter from Frank Lloyd Wright to Frankl, 23 April 1934, Collection Paulette Frankl.

61 Letter from Peter Boulton to Paulette Frankl, 30 June 1998, Collection Paulette Frankl.

62 FA, 84–86.

CHAPTER 10. West and East

1 Letter from Frankl to Frank Lloyd Wright, 15 August 1934, Collection Paulette Frankl.

2 Paul T. Frankl, autobiography (unpublished), c. 1954, Collection Paulette Frankl, 93 (hereafter, FA).

3 Chouinard Art Institute, *Catalogue for 1934–35* (Los Angeles, 1934), frontispiece.

4 Letter from Frankl to Olgivanna Wright, 9 July 1934, Collection Paulette Frankl.

5 FA, 93–94.

6 Letter from Frankl to Frank Lloyd Wright, 30 August 1934, Collection Paulette Frankl.

7 FA, 95.

8 Letters from Frank Lloyd Wright to Frankl, 20 September 1934, 22 April 1935, and 4 May 1935, Collection Paulette Frankl.

9 Ralph Hancock, *Fabulous Boulevard* (New York: Funk and Wagnalls, 1949), 239 306; and Thomas S. Hines, "Wilshire Boulevard, Los Angeles, California," in *The Grand American Avenue, 1850–1920*, ed. Jan Cigliano and Sarah Bradford Landau (San Francisco: Pomegranate, 1994): 307–63.

10 FA, 96.

11 FA, 97, 112–13.

12 Peter Boulton, interview by Paulette Frankl, San Francisco, 15 September 1987, Collection Paulette Frankl.

13 On the émigré Austrian architects and designers in Southern California, see, for example, Matthias Boeckl, ed., *Visionäre und Vertriebene: Österreichische Spuren in der modernen amerikanischen Architektur*, exhibition catalog (Berlin: Ernst and Sohn, 1995), 333, 339–40, 342–43.

14 Karl A. Bieber (Schindler's cousin), interview by author, Graz, Austria, 1 July 1986; and Cis Zoltowska, interview by author, Los Angeles, 31 May 1999.

15 FA, 94.

16 Cis Zoltowska interview.

17 "Another Mediterranean Villa of the Glorious 20's Bites the Dust: Residence of Mr. and Mrs. George Kuhrts, Jr., Los Angeles, California, Milton Black, Architect," *California Arts and Architecture* 49 (April 1936): 30–31. The Kuhrts House was not the first time Frankl's work appeared in California; he had been selling furniture on the West Coast since the 1920s. Glendon Allvine, head of advertising and publicity for the Fox Film Corporation, and his wife, Louise, for example, bought a number of his pieces for their "modernistic" house in Long Beach in 1929, and Frankl did several complete interiors in Los Angeles and San Francisco in the early 1930s. On the Allvine House, see *Furniture from America's First Modernistic House: The de Lorenzo Collection*, auction catalog (New York: Christie's, 1980).

[18] Frankl, "What Does Modern Art Owe Japan?" *California Arts and Architecture* 51 (March 1937): 16–18.

[19] FA, 103–5.

[20] FA, 114.

[21] Paulette Frankl, interview by author, Santa Fe, 5 August 2002.

[22] FA, 117–21.

[23] FA, 121–25.

[24] FA, 126–28; and "Noted Architect Buys P.I. Rattan Furniture," *Manila Herald*, 9 September 1936.

[25] FA, 128.

[26] FA, 129.

[27] "Rattan Furniture Has Big Prospects, U.S. Visitor Says," *Manila Tribune*, 10 September 1936.

[28] FA, 140–41.

[29] FA, 141–42.

[30] FA, 143–44.

[31] Frankl's rattan furniture, for example, appears prominently in Francis Ford Coppola's *The Godfather, Part 2*, released by Paramount in 1974.

[32] FA, 144–45.

[33] Frankl, "In California Every Room a Sun Room," *California Arts and Architecture* 51 (June 1937): 18–19.

[34] "Reflected Modern," *House Beautiful* 80 (July 1938): 36–37.

[35] For a comparison with other contemporary bar designs, see "'At Home' with 'Sweet Adeline,'" *California Arts and Architecture* 54 (December 1938): 26–27.

[36] Frankl, "Modern Will Live," *California Arts and Architecture* 53 (March 1938): 19.

[37] Robert C. Twombly, *Frank Lloyd Wright: An Interpretive Biography* (New York: Harper and Row, 1973), 235–36.

[38] Frankl, "Modern Will Live," 19.

[39] Frankl, "Modern Will Live," 17.

CHAPTER 11. Hollywood Designer

[1] Elizabeth A. T. Smith, "Arts and Architecture and the Los Angeles Vanguard," in Elizabeth A. T. Smith, ed., *Blueprints for Modern Living: History and Legacy of the Case Study Houses*, exhibition catalog (Cambridge, Mass.: MIT Press, 1989), 145–65.

[2] Paul J. Karlstrom, "Modernism in Southern California, 1920–1956: Reflections on the Art and the Times," in *Turning the Tide: Early Los Angeles Modernists, 1920–1956*, exhibition catalog, ed. Paul J. Karlstrom and Susan Ehrlich (Santa Barbara, Calif.: Santa Barbara Museum of Art, 1990), 13–21.

[3] Letter from Peter Boulton to the author, 1 October 2001.

[4] Otto Lang, *A Bird of Passage: The Story of My Life* (Seattle: Sky House, 1994), 336.

[5] See, for example, the advertisement for Heywood-Wakefield in *House Beautiful* 80 (June 1938): 5; the advertisement for the Grand Central Wicker Shop in *House Beautiful* 80 (June 1938): 5; and the advertisement for the Rattan Manufacturing Company in *California Arts and Architecture* 54 (December 1938): 9.

[6] Paul T. Frankl, autobiography (unpublished), c. 1954, Collection Paulette Frankl, 106, 110–12, 145–46 (hereafter, FA).

[7] Frankl, *Space for Living: Creative Interior Decoration and Design* (New York: Doubleday, Doran, 1938), 40.

[8] See, for example, Lin Yutang, "China Sets a Trend: Modern Decoration Owes Much to China," *House and Garden* 92 (July 1942): 10–17.

[9] Mary Schoeser, "Textiles: Surface, Structure, and Serial Production," in *Craft in the Machine Age: 1920–1945*, vol. 3 of *The History of Twentieth-Century American Craft*, exhibition catalog (New York: American Craft Museum/ Harry N. Abrams, 1995), 116–17.

[10] L. S. Gosliner, "Brief Biographies: Paul T. Frankl," *California Arts and Architecture* 51 (March 1937): 7.

[11] Frankl, *Space for Living*, 18, 32.

[12] Frankl, *Space for Living*, 104. Frankl does not mention the name of the client in the book, but the chair was in fact part of a larger commission he carried out for Peter R. L. Brooks and his wife, Pat, on New York's East Side. As Frankl notes in his autobiography, Brooks and his wife were "both seasoned flyers," and asked him "to do their apartment at the corner of Fifty-fifth and First Avenue. Both were aviation enthusiasts, and I was to carry out Pete's dream of an aviation room.

Suspended from the ceiling were diminutive airplane models, exact replicas of the famous ships that had made aviation history. From a loudspeaker hidden in the wall came a drone of their roaring engines. The curtains in that room were made of parachute silk, and all the furniture constructed of airplane parts." FA, supplement, 8.

[13] Frankl, *Space for Living*, 54.

[14] See the photographs of the George Frank House in Encino (1938) and the Norman McLeod House in Tolucca Lake (1939) in "The New Home of Mr. and Mrs. George Frank," *California Arts and Architecture* 54 (July 1938): 16–17; and Walter Rendell Storey, "Interior Decorators of Today: Paul T. Frankl," *The Studio* 117 (April 1939): 164–66.

[15] FA, 97.

[16] "Linen Shop: Paul T. Frankl, Designer, Morris Ketchum, Jr., Associate, Mosse, Inc., New York City," *Architectural Forum* 71 (December 1939): 433.

[17] "The New Building of Myron Selznick and Company, Inc. in Beverly Hills, California," *California Arts and Architecture* 56 (August 1939): 22–23.

[18] FA, 147.

[19] FA, 147–48.

[20] FA, 152–53.

[21] FA, 158–59.

[22] FA, 160–61.

[23] FA, 160–64.

[24] FA, 167.

[25] FA, 168.

[26] FA, 169–70.

[27] FA, 171–72.

[28] "The Residence of Mr. and Mrs. Paul T. Frankl," *California Arts and Architecture* 57 (November 1940): 28. On the design of the house, see also "Distinguished Modern Design in California," *Interior Design and Decoration* 16 (June 1941): 12–17, 38; and "House in Beverly Hills," *Architectural Forum* 73 (September 1940): 184–85.

[29] Frankl's use of the low mahogany partition to simultaneously screen and divide the two spaces recalls several of Schindler's designs from around the same time, including the living room of the Guy C. Wilson House in Los Angeles (1935–38). The arrangement is reminiscent, too, of Loos's *Raumplan*, or space-plan, villas from a decade before—which had influenced Schindler. Frankl was undoubtedly familiar with the work of both men, though it is uncertain if he drew on them here directly.

[30] Julius Shulman, interview by author, Los Angeles, 15 August 2001.

[31] Julius Shulman interview.

[32] "Seven Commercial Units, Including an Office, Photographer's Studio, and a Variety of Retail Shops, Designed by Architects Douglas Honnold and George Vernon Russell for Hollywood's New 'High Style' Street," *Architectural Forum* 78 (June 1943): 97–101.

[33] An advertisement officially announcing the opening of the shop appeared in *California Arts and Architecture* 57 (December 1940): 6. The impact of the new shop, as Honnold said, was dramatic: "A perceptible increase in traffic was noticed immediately," the architects reported in an article on the project. "This might have been due to the vigorous design of his shop, to the distinction of the furnishings within, or to the huge cage of white pigeons he used for a Christmas display.... Very soon two more shops opened next to Frankl's. Our office did a café across the street for 'Prince' Mike Romanoff. This has become a very fashionable place indeed. At lunch and dinner time, cars deposit movie stars and other celebrities at a rate of four a minute." "Seven Commercial Units," 98.

[34] Julius Shulman interview; and "Designing with Spirit: Paul László," transcript of an interview by Marlene L. Laskey, Oral History Program, University of California, Los Angeles, 1986. William Krisel, who worked in László's studio in the years after the war, remembered that Frankl's name was rarely mentioned around the office; each man preferred to ignore the other's existence. Krisel, interview by author, Los Angeles, 8 December 2003.

[35] "In the Far Eastern Manner," *California Arts and Architecture* 58 (December 1941): 24–25; and FA, 104.

[36] David Gebhard and Harriette Von Breton, *L.A. in the Thirties, 1931–1941*, exhibition catalog (Layton, Utah: Peregrine Smith, 1975), 116.

[37] "Colorful California Modern," *House and Garden* 80 (November 1941): 26.

CHAPTER 12. Mass Modern

1 Paul T. Frankl, autobiography (unpublished), c. 1954, Collection Paulette Frankl, 183 (hereafter, FA).

2 FA, 184.

3 Advertisement for Brown-Saltman, *California Arts and Architecture* 58 (October 1941): 3.

4 FA, 185; and "Obituaries," *Los Angeles Times*, 17 June 1942.

5 Among Frankl's few documented commissions of this period was the home for John F. McCarthy. See "House in the Hills," *California Arts and Architecture* 60 (February 1943): 30–31.

6 Although Frankl thought moving away from the city a sound decision, the location in Palos Verdes "was in fact closer to the San Pedro and Long Beach harbors," as his daughter Paulette later remembered, which in the event of a Japanese invasion would have been "major targets." The small cottage they rented had an ocean view, and she and her father would sometimes sit on the terrace and watch the U.S. warships come and go. Letter from Paulette Frankl to the author, 7 November 2005.

7 Elin Vanderlip, interview by Paulette Frankl, Los Angeles, 14 July 1987.

8 Peter Boulton, interview by author, San Diego, 25 August 2001. Henry Boulton formally adopted Peter in the later 1930s, and Peter took his surname.

9 Paulette Frankl, interview by author, Santa Fe, 23 July 2003.

10 Paulette Frankl, interview by author, Austin, 19 October 2003.

11 Elin Vanderlip interview.

12 Barbara Dee, who worked in the Frankl Galleries during the war, recalled that among Frankl's clients at the time were Alfred Hitchcock, Elsa Lancaster, and Igor Sikorsky. Barbara Dee, interview by author, Avalon, California, 7 October 2005.

13 Paulette Frankl, interview by author, Santa Fe, 23 July 2003.

14 "Designer Strikes Pay Dirt," *Interiors* 102 (April 1943): 34–35.

15 Frankl was still making a small number of custom pieces for individual clients, and he designed a line for Baker Brothers, a home furnishings store in Los Angeles. Barbara Dee interview.

16 "Design," *California Arts and Architecture* 57 (March 1940): 15.

17 See, for example, the reprint of the 1939 Herman Miller catalog, *Herman Miller 1939 Catalog: Gilbert Rohde Modern Design* (Atglen, Pa.: Schiffer, 1998); and Donald Albrecht, Robert Schofeld, and Lindsay Stamm Shapiro, *Russel Wright: Creating American Lifestyle*, exhibition catalog (New York: Cooper-Hewitt National Design Museum/Harry N. Abrams, 2001). On the development of the popular modernism of the 1930s, see Kristina Wilson, *Livable Modernism: Interior Decoration and Design during the Great Depression*, exhibition catalog (New Haven: Yale University Art Gallery/Yale University Press, 2004).

18 At the time, the area was mostly residential and underdeveloped. Frankl's daughter recalled that her father's "exotic remodel stood like an exclamation mark" on a street that was otherwise unremarkable. Again, as with his move to Rodeo Drive, his relocation there sparked a development boom in what became the "Golden Triangle." Letter from Paulette Frankl to the author, 7 November 2005.

19 "Studio and Sanctuary," *Interiors* 107 (September 1947): 90.

20 Paulette Frankl, interview by author, Las Vegas, 28 February 1998.

21 Peggy Galloway was born Noreen Louise Phillips in 1914. She attended the Girl's Collegiate School in Glendora, California, before entering the University of Southern California in the fall of 1931. She died in Los Angeles County in 1962. Barbara Bradac (Galloway's daughter), interview by author, Rock Island, Ill., 5 September 2005; and Barbara Dee (Galloway's sister), interview by author, Avalon, California, 7 October 2005.

22 FA, 185.

23 Christian G. Carron, *Grand Rapids Furniture: The Story of America's Furniture City* (Grand Rapids, Mich.: The Public Museum of Grand Rapids, 1998), 171–72.

24 Peter Boulton interview.

25 Cliff May, interview by Paulette Frankl, Los Angeles, 20 July 1987.

26 See, for example, David Bricker, "Cliff May and the California Ranch House after 1945" (M.A. thesis, University of California, Santa Barbara, 1983).

[27] "Streamlining the Ranch House," *House and Garden* 80 (November 1941): 20–21; and David E. Clark, ed., *Western Ranch Houses by Cliff May* (Menlo Park, Calif.: Lane Books, 1958), 24–39. Frankl had also designed the interiors for May's previous house in Mandeville Canyon, California. See "The Rancheria of Mr. and Mrs. Cliff May," *California Arts and Architecture* 56 (August 1939): 24–25.

[28] Frances Heard, "The Station Wagon Way of Life," *House Beautiful* 92 (June 1950): 103–9.

[29] On Frankl's bleached-cork designs, see "Furniture News," *Interiors* 109 (March 1950): 123; and "Frankl Bleaches Cork and Creates Moods," *Interiors* 109 (May 1950): 112–13.

[30] *Contemporary Designs by Paul T. Frankl*, sales catalog from the Johnson Furniture Company, Grand Rapids, Mich., c. 1950.

[31] "Designed by Paul Frankl, This Furniture Can Be Used Interchangeably in All Rooms of the House," *House and Garden* 97 (April 1950): 133–35; and Heard, "The Station Wagon Way of Life," 103–9. See also Frances Heard, "American Taste Has an Unmistakable Flavor," *House Beautiful* 92 (May 1950): 140–43; Betty Pepis, "Modern Moves Ahead," *New York Times*, 26 February 1950, 36–37; and Francis de N. Schroeder, "Designers Are Important People," *Interiors* 110 (November 1950): 96–99.

[32] "Fast Selling California Ranch Houses by Cliff May," *House and Home* 2 (October 1952): 90–97.

[33] FA, 187.

[34] Paulette Frankl, interview by author, Santa Fe, 24 July 2003.

[35] Paulette had begun to learn Spanish the previous summer during their stay in Mexico City; the parents thought their daughter could learn a more cultivated version of the language in Spain. Letter from Paulette Frankl to the author, 7 November 2005.

[36] Paulette Frankl, interview by author, Austin, 19 October 2003.

[37] Paulette Frankl, interview by author, Austin, 20 October 2003.

[38] "Nothing in Europe for Us," *Grand Rapids (Mich.) Herald*, 26 July 1953, 23. The same interview, substantially unaltered, was reprinted in Grace Holm, "Pace Setter in Good Design: Paul Frankl—Austrian Native Revisits Europe, Analyzes Furniture Design Trend," *The Oregonian*, 20 June 1954, 14.

[39] "Nothing in Europe for Us."

[40] Letter from Peter Boulton to the author, 8 March 2000.

[41] Frankl, *American Textiles* (Leigh-on-Sea, England: Lewis, 1954), 9–10.

[42] Letter from Frankl to Manuel Komroff, 15 November 1954, Collection Paulette Frankl.

[43] Letter from Frankl to Manuel Komroff.

[44] Letter from Frankl to Manuel Komroff.

[45] Peter Boulton interview by author.

[46] Paulette Frankl, interview by author, Santa Fe, 10 May 2004. (When the Frankl family stopped in Italy, Leanne Boccardo returned to California.)

[47] Jane Boulton, "Memories of Paul Frankl," unpublished manuscript, n.d., Collection Jane Boulton.

[48] Paulette Frankl, interview by author, Santa Fe, 10 May 2004.

[49] "Paul Frankl, Furniture Expert, Dies," *Los Angeles Times*, 22 March 1958, 6; and "Paul T. Frankl, 1887–1958," *Interiors* 117 (April 1958): 156. See also "Death Takes Designer: Paul T. Frankl, 71, Served Local Firms," *Grand Rapids (Mich.) Press*, 24 March 1958, 21.

EPILOGUE

[1] Frankl, *New Dimensions: The Decorative Arts Today in Words and Pictures* (New York: Payson and Clarke, 1928), 79–80.

[2] Frank Lloyd Wright, foreword to *New Dimensions*, 7.

Bibliography

ARCHIVAL SOURCES

Baupolizei, Vienna, MA 37 (drawings and property records of the Frankl villa in Vienna-Hietzing).

Beinecke Library, Yale University, New Haven (scrapbooks and other materials of the Washington Square Players).

Du Grummond Collection, McCain Library and Archives, University Libraries, University of Southern Mississippi (Maud and Miska Petersham Papers).

Ellis Island Foundation, New York (ship manifests documenting the Frankl family's travels).

Harry Ransom Humanities Research Center, University of Texas at Austin (photographs of Frankl's set designs for the Washington Square Players).

Österreichische Nationalbibliothek, Bildarchiv, Vienna (photographs of Viennese architecture).

Österreichisches Staatsarchiv-Kriegsarchiv (Frankl's military service records).

Rare Book and Manuscript Collection, Columbia University, New York (Joseph Urban Collection).

Státní okresní archiv, Sokolov, Czech Republic (Frankl's Realschule records).

Technische Universität Berlin, Hochschularchiv (Frankl's university records).

Technische Universität Berlin, Universitätsbibliothek (history of the architecture faculty at the university).

Technische Universität Vienna, Universitätsarchiv (Frankl's university records).

Theater Collection, New York Public Library at Lincoln Center (photographs of Frankl's set designs for the Washington Square Players).

Wiener Stadt- und Landesarchiv, Vienna (Vienna registration archives).

FRANKL'S WRITINGS

1913

"Der Stil unserer Zeit." *Der Baumeister* 12 (November 1913): 15–16.

1914

"Die Industrie als Kulturträger." *Der Baumeister* 12 (March 1914): 46–48.

1915

"The Modern Art of Interior Decoration." *Arts and Decoration* 5 (May 1915): 268–70.

1918

"Wie wohnt man in Amerika?" *Innen-Dekoration* 29 (1918): 27–31, 33–38, 40–43, 76.

"Wie wohnt man in Amerika? Vortrag am 27. November 1917 im Österreichischen Ingenieur- und Architektenverein Wien." *Zeitschrift des Österreichischen Ingenieur- und Architektenverein* 70, no. 35 (1918): 387.

1927

"Baths and Bath-Dressing Rooms: The Newest Interiors of This Kind Reveal a Pleasing Use of Decorative Wall Treatments." *House and Garden* 52 (August 1927): 51–55, 102.

"Furniture of the Fourth Dimension: Designed for the New Interior." *House and Garden* 51 (February 1927): 76–77, 140.

Skyscraper Furniture. Sales catalog. New York: Frankl Galleries, c. 1927.

1928

The Arts and Decoration Home Study Course Covering the Modern Movement as Applied to Interior Decoration and Kindred Subjects. Six parts. New York: Arts and Decoration, 1928.

"How to Blend Modernistic and Period Furniture." *Women's Wear Daily*, 26 May 1928.

"Just What Is This Modernistic Movement?" *Arts and Decoration* 29 (May 1928): 56−57, 108, 117−18.

"Logic in Modernistic Decoration." *Arts and Decoration* 29 (July 1928): 54−55, 82−83.

"Merchandising the Modern Idea in Decoration." *Advertising and Selling* 12 (26 December 1928): 36, 38, 63.

New Dimensions: The Decorative Arts of Today in Words and Pictures. New York: Payson and Clarke, 1928.

"The Six Fundamentals of Modernism." *Display World* (Cincinnati), 6 June 1928, 5−7.

"Why We Accept Modernistic Furniture." *Arts and Decoration* 29 (June 1928): 58−59, 90, 99.

1929

"Away from Awkwardness." *New York Herald-Tribune*, 17 November 1929.

"Form and Re-Form." *The Guidon* (National Women's Republican Club), December 1929, 4−5.

1930

Form and Re-Form: A Practical Handbook of Modern Interiors. New York: Harper and Brothers, 1930.

"The Home of Yesterday, To-day, and To-morrow." In *Annual of American Design*, ed. R. L. Leonard and C. A. Glassgold, 25−27. New York: Ives Washburn, 1930. Reprinted as *Modern American Design*, 1933.

"Modern College Rooms." *College Humor* 73 (January 1930): 20−21, 127.

1932

Machine-Made Leisure. New York: Harper and Brothers, 1932.

1934

"Furniture for the House of Tomorrow." *Architecture* 69 (April 1934): 189−96.

1937

"In California Every Room a Sun Room." *California Arts and Architecture* 51 (June 1937): 18−19.

"What Does Modern Art Owe Japan?" *California Arts and Architecture* 51 (March 1937): 16−18.

1938

"Acanthus." *California Arts and Architecture* 54 (July 1938): 2.

"Modern Will Live." *California Arts and Architecture* 53 (March 1938): 16−19.

1940

"Design." *California Arts and Architecture* 57 (March 1940): 15.

"House in Beverly Hills." *Architectural Forum* 73 (September 1940): 184−85.

1943

"Time Is Now Ripe for Radical Change in the Furniture Industry." *Retailing Home Furnishings*, 27 December 1943, 28.

1954

American Textiles. Leigh-on-Sea, England: Lewis, 1954.

Autobiography (unpublished), c. 1954. Collection Paulette Frankl.

"It Takes Creative Ability to Bring Life to Furniture." *Upholstering* 21 (October 1954): 76−79, 160.

"Modern Design Expresses Age, Writes Frankl." *Chicago Market News*, 22 June 1954, 17.

1956

"My Favorite Design . . ." *Chicago Market News*, 17 January 1956, 3.

WORKS ABOUT FRANKL

1915

Osborn, Max. "Das Hohenzollern-Kunstgewerbehaus in Berlin." *Innen-Dekoration* 26 (1915): 55−84.

van Houghton, Rebecca. "Modern Influences in Interior Decoration." *Town and Country* 70 (November 1915): 25.

1916

Frey, Dagobert. "Arbeiten eines österreichischen Architekten in Amerika (Paul Theodor Frankl)." *Der Architekt / Die bildenden Künste* 1, no. 12 (1916/1918): 137−48.

1917

Herts, B. Russell. "What Is Modern Decoration?" *House and Garden* 31 (April 1917): 19–21, 92, 94.

1925

"Seen in New York: At the Frankl Galleries." *Good Furniture Magazine* 25 (October 1925): 173–74.

1926

"American Modern Art: Its History and Characteristics." *Good Furniture Magazine* 27 (October 1926): 172–74.

Clute, Eugene. *The Treatment of Interiors*. New York: Pencil Point Press, 1926, 62, 93-96.

"Fanciful Scenes Depicted on Printed Mohairs." *New York Daily News Record*, 15 April 1926.

"Frankl Galleries Displaying Attractive Hand Blocked Linens." *New York Daily News Record*, 26 January 1926.

"Hand-Blocked Decorative Linens of Extreme Design Imported for Apparel." *Women's Wear Daily*, 27 April 1926.

"Modern Art and Style Dictate in Furniture Field, Declares P. T. Frankl, American Authority Now Here." *New York Herald* (Paris), 7 August 1926.

"Modernist Furniture and Accessories." *House and Garden* 50 (October 1926): 98–99.

1927

"American Modernist Furniture Inspired by Sky-Scraper Architecture." *Good Furniture Magazine* 29 (September 1927): 119–21.

Catalogue of the Exposition of Art in Trade at Macy's, May 2 to May 7, 1927. New York: R. H. Macy, 1927.

Chase, Joseph Cummings. "What Is This Art Game?" *Saturday Evening Post*, 15 October 1927, 16–17, 205–6, 209.

"Christmas Greetings Take New and Sophisticated Modes of Expression: Sentimentality Gone—Decorative Idea Rules Lovely Paper of Smart Colors." *New York Evening Sun*, 10 December 1927.

Crawford, M. D. C. "Cretonnes and Their Use from the Frankl Galleries." *New York Daily News Record*, 3 November 1927.

———. "Rodier Fabrics Designed for the Frankl Galleries." *New York Daily News Record*, 1 December 1927.

"The Dining Room Done in White." *House and Garden* 52 (November 1927): 108–9.

"Furniture." *Time*, 14 November 1927, 24.

Johnson, Nunnally. "The New Furniture Gives Every One His Own Skyline." *New York Evening Post*, 19 May 1927.

"The Last Word in Interior Furnishings: A Modern Library." *New York Times*, 8 May 1927.

"Linen Prints Outstanding in Frankl Collection." *New York Daily News Record*, 16 October 1927.

A Message for Moderns. Pamphlet for an exhibition of Frankl furniture. New York: Lozelle and Lozant Leathers, 1927.

"Modern Furniture." *Brooklyn Times*, 4 February 1927.

"The New Modernist Lights." *House and Garden* 52 (September 1927): 86–87.

Park, Edwin Avery. *New Backgrounds for a New Age*. New York: Harcourt, Brace, 1927, 167–68.

"Two Hand-Blocked Linens Shown by Frankl Galleries." *New York Daily News Record*, 31 December 1927.

"Unusually Handsome Coffee Set from the Frankl Galleries." *Dry Goods Economist*, 19 November 1927, 73.

1928

"About the House." *New Yorker*, 18 February 1928, 55–58.

"American Architecture and the Decorative Arts." *Waterbury (Conn.) Democrat*, 27 May 1928.

"American Designers' Gallery to Have Their First Modern Art Exhibit." *Dry Goods Economist*, 22 September 1928, 223–24.

"American Modern Art to Be Shown." *New York World*, 25 August 1928.

"The Answer to Modern Art Is 'Be Yourself.'" *Printers Ink*, 17 May 1928.

"The Art Gallery." *Brooklyn Life*, 11 February 1928.

"Avers Venus de Milo Would Lose Modern Beauty Contest." *Brooklyn Eagle*, 15 November 1928.

Bauer, Catherine. "And Then What?" *New York Herald-Tribune*, 17 June 1928.

"Boudoir in A. & S. Model House." *Brooklyn Times*, 9 February 1928.

Breuning, Margaret. "Modern Tendencies in Interior Decoration Shown." *New York Post*, 11 February 1928.

Brock, H. I. "Bringing the Skyscraper Indoors: 'New Dimensions' States the Case for the Innovators Who Seek to Establish a Modern Style of Interior Decoration." *New York Times Book Review*, 17 June 1928.

Brooks, Walter R. "Ivory, Apes and Peacocks." *New York Outlook*, 22 August 1928.

——. "Picked at Random." *New York Outlook*, 11 July 1928.

"Comfort with the Exotic." *New York Evening World*, 22 June 1928.

"Comfort with the Exotic." *Norwalk (Conn.) Sentinel*, 25 June 1928.

"Conservative Modernism." *Memphis Evening Appeal*, 7 June 1928.

"Course of Lectures for Art Directors' Exhibition." *Printers Ink*, 19 April 1928.

"Cubist and Other Designs Bid for Favor." *Springfield (Mass.) Republican*, 30 May 1928.

"Decorative Art." *Cleveland Time*, 27 August 1928.

"The Decorative Arts." *The Arts* 14 (December 1928): 339–43, 361–63.

"A Dissertation on the Future of Decorative Art." *Philadelphia Inquirer*, 18 August 1928.

E. C. S. [?]. "For the Skyscraper Age." *Christian Science Monitor*, 9 July 1928.

"Elegance and Modernism." *Furnishing Trades' Organizer* (London), February 1928, 93.

Erler, Diana D. "Our Most Modern Ideas Are the Most Ancient." *Brooklyn Eagle*, 15 April 1928.

"Extensive Modern Art Exhibit." *Women's Wear Daily*, 2 September 1928.

"Fabrics with a Modern Flavor." *House and Garden* 53 (March 1928): 127.

"Famous Designer to Give Address." *San Francisco Bulletin*, 3 October 1928.

Fisher, Irene. "Interior Decoration Has Moved to New York after Flowering as Paris Art." *Albuquerque Tribune*, 14 February 1928.

"Frankl Drops Trip to Japan; Resuming Tour." *Women's Wear Daily*, 16 July 1928.

"Frankl Sees Style Element in Modernistic Furniture as Means of Increased Turnover." *Women's Wear Daily*, 30 June 1928.

"Frankl to Address Women." *New York Post*, 28 March 1928.

"Frankl to Continue U.S. Lecture Tour." *New York Daily News Record*, 17 July 1928.

"Frankl's Art Course for N.Y.U. Opens." *Women's Wear Daily*, 6 October 1928.

"Furnishings for the New Interior." *House and Garden* 53 (February 1928): 81.

Glassgold, C. Adolph. "The Modern Note in Decorative Arts, Part 2." *The Arts* 13 (April 1928): 221–35.

——. Review of *New Dimensions: The Decorative Arts Today in Words and Pictures*, by Paul T. Frankl. *The Arts* 14 (September 1928): 167–68.

Hansen, Harry. "Modern Art Becomes a Movement, Says Paul Frankl in 'New Dimensions.'" *New York World*, 27 May 1928.

"Herron Institute Displays Exquisite Home Decorations." *Indianapolis Star*, 1 October 1928.

Hitchcock, Henry-Russell, Jr. "Some American Interiors in the Modern Style." *Architectural Record* 64 (September 1928): 235–43.

Holbrook, Christine. "Modern Furniture Is Described as Definite Style Period." *Des Moines Register*, 1 July 1928.

"Home Study Course in Modern Art to Be Given Publication." *Women's Wear Daily*, 2 May 1928.

"House and Garden's Modern House." *House and Garden* 54 (November 1928): 98–99.

"How to Blend Modernistic and Period Furniture: Expressions by Lescaze, Paul T. Frankl, Carl Schmieg, Eugene Schoen, and Kem Weber." *Women's Wear Daily*, 26 May 1928.

"Issue Brochure on Modern Art." *Women's Wear Daily*, 14 July 1928.

Laganke, Florence. "About These New Pianos, Do You Like Their Style?" *Cleveland Plain Dealer*, 7 October 1928.

L[ang, Hugo]. "Neue Kunst in Amerika: Arbeiten von Paul T. Frankl—New York." *Innen-Dekoration* 39 (1928): 56–62.

Lennon, R. A. "Skyscraper and Flapper Seen as Influence in Modern Design." *Chicago Post*, 18 September 1928.

"'Livable House' Opens to Public View Tomorrow." *Brooklyn Standard Union*, 7 February 1928.

"Manufacturers and Artists Should Combine to Protect Design Rights, Frankl Says." *New York Journal of Commerce*, 12 June 1928.

McCampbell, Coleman W. "With the New York Displaymen: Screens of All types Are Experiencing a Revival, but They Differ Widely from Styles of Earlier Months." *Display World* (Cincinnati), July 1928, 14–15.

"Merchandising the Modern Idea in Decoration." *Advertising and Selling*, 26 December 1928.

Migennes, Pierre. "Un artiste décorateur américain: Paul Th. Frankl." *Art et Décoration* 53 (January 1928): 49–56.

"Modern American Art in New York." *Springfield (Mass.) Union and Republic*, 2 September 1928.

"Modern Art Course Finds Favor." *Women's Wear Daily*, 18 August 1928.

"Modern Art Exponent Will Lecture in City Wednesday." *Indianapolis News*, 1 October 1928.

"Modern Art Influencing Interior Decoration Exhibition Discloses; Outcome of New Movement Difficult to Forecast; Wide Variety of Articles Displayed." *Waterbury (Conn.) Republican*, 20 August 1928.

"Modern Art Prophet Opens Herron Exhibition." *Indianapolis News*, 4 October 1928.

"Modern Decorative Art Applied in Brooklyn." *New York Sun*, 11 February 1928.

"Modern Furniture Is Shown at A. & S." *Brooklyn Times*, 7 February 1928.

"Modern Home Decoration Exposition." *San Francisco Call-Post*, 15 September 1928.

"Modernism in the Home." *New York Herald-Tribune*, 26 June 1928.

"Modernism in the Library." *House and Garden* 53 (February 1928): 60.

"Modernism Is Entering the Home." *South Bend (Ind.) Tribune*, 16 December 1928.

"Modernism May Be Conservative: Fine Feeling in Furniture Seen in New Designs." *St. Louis Star*, 31 October 1928.

"'Modernism' Subject of Frankl's Talk in Store Lecture Tour." *New York Daily News Record*, 3 May 1928.

"Modernist Room at Ayres Store: Frankl Designs in Furniture Make Brilliant and Attractive Display for Department." *Philadelphia Retail Ledger*, 14 August 1928.

"Modernistic Designs Oust Prized Antiques." *Springfield (Mass.) Union and Republic*, 6 May 1928.

"The Modernistic Trend: Ideals and Merchandise That Will Appeal to Those Who Follow the New Style in Decoration." *National Decorative Trade Service*, July 1928, 17, 20.

"Modernistic Vogue a Factor in Latest Fall Rug Design." *New York Journal of Commerce*, 10 April 1928.

Moore, Jennie. "Modernism, Seen in Many Fields, Now Enters the Home." *New York Herald-Tribune*, 9 December 1928.

Morehouse, Lucille E. "Exhibition of Modernistic Furniture Will Be Shown at Herron Art Institute." *Indianapolis Star*, 30 September 1928.

———. "Herron Institute Displays Exquisite Home Decorations." *Indianapolis Star*, 14 October 1928.

———. "Will You Let 'Furniture Moderne' Excite You, Too?" *Indianapolis Star*, 7 October 1928.

"New Modern Dress of Livable House Is Shown by A. & S." *Brooklyn Eagle*, 7 February 1928.

"P. T. Frankl to Give Course on Styling." *Women's Wear Daily*, 22 December 1928.

"Paul Frankl Answers Many Questions on Modern Art Movement in His New Book." *Women's Wear Daily*, 2 June 1928.

"Paul Frankl Cheers the New Art." *Providence (R.I.) Journal*, 10 June 1928.

"Paul Frankl Plans Store Lecture Tour." *Women's Wear Daily*, 20 April 1928.

"Paul Frankl Speaker at Second Citivas Meeting." *Brooklyn Times*, 15 November 1928.

"Paul T. Frankl to Give Course in Art." *Women's Wear Daily*, 22 September 1928.

"Paul T. Frankl to Sail for Japan July 12." *Women's Wear Daily*, 18 May 1928.

Perkins, Harely. "New Dimensions in Decorative Arts: Phenomenal Interest in a New York Department Store's Modernistic Furniture." *Boston Transcript*, 26 May 1928.

"Program of Events at Metropolitan Museum." *New York Sun*, 6 October 1928.

Ries, Estelle. "Modernistic Decoration." Part 9 of "Great Epochs in Fine Furniture." *New York World Traveller*, 14 September 1928, 26–27.

"Rike-Kumler Co., Dayton, O. Staging Extensive Modern Art Exhibit: Prominent Names in New Art Movement on Store's Lecture Schedule in Connection with Showing—Rooms by Frankl and Kem Weber Designed for Occasion." *Women's Wear Daily*, 8 September 1928.

Sanford, Nellie C. "The Livable House Transformed: Abraham and Straus Present the Modern House." *Good Furniture Magazine* 30 (April 1928): 174–76.

"Schuster's Stage Successful Modern Exhibit at Milwaukee 'Home Show.'" *Women's Wear Daily*, 7 April 1928.

"Skyscraper Furniture Has 'It.'" *Milwaukee News*, 20 March 1928.

"Skyscraper Inspires Modernistic Art." *Newark Star-Eagle*, 7 November 1928.

S[mith], M[ary Byers]. "What I See in New York." *House Beautiful* 64 (November 1928): 517.

Southworth, Clara. "Modernism in Decorative Arts." *Portland (Ore.) Evening News*, 31 July 1928.

Storey, Walter Rendell. "Modernism Enters the Business World." *New York Times*, 18 March 1928.

———. "Modernism Enters the Small House." *New York Times Magazine*, 26 February 1928.

Strauss, Frances. "But Is It Art? Modernists Distinguish Themselves From Modern Art 'Running Wild.'" *Brooklyn Citizen*, 2 September 1928.

"Tall Buildings Set New Style." *Milwaukee Journal*, 18 March 1928.

"Tea Given in Livable House for Art Critics and Museum Directors Yesterday." *Brooklyn Eagle*, 7 February 1928.

"Three Modern Rooms for the Rike-Kumler Co." *Women's Wear Daily*, 25 August 1928.

"Throngs at A. & S. View Livable House." *Brooklyn Times*, 8 February 1928.

"Walls in Black and White: A New Decorative Scheme." *House and Garden* 53 (April 1928): 94–95.

"Watch the Modern Vogue in Fabrics!" *Good Furniture Magazine* 30 (May 1928): 234–38.

"What Is Modernism?—Read 'New Dimensions.'" *American Carpet and Upholstery Journal* 46 (July 1928): 65–66.

"Where Ancient and Modern Meet." *Boston Post*, 2 December 1928.

Yust, Walter. "Of Making Many Books—." *Philadelphia Public Ledger*, 29 May 1928.

1929

Adair, Doris. "Explaining Modern Art." *New York Herald-Tribune*, 29 December 1929.

"Architekt Paul Th. Frankl—New York: 'Runder Frisier-Spiegel.'" *Innen-Dekoration* 40 (1929): 235.

"Artists' Luncheon at Casino." *New York World*, 12 October 1929.

Beede, Carl Greenleaf. "Fifth Avenue and Thereabouts." *Christian Science Monitor*, 9 November 1929.

"Designers—European and American." *Good Furniture Magazine* 32 (April 1929): 167, 172.

"Dramatizing Fabric Printing." *Women's Wear Daily*, 15 June 1929.

"Enterprising Hotel Men Embrace Modernistic Plan." *Hotel Industry* 23 (May 1929): 5–9.

"Frankl Writes Sanely about Modernism." *Detroit Free Press*, 2 June 1929.

Glassgold, C. Adolph. "The Decorative Arts." *The Arts* 15 (May 1929): 343–46, 358.

Holme, C. Geoffrey, and S. B. Wainright, eds. *Decorative Art 1929: Yearbook of Creative Art*. London: The Studio, 1929, 148–50.

Hutchinson, James L. Review of *New Dimensions: The Decorative Arts Today in Words and Pictures*, by Paul T. Frankl. *House Beautiful* 65 (June 1929): 772–73.

Lang, Hugo. "Luxus-Räume in New York." *Innen-Dekoration* 40 (1929): 358–59.

"A Living Room Decorated and Furnished in the Modern Manner." *New York Times*, 6 October 1929.

"Living Room in the Modern Manner." *New York World*, 5 May 1929.

MacMaster, Amy. "The Father of Modern Decoration: Paul T. Frankl, Designer of the First Modern Stage Settings in America, Says Elimination Is Essence of New Art." *Brooklyn Eagle*, 3 November 1929.

"Modernism—A New Era or a Passing Fad?" *Allentown (Pa.) Call*, 15 January 1929.

"Modernism in Furniture, Simply Simplicity, Frankl Says." *Pittsburgh Press*, 2 February 1929.

"Modernism Seen in Many Fields, Now Enters the Home." *New York Herald-Tribune*, 9 December 1929.

"Modernist Designer to Talk Tomorrow." *Pittsburgh Sun-Telegraph*, 24 January 1929.

"Modernist to Speak." *Pittsburgh Post Gazette*, 25 January 1929.

Moore, Jennie. "Spirit of the Times Being Expressed: Greater Simplicity of Interior Is One Evidence of It, Declares Paul T. Frankl." *Hartford Times*, 12 January 1929.

"Newest Furniture Follows Line of Simplicity." *Chicago Tribune*, 18 September 1929.

"P. T. Frankl Holds Showing of New Modern Furniture." *Women's Wear Daily*, 6 April 1929.

"P. T. Frankl Sails for Algiers June 26." *Women's Wear Daily*, 17 June 1929.

Sprackling, Helen. "Modern Art and the Artist: The Farseeing Manufacturer Is Proving That He Appreciates the Value of the Artist." *House Beautiful* 65 (February 1929): 151–55.

"Stage Leaning to Symbolism." *New York Sun*, 11 July 1929.

Storey, Walter Rendell. "Mosaics Find New Uses in Decoration." *New York Times*, 22 September 1929.

——. "Strange Motifs in Furniture Design: Modern Architecture Leads Decorators to Construct Some Novel Pieces—Old Moldings and New Silver." *New York Times*, 28 April 1929.

"Vanity Mirrors in a Practical Age." *Art-In-Trade*, August 1929, 42, 48, 74.

Vreeland, Alida. "What the New Furniture Is All About." *High Point (N.C.) Enterprise*, 1 January 1929.

Weeks, Edward. "Trophy Rooms: Whether Hunter's or Bookman's, These Rooms Bear the Impress of Hobbies Pursued." *House Beautiful* 66 (1929): 577–80, 620–22.

Weigle, Edith. "Newest Furniture Follows Line of Simplicity." *Chicago Tribune*, 18 August 1929.

Zaiss, Alma. "Beautiful Homes for Every Income." *New York World*, 8 October 1929.

——. "Intriguing Decorative Notes Furnished by Modern Screens." *New York Evening World*, 8 October 1929.

——. "You Can't Write Bad News When Sitting at This Table." *Boston Post*, 13 January 1929.

1930

Auerbach, Alfred. "A New Book on Modern Art: P. T. Frankl Explains the Principles Which Are Guiding Contemporary Designers for Their Work." *Women's Wear Daily*, 1 February 1930.

Bonney, Louise. "Books and Interior Decoration." *Publishers Weekly*, 18 January 1930, 297–98.

——. "New Metal Furniture for Modern Schemes." *House and Garden* 57 (April 1930): 82–83, 142.

Bulliet, C. J. "Artless Comment on the Seven Arts." *Chicago Post*, 11 February 1930.

Clearage, Eleanor. "Main Street Meditations." *Cleveland Plain Dealer*, 8 February 1930.

Corby, Jane. "Suit Yourself Is the Slogan Suggested by Exhibit of 1930 Furniture." *Brooklyn Eagle*, 6 February 1930.

Davies, Florence. Review of *Form and Re-Form: A Practical Handbook of Modern Interiors*, by Paul T. Frankl. *Detroit News*, 16 February 1930.

Davis, Maxine. "Backs Intellectual Appeal in Modern House Furniture: Paul Frankl Decries Sentimentality in So Practical a Matter, Says Artistic Notions Need Not Suffer in Selections." *New York Telegram*, 6 February 1930.

Deskey, Donald. "Style in Summer Furniture." *Good Furniture and Decoration* 34 (April 1930): 201–6.

Drake, Ethel. "Austere Lines Emphasized by Paul Frankl." *New York World*, 26 January 1930.

"'Form and Re-Form.'" *New York Evening Post*, 1 February 1930.

"Frankl Urges Ban on Old Type Homes: New York Designer Insists on Modernism in Buildings, Furnishing." *Minneapolis Tribune*, 11 February 1930.

Glassgold, C. Adolph. Review of *Form and Reform: A Practical Handbook of Modern Interiors*, by Paul T. Frankl. *Creative Art* 6 (June 1930): supplement, 137–38.

———. "Some Modern Furniture Designers." *House Beautiful* 67 (February 1930): 163–66, 214.

Harbeson, John F. "Design in Modern Architecture: The Modern Interior." *Pencil Points* 11 (April 1930): 258–64.

Hitchcock, Henry-Russell, Jr. Review of *Form and Reform: A Practical Handbook of Modern Interiors*, by Paul T. Frankl. *International Studio* 96 (May 1930): 110.

Holme, C. Geoffrey, and S. B. Wainright, eds. *Decorative Art 1930: Yearbook of Creative Art*. London: The Studio, 1930, 142.

"Horizontalism Is Keynote of Modernism in Decorative Arts." *Dallas Morning News*, 23 March 1930.

Lyon, Jean. "American Designers Play with the Modern in Interiors." *New York Sun*, 27 February 1930.

"Manufacturers and Artists Should Combine to Protect Design Rights." *New York Journal of Commerce*, 6 February 1930.

McCarroll, Marion Clyde. "New Book on Modern Decoration and Design Interprets Present-Day Ideas for Practical Use of Home-Makers." *New York Post*, 13 February 1930.

"Modern Designs in Furniture Urged." *Indianapolis News*, 11 February 1930.

"Modern Designs in Furniture Urged: Frankl Declares Americans Should Furnish Homes as They Choose." *Minneapolis Journal*, 11 February 1930.

"Modern Interiors." *Boston Transcript*, 15 February 1930.

"Modern Manifestations." *Buffalo News*, 2 February 1930.

"Modernistic Art for Interiors Well Exhibited." *San Francisco Chronicle*, 9 February 1930.

"Modernistic Art Is Expressed in Straight Lines." *Indianapolis News*, 10 February 1930.

"New and Old Uses for Leather." *Good Furniture and Decoration* 34 (March 1930): 149–52.

"Notes on Decorating the Hotel Westover's Lobby in New York by Paul T. Frankl." *Women's Wear Daily*, 27 July 1930.

P. R. [?]. Review of *Form and Reform: A Practical Handbook of Modern Interiors*, by Paul T. Frankl. *Connoisseur* 85 (May 1930): 321–22.

"Paul Frankl on Trip." *Women's Wear Daily*, 11 February 1930.

"Paul Frankl Speaks on the Modern Art." *Minneapolis Tribune*, 9 February 1930.

Review of *Form and Reform: A Practical Handbook of Modern Interiors*, by Paul T. Frankl. *American Magazine of Art* 21 (April 1930): 239–40.

Soskin, William. "A Modernist Book on Modernist Furniture." *New York Evening Post*, 28 January 1930.

Storey, Walter Rendell. "The Decorator's Art in the New Age." *New York Times*, 23 February 1930.

———. "A New Display of Modern Furniture." *New York Times*, 7 December 1930.

Winn, Lucy. "A Roof Terrace May Very Well Go Modern." *New York Sun*, 19 May 1930.

1931

K. G. S. [?]. "Clever Drawings by Frankl." *New York Times*, 6 December 1931.

Linsley, Everett Gray. "Dark Backgrounds—A Dramatic Note in Decoration." *House and Garden* 59 (February 1931): 53–56.

"New Developments in Modern Furnishing by Eight Leading Designers in America." *House and Garden* 59 (April 1931): 70–72.

1932

"Art of Shop Window Put above Museum's: Paul T. Frankl Says Great Work of Past Was Commercial—Mass Production of Designs Hailed." *New York Times*, 17 March 1932.

Duffus, R. L., "The Artist in the Machine Age: Mr. Frankl Discusses Some of the Problems Which Confront the

Designer at the Present Time." *New York Times Book Review*, 24 April 1932, 6.

Mussey, June Barrows. Review of *Machine-Made Leisure*, by Paul T. Frankl. *Creative Art* 10 (June 1932): 490.

Review of *Form and Re-Form: A Practical Handbook of Modern Interiors*, by Paul T. Frankl. *Arts and Decoration* 37 (May 1932): 69.

"Taste in Mass Production: Problem Now Is to Master the Leisure It Creates, Paul T. Frankl Says in Book." Review of *Machine-Made Leisure*, by Paul T. Frankl. *New York Times*, 23 April 1932.

1933

"Attractions in the Galleries." *New York Sun*, 18 March 1933.

Burrows, Carlyle. "Studies in Drawing and Water Color." *New York Herald-Tribune*, 19 March 1933.

"Exhibition of Frankl Drawings at Knoedler Galleries." *New York Sun*, 11 March 1933.

Holme, C. G., ed. *Decorative Art 1933: The Studio Yearbook*. London: The Studio, 1933, 87−88.

"In the Galleries." *New York Times*, 9 March 1933.

"In the Market: 'New York, by Paul T. Frankl.'" *Creative Art* 12 (April 1933): 310.

"Paul T. Frankl Takes Up Painting." *Art Digest*, 1 March 1933.

1934

"The Apartment of Roger Wolfe Kahn, by Paul T. Frankl." *House and Garden* 66 (July 1934): 54−55.

"Furniture for the House of Tomorrow." *Architecture* 69 (April 1934): 189−90.

Genauer, Emily. "The Current Vogue for Streamlining Captures the Modern Interior." *New York World-Telegram*, 3 March 1934.

"Machine Age's Contributions." *New York World-Telegram*, 31 March 1934.

"Modern Room in Newark Industrial Exhibit." *New York Sun*, 3 April 1934.

"A Modernist Celebrates His Twentieth Anniversary." *Retailing* (New York), Home Furnishings Edition, 19 March 1934.

"'Modernist' Paul T. Frankl." *California Art News* (11 December 1934): 2.

Storey, Walter Rendell. "The Chemist Aids the Decorator: Plastic Products and Synthetic Fabrics Lend a New Tone to the Interior." *New York Times*, 8 April 1934.

"A Twentieth Anniversary in Modern Shows How Tastes Change with the Years." *House and Garden* 66 (July 1934): 53.

Wingert, Dorothea. "Chemistry and Interior Decoration Mix Well, Exhibit Reveals: Paul T. Frankl, American Decorator, Is Responsible for Scientific Room Now on Display at Museum." *Newark Evening News*, 6 April 1934.

1935

Miller, Arthur. "Brush Strokes." *Los Angeles Times*, 21 July 1935.

"Paul T. Frankl Will Deliver Lecture Here." *Long Beach Press*, 4 January 1935.

"Retreat for This Modern Man Styled by One of His Fellows." *House and Garden* 67 (March 1935): 65.

Wright, Frank Lloyd. "Form and Reform." *Daily Cardinal*, 1935. Reprinted in *Frank Lloyd Wright: Collected Writings*, vol. 3, ed. Bruce Brooks Pfeiffer. New York: Rizzoli, 1993, 183−84.

1936

"Another Mediterranean Villa of the Glorious 20's Bites the Dust: Residence of Mr. and Mrs. George Kuhrts, Jr., Los Angeles, California, Milton Black, Architect." *California Arts and Architecture* 49 (April 1936): 30−31.

"Bumabalangkasng Kagamitang yari sa yantak." *Taliba* (Manila, Philippines), 10 September 1936.

"Un Gran pedido de muebles de bejuo para Hollywood." *Vanguardia* (Manila, Philippines), 10 September 1936.

"Noted Architect Buys P.I. Rattan Furniture." *Manila Herald*, 9 September 1936.

"A Puff for Frankl." *Retailing* (New York), 15 June 1936.

"Rattan Furniture Has Big Prospects, U.S. Visitor Says." *Manila Tribune*, 10 September 1936.

1937

Cook, Alma May. "Paints Picture with Powder Puff: Talcum and Sun-Tan Give Tint: U.S.C. Professor Invents New Art for Moderns." *Los Angeles Evening Herald*, 25 May 1937.

Gosliner, L. S. "Brief Biographies: Paul T. Frankl." *California Arts and Architecture* 51 (March 1937): 7.

"Iron as Light as Lace." *House and Garden* 71 (May 1937): 80.

Killoran, Patricia. "Ideal 'Space House' Brings Outdoors In." *Los Angeles Citizen*, 11 December 1937.

"Summer Screens." *House and Garden* 72 (July 1937): 40–41.

"Two Eminent Industrial Designers." *Design* 39 (May 1937): 12–13.

1938

"'At Home' with 'Sweet Adeline.'" *California Arts and Architecture* 54 (December 1938): 26–27.

Bogner, Walter F. "One Man's Concept of Architecture." *Boston Transcript*, 31 December 1938.

Hodel, Emilia. "Ways to Decorate Homes Shown in Exhibit at Museum of Art: Gallery Made in Eight Rooms for Display." *San Francisco News*, 14 May 1938.

"The Home of Miss Miriam Hopkins in Beverly Hills, California." *California Arts and Architecture* 53 (June 1938): 24–25.

"The New Home of Mr. and Mrs. George Frank." *California Arts and Architecture* 54 (July 1938): 16–17.

"The New Home of Mr. and Mrs. George Frank in Encino, California, Leland Fuller, Architect, Paul T. Frankl, Interior Decorator." *California Arts and Architecture* 53 (March 1938): 16–19.

"Paul Frankl Writes Books on Modern." *Retailing* (New York), 19 December 1938.

"Reflected Modern." *House Beautiful* 80 (July 1938): 36–37.

Review of *Space for Living: Creative Interior Decoration and Design*, by Paul T. Frankl. *California Arts and Architecture* 54 (July 1938): 39.

"'Space for Living.'" *Los Angeles Times*, 4 December 1938.

1939

Beede, Carl Greenleaf. "A Modernist's Credo and Method." *Christian Science Monitor*, 7 March 1939.

"Color and Texture May Puzzle You." *Los Angeles Times*, Home and Garden Issue, 1 January 1939.

Holme, C. G., ed. *Decorative Art 1939: The Studio Yearbook*. London: The Studio, 1939, 37, 65, 137.

"Linen Shop: Paul T. Frankl, Designer, Morris Ketchum, Jr., Associate, Mosse, Inc., New York City." *Architectural Forum* 71 (December 1939): 433.

McLane, Robert C. "Notes of a Ragman." *California Arts and Architecture* 55 (March 1939): 28–31.

"The Modern Room." *New York Times*, 5 February 1939.

"The New Building of Myron Selznick and Company, Inc., in Beverly Hills, California." *California Arts and Architecture* 56 (August 1939): 22–23.

"The Rancheria of Mr. and Mrs. Cliff May." *California Arts and Architecture* 56 (August 1939): 24–25.

Storey, Walter Rendell. "Interior Decorators of Today: Paul T. Frankl." *The Studio* 117 (April 1939): 164–66.

1940

"House in Beverly Hills, California, Paul T. Frankl, Designer." *Architectural Forum* 73 (September 1940): 184–85.

"The Residence of Mr. and Mrs. Paul T. Frankl." *California Arts and Architecture* 57 (November 1940): 28–29.

1941

"Colorful California Modern." *House and Garden* 80 (November 1941): 26.

"Country House in Town." *California Arts and Architecture* 58 (October 1941): 26–27.

"Distinguished Modern Design in California." *Interior Design and Decoration* 16 (June 1941): 12–17, 38.

Holme, C. G., ed. *Decorative Art 1941: The Studio Yearbook*. London: The Studio, 1941, 79, 94, 96.

"In the Far Eastern Manner." California Arts and Architecture 58 (December 1941): 24–25.

"New Furniture Designs." *California Arts and Architecture* 58 (September 1941): 23.

"Recent Work by Edward D. Stone." *Architectural Forum* 76 (July 1941): 13–30.

"Streamlining the Ranch House." *House and Garden* 80 (November 1941): 20–21.

"The Year's Work." *Interiors* 101 (August 1941): 25–48, 62–65.

1942

Ford, James, and Katherine M. Ford. *Design of Modern Interiors*. New York: American Book, 1942, 34.

Holme, C. G., ed. *Decorative Art 1942: The Studio Yearbook*. London: The Studio, 1942, 67, 73.

"The Year's Work." *Interiors* 102 (August 1942): 29–54.

Yutang, Lin. "China Sets a Trend: Modern Decoration Owes Much to China." *House and Garden* 92 (July 1942): 10–17.

1943

"Designer Strikes Pay Dirt." *Interiors* 102 (April 1943): 34–35.

"House in the Hills." *California Arts and Architecture* 60 (February 1943): 30–31.

"Seven Commercial Units, Including an Office, Photographer's Studio, and a Variety of Retail Shops, Designed by Architects Douglas Honnold and George Vernon Russell for Hollywood's New 'High Style' Street." *Architectural Forum* 78 (June 1943): 97–101.

1944

"House in West Los Angeles, Calif." *Architectural Forum* 81 (December 1944): 134–35.

1945

"A Genuine Aid to Medical Practice—Efficiency and Psychological Boost for a Physician's Office." *Interiors* 105 (September 1945): 76–77.

1947

"California Scrapbook: West Coast Artists Set Decorative Trends in Motion." *House and Garden* 92 (December 1947): 123–25.

"Studio and Sanctuary." *Interiors* 107 (September 1947): 90–91.

"Taste in Our Time: A Collection of Distinguished American Interiors." *House and Garden* 91 (April 1947): 72–85.

1948

Holme, Rathbone, and Kathleen M. Frost, eds. *Decorative Art: The Studio Yearbook, 1943–1948*. London: The Studio, 1948, 35.

Rosenthal, Rudolph, and Helena L. Ratzka. *The Story of Modern Applied Art*. New York: Harper and Brothers, 1948, 172–73.

"They Design Tomorrow's Traditional." *House Beautiful* 90 (October 1948): 158–63.

1949

Dillard, Katherine. "Overscaling, Naturalism in Evidence." *Dallas Morning News*, 18 January 1949.

Holme, Rathbone, and Kathleen M. Frost, eds. *Decorative Art: The Studio Yearbook, 1949*. London: The Studio, 1949, 28, 32, 36.

"Model Office to Be Shown for Southwest Executives." *Dallas Morning News*, 16 January 1949.

1950

Contemporary Designs by Paul T. Frankl. Johnson Furniture Company: Grand Rapids, Mich., c. 1950.

"Designed by Paul Frankl, This Furniture Can Be Used Interchangeably in All Rooms of the House." *House and Garden* 97 (April 1950): 133–35.

"Frankl Bleaches Cork and Creates Moods." *Interiors* 109 (May 1950): 112–13.

"Furniture News." *Interiors* 109 (March 1950): 123.

Heard, Frances. "American Taste Has an Unmistakable Flavor." *House Beautiful* 92 (May 1950): 140–43.

———. "The Station Wagon Way of Life." *House Beautiful* 92 (June 1950): 103–9.

"Ideas That Work." *House and Garden* 97 (March 1950): 4.

Pepis, Betty. "Modern Moves Ahead." *New York Times*, 26 February 1950.

Schroeder, Francis de N. "Designers Are Important People." *Interiors* 110 (November 1950): 96–99.

"Tables and Racks Provide More Room for Magazines." *Milwaukee Journal*, 7 May 1950.

"Toward Lovelier Homes and Easier Living." *Milwaukee Journal*, 19 March 1950.

1951

"Furniture for the Many." *Grand Rapids (Mich.) Herald*, 18 March 1951.

Hoffman, Marylin. "Paul Frankl Incorporates Stately Elegance in Designs for Modern Furniture." *Christian Science Monitor*, 21 March 1951, 11.

La Barbera, Louis. "Paul T. Frankl: A Chronological Survey of His Works." M.A. thesis, University of Southern California, 1951.

1952

"Fast Selling California Ranch Houses by Cliff May." *House and Home* 2 (October 1952): 90–97.

1953

"Nothing in Europe for Us." *Grand Rapids (Mich.) Herald*, 26 July 1953, 23.

1954

Holm, Grace. "Pace Setter in Good Design: Paul Frankl—Austrian Native Revisits Europe, Analyzes Furniture Design Trend." *The Oregonian*, 20 June 1954, 14.

Holme, Rathbone, and Kathleen Frost, eds. *Decorative Art: Studio Yearbook of Furnishing and Decoration, 1953–1954*. London: The Studio, 1954, 27, 63.

1955

"Reply to a Letter to *Kagu Taimuzu*." *Kagu Taimuzu* (Tokyo), 1 January 1955, 13.

1956

Holme, Rathbone, and Kathleen Frost, eds. *Decorative Art: Studio Yearbook of Furnishing and Decoration, 1955–1956*. London: The Studio, 1956, 54–55.

1957

Holme, Rathbone, and Kathleen Frost, eds. *Decorative Art: Studio Yearbook of Furnishing and Decoration, 1956–1957*. London: The Studio, 1957, 35, 53, 60.

"Paul Frankl . . . Look for a Modern German Comeback." *Marketing* 4 (Fall 1957): 38.

1958

Clark, David E., ed. *Western Ranch Houses by Cliff May*. Menlo Park, Calif.: Lane Books, 1958, 32–39, 69–73.

"Death Takes Designer: Paul T. Frankl, 71, Served Local Firms." *Grand Rapids (Mich.) Press*, 24 March 1958, 21.

"Paul Frankl, Furniture Expert, Dies." *Los Angeles Times*, 22 March 1958.

"Paul T. Frankl." *New York Times*, 22 March 1958.

"Paul T. Frankl, 1887–1958." *Interiors* 117 (April 1958): 156.

1985

Keating, Grace. "Frankl Says 'I Made Junk Sing!' The Career of Paul Theodore Frankl." M.A. thesis, Parsons School of Design / Cooper-Hewitt Museum, 1985.

1989

Boeckl, Matthias. "Paul Theodore Frankl: Wolkenkratzermöbel und Fünfzig-Dollar-Uhren." *Parnass* 4 (1989): 36–40.

1990

Algozer, Sharon Ann. "Paul Theodor Frankl: American Interior and Furniture Designer." M.A. thesis, University of California at Riverside, 1990.

Potter, Durwood. "The Skyscraper Furniture of Paul T. Frankl." M.A. thesis, University of Virginia, 1990.

1991

Keating, Grace. "Practical Solutions: Paul T. Frankl's Approach to Modern Interior Design." In *Merchandising Interior Design: Methods of Furniture Fabrication in America between the World Wars*, ed. Lisa W. Baldauf, 36–47. New Haven: Yale University School of Architecture, 1991.

1995

Boeckl, Matthias. "Die Reform der Form: New Yorker Art Déco-Design am Beispiel von Paul Theodore Frankl and Wolfgang Hoffmann." In *Visionäre und Vertriebene: Österreichische Spuren in der modernen amerikanischen Architektur*, ed. Matthias Boeckl, 86–95, 331. Exhibition catalog. Berlin: Ernst and Sohn, 1995.

Property from Mar-a-Lago, sold by Donald J. Trump. Auction catalog. New York: Christie's, 1995.

1996

Hobik, Claudia. "'Ein Wiener in New York': Paul Theodore Frankl (1886–1958)—Pionier des modernen Designs in den USA—Theorie und Praxis." M.A. thesis, Leopold-Franzens Universität Innsbruck, 1996.

1997

Smith, Mary Peskett. "Frankl, Paul." In *Encyclopedia of Interior Design*, vol. 1, ed. Joanna Banham, 462–64. London: Fitzroy Dearborn, 1997.

2001

Barter, Judith A., and Jennifer M. Downs. "Shaping the Modern: American Decorative Arts at The Art Institute of Chicago, 1917–65." *Museum Studies* 27, no. 2 (2001): 30–32.

2002

Long, Christopher. "The New Interior: Paul T. Frankl in New York, 1914–1917." *Studies in the Decorative Arts* 9 (Spring–Summer 2002): 2–32.

2003

Long, Christopher. "The Business of Beauty: Paul T. Frankl." In *Over the Top: Helene Rubinstein: Extraordinary Style, Beauty, Art, Fashion Design*, ed. Suzanne Slesin, 38–39. New York: Pointed Leaf Press, 2003.

OTHER SOURCES

Adams, Maurice S. R. *Modern Decorative Art*. Philadelphia: J. B. Lippincott, 1930.

Adler, Hazel H. *The New Interior: Modern Decorations for the Modern Home*. New York: Century, 1916.

Albrecht, Donald, Robert Schofeld, and Lindsay Stamm Shapiro. *Russel Wright: Creating American Lifestyle*. Exhibition catalog. New York: Cooper-Hewitt National Design Museum/Harry N. Abrams, 2001.

"All Glass Room." *New York Times*, 8 May 1928.

Alofsin, Anthony. *Frank Lloyd Wright: The Lost Years, 1910–1922*. Chicago: University of Chicago Press, 1993.

———. "Wright, Influence, and the World at Large." In *Frank Lloyd Wright: Europe and Beyond*, ed. Anthony Alofsin, 1–23. Berkeley: University of California Press, 1999.

"American Union of Decorative Artists and Craftsmen." *Creative Art* 6 (March 1930): supplement, 52–53.

Anderson, Stanford. "Deutscher Werkbund—The 1914 Debate: Hermann Muthesius versus Henry van de Velde." In *Companion to Contemporary Architectural Thought*, ed. Ben Farmer and Hentie Louw, 462–67. London: Routledge, 1993.

———. "The Legacy of German Neoclassicism and Biedermeier: Behrens, Tessenow, Loos, and Mies." *Assemblage* 15 (August 1991): 63–87.

Annual of American Art, vol. 30. Washington, D.C.: American Federation of Arts, 1933.

Appel, Erika. "Vom Oswaldhof zum Dr. Karl Renner-Institut." *Meiding—Blätter des Bezirksmusems* 27 (1991): 6–40.

The Architect and the Industrial Arts: An Exhibition of Contemporary American Design. Exhibition catalog. New York: The Metropolitan Museum of Art, 1929.

"The Architect and the Industrial Arts: An Exhibition of Contemporary American Design, Metropolitan Museum of Art." *American Magazine of Art* 20 (April 1929): 201–12.

Aronson, Arnold, ed. *Architect of Dreams: The Theatrical Vision of Joseph Urban*. Exhibition catalog. New York: Miriam and Ira D. Wallach Art Gallery, Columbia University, 2000.

Asenbaum, Paul, Stefan Asenbaum, and Christian Witt-Dörring, eds. *Moderne Vergangenheit: Wien 1800–1900*. Exhibition catalog. Vienna: Künstlerhaus, 1981.

"AUDAC News: Protection of Design." *Creative Art* 6 (April 1930): supplement, 76–77.

"The Austrian Exhibition." *Bulletin of the Art Institute of Chicago* 16, no. 6 (November 1922): 84–85.

Bab, Julius, and Willi Handel. *Wien und Berlin: Vergleichendes zur Kulturgeschichte der beiden Hauptstädte Mitteleuropas*. Berlin: Osterheld, 1918.

Bach, Richard F. "A Note on Producers of Industrial Art and Their Relation to the Public." *Arts and Decoration* 18 (December 1922): 82, 84, 96.

———. "Styles A-Borning: Musings on Contemporary Industrial Art and Decoration." *Creative Art* 2 (June 1928): 36–40.

———. "What Is the Matter with Our Industrial Art?" *Arts and Decoration* 18 (January 1923): 14, 15, 46, 49.

Baldauf, Lisa W., ed. *Merchandising Interior Design: Methods of Furniture Fabrication in America between the World Wars*. New Haven: Yale University School of Architecture, 1991.

Barron, Stephanie, Sheri Bernstein, and Ilene Susan Fort, eds. *Made in California: Art, Image, and Identity,*

1900—2000. Exhibition catalog. Berkeley: University of California Press, 2000.

Bauer, Helmut, and Elisabeth Tworek, eds. *Schwabing, Kunst und Leben um 1900: Essays*. Munich: Münchner Stadtmuseum, 1998.

Bauten und Entwürfe von Carl König herausgegeben von seinen Schülern. Vienna: Gerlach and Wiedling, [1910].

Benedict, Burton, ed. *The Anthropology of World's Fairs: San Francisco's Panama Pacific International Exposition of 1915*. Exhibition catalog. Berkeley: The Lowie Museum of Anthropology/London: Scolar Press, 1983.

Bent, Dorothy. "Small Tables Essential in Modern Decoration." *Arts and Decoration* 27 (August 1927): 47—49, 76.

Benton, Charlotte, Tim Benton, and Ghislaine Wood, eds. *Art Deco, 1910—1939*. Exhibition catalog. Boston: Bulfinch Press, 2003.

Bernstorff, Johann Heinrich von. *The Memoirs of Count Bernstorff*. London: William Heinemann, 1936.

———. *My Three Years in America*. New York: Charles Scribner's Sons, 1920.

Birnbaum, Martin. *Introductions: Painters, Sculptors, and Graphic Artists*. New York: Frederic Fairchild Sherman, 1919.

Boeckl, Matthias, ed. *Visionäre und Vertriebene: Österreichische Spuren in der modernen amerikanischen Architektur*. Exhibition catalog. Berlin: Ernst and Sohn, 1995.

Bogner, Dieter, ed. *Friedrich Kiesler: Architekt—Maler—Bildhauer, 1890—1965*. Exhibition catalog. Vienna: Museum des 20. Jahrhunderts/Löcker, 1988.

Bonney, Claire. "Le Service Bonney: Fotojournalismus in 'Paris Moderne', 1925—1935." *Archithese* 24 (July—August 1994): 54—56.

———. *Thérèse Bonney: The Architectural Photographs*. Ph.D. dissertation, Universität Zürich, 1995.

Bott, Gerhard, ed. *Sitz-Gelegenheiten: Bugholz- und Stahlrohrmöbel von Thonet*. Exhibition catalog. Nuremberg: Germanisches Nationalmuseum, 1989.

Bredt, Ernst Wilhelm. "Bruno Paul—Biedermeier—Empire." *Dekorative Kunst* 8 (March 1905): 217—29.

Bricker, David. "Cliff May and the California Ranch House after 1945." M.A. thesis, University of California, Santa Barbara, 1983.

Brigham, Louise. *Box Furniture: How to Make a Hundred Useful Articles for the Home*. New York: Century, 1910.

Broussard, Juliette. "Art Moderne." *Talk of the Town* 6 (April 1930): 19—22.

Brown, Ashley. "Ilonka Karasz: Rediscovering a Modernist Pioneer." *Studies in the Decorative Arts* 8 (Fall—Winter 2000—2001): 69—91.

Buddensieg, Tilmann, ed. *Berlin 1900—1933: Architecture and Design*. Exhibition catalog. New York: Cooper-Hewitt Museum/Berlin: Gebr. Mann, 1987.

Burckhardt, Lucius, ed. *The Werkbund: Studies in the History and Ideology of the Deutscher Werkbund, 1907—1933*. London: The Design Council, 1980.

Campbell, Joan. *The German Werkbund: The Politics of Reform in the Applied Arts*. Princeton: Princeton University Press, 1978.

Candee, Helen Churchill. *Decorative Styles and Periods in the Home*. New York: Frederick A. Stokes, 1906.

Carron, Christian G. *Grand Rapids Furniture: The Story of America's Furniture City*. Grand Rapids, Mich.: The Public Museum of Grand Rapids, 1998.

Carter, Randolph, and Robert Reed Cole. *Joseph Urban: Architecture, Theater, Opera, Film*. New York: Abbeville Press, 1992.

Catalogue of the Exposition of Art in Trade at Macy's, May 2 to May 7, 1927. New York: R. H. Macy, 1927.

Cheney, Sheldon, and Martha Candler Cheney. *Art and the Machine: An Account of Industrial Design in Twentieth-Century America*. New York: Whittlesey House, 1936.

Clark, Robert Judson. "The German Return to Classicism after Jugendstil." *Journal of the Society of Architectural Historians* 29 (October 1970): 273.

Cleary, Richard. *Merchant Prince and Master Builder: Edgar J. Kaufmann and Frank Lloyd Wright*. Exhibition catalog. Pittsburgh: Heinz Architectural Center, Carnegie Museum of Art, in association with University of Washington Press, 1999.

Clute, Eugene. *The Treatment of Interiors*. New York: Pencil Point Press, 1926.

"Colors and Forms from the Chinese." *Arts and Decoration* 41 (May 1934): 4–7.

Contempora Exposition of Art and Industry. Exhibition catalog. New York: Contempora, 1929.

"Contemporary Art in Current Exhibitions." *Good Furniture Magazine* 32 (May 1929): 241–48.

Corn, Wanda M. *The Great American Thing: Modern Art and National Identity, 1915–1935*. Berkeley: University of California Press, 1999.

Cram, Ralph Adams. "Will This Modernism Last?" *House Beautiful* 65 (January 1929): 45, 88.

Davies, Karen. *At Home in Manhattan: Modern Decorative Arts, 1925 to the Depression*. Exhibition catalog. New Haven: Yale University Press, 1983.

"Decorated Interiors in Retail Stores." *Good Furniture Magazine* 29 (June 1927): 326.

"Decorative Artists Form Union." *Architectural Record* 64 (August 1928): 164.

Department of Overseas Trade. *Reports on the Present Position and Tendencies of the Industrial Arts as Indicated at the International Exhibition of Modern Decorative and Industrial Arts, Paris, 1925*. Harrow, England: HMSO, 1927.

"Designers—European and American." *Good Furniture Magazine* 32 (April 1929): 167, 172.

Deutscher Werkbund. *Die Kunst in Industrie und Handel: Jahrbuch des Deutschen Werkbundes, 1913*. Jena: Eugen Diederichs, 1914.

Deutsches Kunstgewerbe. Exhibition catalog. St. Louis: City Art Museum of St. Louis, 1912.

Duncan, Alastair. *American Art Deco*. New York: Harry N. Abrams, 1986.

——. *Art Deco Furniture*. New York: Holt, Rinehart and Winston, 1984.

——. *The Encyclopedia of Art Deco: An Illustrated Guide to a Decorative Style from 1920 to 1939*. New York: E. P. Dutton, 1988.

Eidelberg, Martin. *Eva Zeisel: Designer for Industry*. Exhibition catalog. Montreal: Le Château Dufresne, Musée des Arts Décoratifs de Montréal / Chicago: University of Chicago Press, 1984.

Eisler, Max, ed. *Österreichische Werkkultur*. Vienna: Anton Schroll, 1916.

Evers, Alf. *Woodstock: History of an American Town*. Woodstock, N.Y.: Overlook Press, 1988.

"Exhibit of American Designers' Gallery: An Ambitious Program in Art Moderne." *Good Furniture Magazine* 32 (January 1929): 40–45.

"Exhibition Brings Viennese Art Here." *New York Times*, 25 June 1922.

An Exhibition of Modern French Decorative Art. Exhibition catalog. New York: Lord and Taylor, 1928.

"Exhibitions of Modern Designs." *Good Furniture Magazine* 21 (November 1923): 204–5.

Exposition internationale des arts décoratifs et industriels modernes. Exhibition catalog. Paris: Larousse, 1925.

"Exposition of Modern French Decorative Art." *American Architect* 133 (5 March 1928): 317–22.

Faville, William B. "Phases of Panama-Pacific International Exposition Architecture." *American Architect* 107 (6 January 1915): 5–10, and plates.

Fawcett, Waldon. "The Future of the Art-in-Trade-Exposition." *Good Furniture Magazine* 31 (November 1928): 285–86.

——. "Stop Thief! Designs Are Entailed! Why Congress Must Enact a New Law to Prevent the Theft of American Industrial Art Ideas." *Arts and Decoration* 18 (December 1922): 94.

"Features of the American Designers' Gallery Exhibition." *Metal Arts* 1 (December 1928): 81–84, 119.

Folnesics, Joseph, ed. *Innenräume und Hausrat der Empire- und Biedermeierzeit in Österreich-Ungarn*. Vienna: Anton Schroll, 1903.

Ford, James L. "The Washington Square Players." *Vanity Fair* 4 (April 1915): 33.

Freiday, Dean. "Modern Design at the Newark Museum: A Survey." *The Museum* 4 (Winter–Spring 1952): 17.

Friedman, Marilyn F. *Selling Good Design: Promoting the Early Modern Interior*. New York: Rizzoli, 2003.

——. "The United States and the 1925 Paris Exposition: Opportunity Lost and Found." *Studies in the Decorative Arts* 13 (Fall–Winter 2005–6): 94–119.

Frohne, Henry W. "Is Modernism a Passing Fancy or a Fact?" *Good Furniture Magazine* 30 (March 1928): 111.

Furniture from America's First Modernistic House: The de Lorenzo Collection. Auction catalog. New York: Christie's, 1980.

G. S. L. [?]. "A Millionaire of Imagination and Refreshing Stream of Art and Craft." *Christian Science Monitor*, 24 July 1922.

Gay, Peter. *Freud: A Life for Our Time.* New York: W. W. Norton, 1988.

———. *Weimar Culture: The Insider as Outsider.* New York: Harper and Row, 1968.

Gebhard, David. "Modern Architecture." *Journal of the Society of Architectural Historians* 31 (October 1972): 230–31.

———. *Tulsa Art Deco: An Architectural Era, 1925–1942.* Tulsa, Okla.: Junior League of Tulsa, 1988.

Gebhard, David, and Harriette Von Breton. *Kem Weber: The Moderne in Southern California, 1920–1941.* Exhibition catalog. Santa Barbara: University of California, Santa Barbara, 1969.

———. *L.A. in the Thirties, 1931–1941.* Exhibition catalog. Layton, Utah: Peregrine Smith, 1975.

Gilman, Roger. "Is This Modernistic Furniture More Than a Fad?" *House Beautiful* 65 (February 1929): 162, 198.

Glassgold, C. Adolph. "AUDAC Exhibit of Modern Industrial and Decorative Art at the Brooklyn Museum." *Creative Art* 8 (June 1931): 436–40.

———. "Decorative Art Notes." *The Arts* 13 (May 1928): 296–301.

———. "The Decorative Arts." *The Arts* 14 (October 1928): 214–17.

———. "The Decorative Arts." *The Arts* 14 (November 1928): 279–83.

———. "The Decorative Arts." *The Arts* 14 (December 1928): 339–43, 361–63.

———. "Modern American Industrial Design." *Arts and Decoration* 35 (July 1931): 30–31, 87.

———. "The Modern Note in Decorative Arts, Part 1." *The Arts* 13 (March 1928): 153–67.

Greenberg, Cara. *Mid-Century Modern: Furniture of the 1950s.* New York: Harmony Books, 1984.

Haddon, Rawson W. "Some Recent Interiors, Art Galleries, and Decorator's Studios." *Architecture* 36 (August 1917): 157–62.

Hamlin, Elizabeth. "The AUDAC Exhibition." *Brooklyn Museum Quarterly* 18 (July 1931): 93–97.

Hancock, Ralph. *Fabulous Boulevard.* New York: Funk and Wagnalls, 1949.

Hanks, David A., with Jennifer Toher. *Donald Deskey: Decorative Designs and Interiors.* New York: E. P. Dutton, 1987.

Hardberger, Linda. *The New Stagecraft: Setting an American Style, 1915–1949.* Exhibition catalog. San Antonio: Marion Koogler McNay Art Museum, 1997.

Harris, William Laurel. "Back to Duncan Phyfe—or Forward to Art Nouveau?" *Good Furniture Magazine* 19 (December 1922): 257–59.

Harrod, W. Owen. *Bruno Paul: The Life and Work of a Pragmatic Modernist.* Stuttgart: Edition Axel Menges, 2005.

Hegger, Grace. "Beauty Bought and Paid For." *Vogue*, 15 November 1915, 68, 116.

Heller, Adele, and Lois Rudnick, eds. *1915, The Cultural Moment: The New Politics, the New Woman, the New Psychology, the New Art and the New Theatre in America.* New Brunswick, N.J.: Rutgers University Press, 1991.

Hennessey, William J. *Russel Wright: American Designer.* Cambridge, Mass.: MIT Press, 1983.

Herts, B. Russell. "What Is Modern Decoration?" *House and Garden* 31 (April 1917): 19–21, 92, 94.

Heskett, John. *German Design, 1870–1918.* New York: Taplinger, 1986.

Hillier, Bevis. *Art Deco.* Exhibition catalog. Minneapolis: The Minneapolis Institute of Arts, 1971.

Hines, Thomas S. *Richard Neutra and the Search for Modern Architecture: A Biography and History.* New York: Oxford University Press, 1982.

———. "Wilshire Boulevard, Los Angeles, California." In *The Grand American Avenue, 1850–1920,* ed. Jan Cigliano and Sarah Bradford Landau, 307–63. San Francisco: Pomegranate, 1994.

Hitchcock, Henry-Russell, Jr. "Some American Interiors in the Modern Style." *Architectural Record* 64 (September 1928): 235–43.

Hobbs, Douglass B. "Aluminum—A Decorative Metal." *Good Furniture and Decoration* 35 (August 1930): 88–94.

Holloway, Edward Stratton. *The Practical Book of Furnishing the Small House and Apartment*. Philadelphia: J. B. Lippincott, 1922.

Hörmann, Marianne. *Vally Wieselthier, 1895–1945: Wien—Paris—New York, Keramik—Skulptur—Design der zwanziger und dreißiger Jahre*. Vienna: Böhlau, 1999.

Hostache, Ellow H. "Reflections on the Exposition des Arts Décoratifs." *Architectural Forum* 44 (January 1926): 11–16.

Hubert, Christian, and Lindsay Stamm Shapiro. *William Lescaze*. Exhibition catalog. New York: Institute for Architecture and Urban Studies/Rizzoli, 1982.

Imperial Royal Ministry for Public Instruction. *Exhibition of Professional Schools of Arts and Crafts, Universal Exhibition St. Louis 1904*. Exhibition catalog. Vienna: Verlag des k. k. Ministeriums, 1904.

Innes, Christopher. *Designing Modern America: Broadway to Main Street*. New Haven: Yale University Press, 2005.

An International Exposition of Art in Industry from May 14 to May 26, 1928 at Macy's. New York: R. H. Macy, 1928.

"The International Exposition of Modern Decorative and Industrial Art." *Good Furniture Magazine* 25 (September 1925): 121.

Jeanneret, Charles-Édouard [Le Corbusier]. *Étude sur le mouvement d'Art Décoratif en Allemagne*. La Chaux-de-Fonds, Switzerland: Haefeli, 1912.

Johnson, J. Stewart. *American Modern, 1925–1940: Design for a New Age*. Exhibition catalog. New York: The Metropolitan Museum of Art/Harry N. Abrams, 2000.

Johnson, Philip. *Machine Art, March 6 to April 30, 1934*. Exhibition catalog. New York: Museum of Modern Art, 1934; repr. New York: Arno Press, 1969.

Junghanns, Kurt. *Der Deutsche Werkbund: Sein erstes Jahrzehnt*. Berlin: Henschelverlag Kunst und Gesellschaft, 1982.

Kahle, Katharine Morrison. *Modern French Decoration*. New York: G. P. Putnam's Sons, 1930.

Kallir, Jane. *Viennese Design and the Wiener Werkstätte*. New York: George Braziller, 1986.

Kaplan, Wendy, ed. *"The Art That Is Life": The Arts and Crafts Movement in America, 1875–1920*. Exhibition catalog. Boston: Museum of Fine Arts/Bulfinch Press, 1987.

——, ed. *Designing Modernity: The Arts of Reform and Persuasion, 1885–1945*. Exhibition catalog. Miami Beach: Wolfsonian, 1995.

Kardon, Janet, ed. *Craft in the Machine Age, 1920–45*. Vol. 3 of *The History of Twentieth-Century American Craft*. Exhibition catalog. New York: American Craft Museum/Harry N. Abrams, 1995.

——, ed. *The Ideal Home, 1900–1920*. Vol. 2 of *The History of Twentieth-Century American Craft*. Exhibition catalog. New York: American Craft Museum/Harry N. Abrams, 1993.

Karlstrom, Paul J., and Susan Ehrlich, eds. *Turning the Tide: Early Los Angeles Modernists, 1920–1956*. Exhibition catalog. Santa Barbara, Calif.: Santa Barbara Museum of Art, 1990.

Keyes, Homer Eaton. "Is This Modernistic Furniture More Than a Fad?" *House Beautiful* 65 (February 1929): 163, 198, 200.

Kiesler, Frederick. *Contemporary Art Applied to the Store and Its Display*. New York: Brentano's, 1930.

Kirkham, Pat, ed. *Women Designers in the United States, 1900–2000: Diversity and Difference*. Exhibition catalog. New York: Bard Graduate Center/New Haven: Yale University Press, 2000.

Kleihues, Josef Paul, and Christina Rathgeber, eds. *Berlin/New York—Like and Unlike: Essays on Architecture and Art from 1870 to the Present*. New York: Rizzoli, 1993.

Kolosek, Lisa Schlansker. *The Invention of Chic: Thérèse Bonney and Paris Moderne*. London: Thames and Hudson, 2002.

Königliche Technische Hochschule zu Berlin. *Program für das Studienjahr 1905–1906*. Berlin, 1905.

Kouwenhoven, John. *Made in America: The Arts in Modern Civilization*. Garden City, N.Y.: Doubleday, 1948.

Kristan, Markus. *Carl König, 1841–1915: Ein neubarocker Großstadtarchitekt in Wien*. Exhibition catalog. Jüdisches Museum der Stadt Wien. Vienna, 1999.

————. *Joseph Urban. Die Wiener Jahre des Jugendstilarchitekten und Illustrators, 1872–1911*. Vienna: Böhlau, 2000.

Lang, Otto. *A Bird of Passage: The Story of My Life*. Seattle: Sky House, 1994.

Langer, Lawrence. *The Magic Curtain*. New York: E. P. Dutton, 1951.

Lanmon, Lorraine Welling. *William Lescaze, Architect*. Philadelphia: Art Alliance Press, 1987.

"The Last Word in Interiors: A Modern Library." *New York Times*, 8 May 1927.

Leach, William. *Land of Desire: Merchants, Power, and the Rise of a New American Culture*. New York: Pantheon Books, 1993.

Lehmanns Allgemeiner Wohnungsanzeiger nebst Handels- und Gewerbe Adreßbuch für die k. u. k. Reichs- Haupt- und Residenzstadt und Umgebung. Vienna, 1886–1910.

Lektionskatalog, Studienpläne und Personalstand der Technischen Hochschule in Wien für das Studienjahr 1904–1905. Vienna, 1904.

Leonard, R. L., and C. A. Glassgold, eds. *Annual of American Design*. New York: Ives Washburn, 1930. Reprinted as *Modern American Design*, 1933.

————. *Modern American Design by the American Union of Decorative Artists and Craftsmen*. New York: American Union of Decorative Artists and Craftsmen, 1928.

Lewis, Alfred Allan, and Constance Woodworth. *Miss Elizabeth Arden*. New York: Coward, McCann and Geoghegan, 1972.

Lichtenstein, Claude. *O. R. Salvisberg: Die andere Moderne*. Zurich: Institut für Geschichte und Theorie der Architektur, Eidgenössische Technische Hochschule, 1995.

Lloyd, David. "A Workshop Background by Urban, with Reflections on the Viennese Revolt." *New York Evening Post*, 17 June 1922.

Loewy, Raymond, and Peter Mayer. *Industrial Design: Raymond Loewy*. Woodstock, N.Y.: Overlook Press, 1979.

Long, Christopher. "An Alternative Path to Modernism: Carl König and Architectural Education at the Vienna Technische Hochschule, 1890–1913." *Journal of Architectural Education* 55 (September 2001): 21–30.

————. *Josef Frank: Life and Work*. Chicago: University of Chicago Press, 2002.

————. "'A Symptom of the Werkbund': The Spring 1912 Exhibition at the Austrian Museum for Art and Industry, Vienna." *Studies in the Decorative Arts* 7 (Spring–Summer 2000): 91–121.

Lorne, Francis. "The New Architecture of a Flamboyant Civilization: The Skyscraper as an Expression of America's Commercial Triumph." *Arts and Decoration* 24 (November 1925): 58–59, 90.

Lucie-Smith, Edward. *A History of Industrial Design*. New York: D. Van Nostrand Reinhold, 1983.

Lux, Joseph August. "Biedermeier als Erzieher." *Hohe Warte* 1 (1904–5): 145–55.

————. *Ingenieur-Ästhetik*. Munich: G. Lammers, 1910.

————. *Das neue Kunstgewerbe in Deutschland*. Leipzig: Klinkhardt and Biermann, 1908.

MacGowan, Kenneth. "Profile: Caprice Viennois." *New Yorker*, 25 June 1927, 21–23.

Machine-Age Exposition. Exhibition catalog. New York: Little Review, 1927.

Makela, Maria. *The Munich Secession: Art and Artists in Turn-of-the-Century Munich*. Princeton: Princeton University Press, 1990.

Mang, Karl, ed. *Kommunaler Wohnbau in Wien: Aufbruch 1923–1934 Ausstrahlung*. Vienna: Presse- und Informationsdienst der Stadt Wien, 1977.

Marchand, Roland. *Advertising and the American Dream: Making Way for Modernity, 1920–1940*. Berkeley: University of California Press, 1985.

Marke, G. Mortimer. "The Informal Note in Summer Furniture." *Arts and Decoration* 5 (April 1915): 232–33.

Marsh, Janet Howison. "Amusing French Furniture in l'Art Moderne." *Arts and Decoration* 27 (May 1927): 74, 76, 91.

Massey, Anne. *Interior Design of the Twentieth Century*. London: Thames and Hudson, 1990.

Matis, Herbert, and Dieter Stiefel. *Mit der vereinigten Kraft des Capitals, des Credits und der Technik: Die Geschichte des österreichischen Bauwesens am Beispiel der Allgemeinen Baugesellschaft A. Porr AG*. Vienna: Böhlau, 1994.

Mayreder, Karl. *Zu Karl Königs siebzigstem Geburtstag*. Vienna: Selbstverlag des Karl König-Komitees, 1912.

McCoy, Esther. *Modern California Houses*. New York: Reinhold, 1962.

McGregor, Donald. "AUDAC in Brooklyn: A Great Museum Host to Moderns." *Good Furniture and Decoration* 36 (June 1931): 322–25.

Mebes, Paul, ed. *Um 1800: Architektur und Handwerk im letzten Jahrhundert ihrer traditionellen Entwicklung*. 2 vols. Munich: F. Bruckmann A.-G., 1908.

Meikle, Jeffrey L. *Twentieth Century Limited: Industrial Design in America, 1925–1939*. Philadelphia: Temple University Press, 1979.

The Metropolitan Museum of Art. *The Architect and the Industrial Arts: An Exhibition of Contemporary American Design*. New York: The Metropolitan Museum of Art, 1929.

"Metropolitan Museum of Art—Exhibition of Contemporary American Industrial Art 1934." *Architectural Forum* 61 (December 1934): 410–20.

"Modern Art? Without Doubt." *Decorative Furnisher* 54 (June 1928): 97.

"Modern Art in a Department Store: Wanamaker's Furnished Rooms Arouse Keen Interest." *Good Furniture Magazine* 30 (January 1928): 35.

Modern Art Makes Its Bow in a Commercial Manner." *Decorative Furnisher* 53 (December 1927): 101.

"'Modern' Interior Decoration in American Homes by E. H. and G. G. Aschermann [*sic*]." *International Studio* 53 (October 1914): 81–85.

"Modern Interiors: A Portfolio." *Arts and Decoration* 39 (September 1933): 19–47.

"Modernists' Dilemma: A Quest for Contemporary Furniture Puts You at the Mercy of Your Own Judgment." *Arts and Decoration* 41 (June 1934): 18–23.

"Mr. and Mrs. Aschermann's [*sic*] Studio Decorations." *New York Times*, 16 April 1914.

Mumford, Lewis. "Modernism for Sale." *American Mercury* 16 (April 1929): 353–55.

Museum of Modern Art. *Machine Art*. Exhibition catalog. New York: Harry N. Abrams, 1934.

Muthesius, Hermann. *Die Werkbund-Arbeit der Zukunft und Aussprache darüber…* Jena: Eugen Diederichs, 1914.

Naylor, Blanche. "American Design Progress." *Design* 33 (September 1931): 82–89.

——. "Decorative Arts Show Stresses Straight Simplicity." *Design* 35 (May 1933): 7, 28.

——. "National Alliance of Art and Industry Shows New Design Trends." *Design* 35 (May 1934): 4–5.

Neiß, Herta. *100 Jahre Wiener Werkstätte: Mythos und ökonomische Realität*. Vienna: Böhlau, 2004.

"New Models in Fascinating Metal Furniture." *Arts and Decoration* 37 (June 1932): 18–19.

"The 'New Style' Popular in France." *Good Furniture Magazine* 21 (November 1923): 204–5.

"A New York Decorator's Opinion of the Paris Exposition." *Good Furniture Magazine* 25 (November 1925): 260.

Nordvold, Robert O. "Showcase for the New Stagecraft: The Scenic Designs of the Washington Square Players and the Theatre Guild, 1915–1929." Ph.D. dissertation, Indiana University, 1973.

"On Her Dressing Table." *Vogue*, 1 May 1915, 82, 84.

"On the Theme of Supreme Modern Comfort." *Arts and Decoration* 40 (November 1933): 16–17.

"1,000 Viennese Artists Show Their Work." *New York Times*, 14 June 1922.

Osborn, Max. "Das Hohenzollern-Kunstgewerbehaus in Berlin." *Innen-Dekoration* 26 (1915): 55–84.

"Otto Rudolf Salvisberg, 1882–1940." *Das Werk* 11 (1941): 289–306.

"Otto Rudolf Salvisberg, 1882–1940." *Werk-Architese* 10 (1977): 4–54.

Owen, Bobbi. *Scenic Design on Broadway: Designers and Their Credits, 1915–1990*. New York: Greenwood Press, 1991.

Park, Edwin Avery. *New Backgrounds for a New Age*. New York: Harcourt, Brace, 1927.

Patterson, Augusta Owen. "What Is Happening to Modern?" *House Beautiful* 79 (September 1937): 37–39, 106.

Phillips, Lisa, ed. *Frederick Kiesler*. Exhibition catalog. New York: Whitney Museum of American Art / W. W. Norton, 1989.

Pietsch, Ludwig. "Das Hohenzollern-Kunstgewerbehaus—Berlin: Aus Anlaß seines 25-jährigen Bestehens." *Deutsche Kunst und Dekoration* 15 (1904–5): 169–76.

"Poiret, Interpreter of His Own Age." *Arts and Decoration* 14 (March 1921): 380.

Posch, Wilfried. "Die Österreichische Werkbundbewegung, 1907–1912." In *Geistiges Leben im Österreich der Ersten Republik*, ed. Isabella Ackerl and Rudolf Neck, 279–312. Vienna: Verlag für Geschichte und Politik, 1986.

Pozzetto, Marco. "Karl König und die Architektur der Wiener Technischen Hochschule." In *Wien um 1900: Kunst und Kultur*, ed. Maria Auböck and Maria Marchetti, 305–6. Exhibition catalog. Vienna: Christian Brandstetter, 1985.

Price, C. Matlack. "The Gothic Style of Interior Decoration: A Question of Non-Adaptability." *Arts and Decoration* 5 (May 1915): 277–78.

———. "Secessionist Architecture in America: Departures from Academic Traditions of Design." *Arts and Decoration* 3 (December 1912): 51–53.

———. "Some Recent Decorative Fabrics." *Arts and Decoration* 5 (September 1915): 440.

———. "Your Home and Its Decoration." *Arts and Decoration* 5 (June 1915): 372.

Price, Renée, ed., with Pamela Kort and Leslie Topp. *New Worlds: German and Austrian Art, 1890–1940*. Exhibition catalog. New York: Neue Galerie/Cologne: DuMont, 2001.

"The Profession and Business of Decorating: The Status of the Profession as Advanced by the Society of Interior Decorators." *Arts and Decoration* 13 (May 1920): 26, 62.

Pulos, Arthur J. *American Design Ethic: A History of Industrial Design to 1940*. Cambridge, Mass.: MIT Press, 1983.

———. "The Restless Genius of Norman Bel Geddes." *Architectural Forum* 133 (January 1970): 46–51.

Purdy, W. Frank. "America Needs Co-operation in Industrial Art: A National School of Design Should Be Developed." *Arts and Decoration* 14 (January 1921): 208, 250, 252.

———. "The Taste of the American People: And the Present Industro-Art Problem in the United States." *Arts and Decoration* 14 (November 1920): 38, 64, 66.

"Queer Bolshevist Art in Berlin." *Arts and Decoration* 18 (April 1923): 87.

"R. H. Macy Hold an Exhibition of Modern Art." *Decorative Furnisher* 54 (June 1928): 95, 114.

Randole, Leo. "The Evolution of Furniture in France: Ruhlmann—Master Furniture Designer." *Arts and Decoration* 15 (August 1921): 226–27.

Read, Helen Appleton. "Modern Decorative Art." *The Arts* 13 (January 1928): 57.

———. "Modern Decorative Art." *The Arts* 13 (February 1928): 120–21.

Richards, Charles R. *Art in Industry*. New York: Macmillan, 1922.

———. *Industrial Art and the Museum*. New York: Macmillan, 1927.

———. "Sane and Insane Modernism in Furniture." *Good Furniture Magazine* 32 (January 1929): 8–14.

Richards, Charles R., Henry Creange, and Frank Grant Holmes. *Report of the Commission Appointed by the Secretary of Commerce to Visit and Report upon the International Exposition of Modern Decorative and Industrial Art in Paris, 1925*. Washington, D.C.: Government Printing Office, 1926.

Roberts, Mary Fanton [Giles Edgerton, pseud.]. "Beauty Combined with Convenience in Some Modernistic Rooms: In a Recent Exhibition of the American Designer's Gallery, the American Point of View toward This Movement Was Brought Out in Interesting Furniture, Fittings and Room Decoration." *Arts and Decoration* 30 (February 1929): 72–73, 112.

———. "Curious and Brilliant New Arts and Crafts from Vienna." *Vogue*, 15 October 1922, 81, 104.

———. "Modernistic Movement in Arts and Crafts." *Arts and Decoration* 28 (April 1928): 60–61, 101.

Robinson, Cervin, and Rosemarie Haag Bletter. *Skyscraper Style: Art Deco New York*. New York: Oxford University Press, 1975.

Rosenthal, Rudolph. "Contemporary Art in Retrospect." *Parnassus* 7 (December 1935): 172–73.

Rosenthal, Rudolph, and Helena L. Ratzka. *The Story of Modern Applied Art*. New York: Harper and Brothers, 1948.

Rubinstein, Helena. *My Life for Beauty*. New York: Simon and Schuster, 1964.

Rürup, Reinhard, ed. *Wissenschaft und Gesellschaft: Beiträge zur Geschichte der Technischen Universität Berlin, 1879–1979*. Berlin: Springer, 1979.

Sanford, Nellie C. "An International Exhibit of Modern Art: Macy's of New York Sponsored Forward-Looking Event." *Good Furniture Magazine* 31 (July 1928): 15–20.

Sayer, Oliver M. *Our American Theater*. New York: Brentano's, 1923.

Scheffler, Karl. *Die Architektur der Großstadt*. Berlin: Cassirer, 1913.

———. *Berlin, ein Schicksalstadt*. Berlin: E. Reiss, 1910.

Schleier, Merrill. *The Skyscraper in American Art, 1890–1931*. New York: Da Capo, 1986.

Schoen, Eugene. "The Design of Modern Interiors." *Creative Art* 2 (May 1928): xl–xliii.

Schönberger, Angela, ed. *Raymond Loewy: Pioneer of American Industrial Design*. Munich: Prestel-Verlag, 1990.

Schwartz, Frederic J. *The Werkbund: Design Theory and Mass Culture before the First World War*. New Haven: Yale University Press, 1996.

Schwarz, Karl, ed. *Von der Bauakademie zur Technischen Universität: 200 Jahre Forschung und Lehre*. Berlin, 1999.

———, ed. *Von der Bauakademie zur Technischen Universität Berlin: Geschichte und Zukunft, 1799–1999*. Exhibition catalog. Berlin: Ernst and Sohn, 2000.

Schweiger, Werner J. *Wiener Werkstätte: Design in Vienna, 1903–1932*. New York: Abbeville Press, 1984.

"Seen and Heard in the Trade." *Good Furniture and Decoration* 34 (March 1930): 167.

"Seen in New York: New Art and the Paris Exposition." *Good Furniture Magazine* 25 (September 1925): 135–36.

"Seen in New York: The Modern Art Shop of Joseph Urban." *Good Furniture Magazine* 19 (August 1922): 98–99.

Sekler, Eduard F. *Josef Hoffmann: The Architectural Work*. Princeton, N.J.: Princeton University Press, 1985.

Seldes, Gilbert, and Henry Dreyfus. "Norman Bel Geddes, 1893–1958." *Industrial Design* 5 (June 1958): 48–51.

A Selected Collection of Objects from the International Exposition of Modern Decorative and Industrial Art, Paris 1925. Exhibition catalog. New York: American Association of Museums, 1926.

"Shall We Succumb to Modern Art?" *Decorative Furnisher* 42 (September 1922): 68–69.

Shifman, Barry. "Design for Industry: The 'German Applied Arts' Exhibition in the United States, 1912–13." *Journal of the Decorative Arts Society* 22 (1998): 19–31.

Shipp, Steve. *American Art Colonies, 1850–1930: A Historical Guide to America's Original Art Colonies and Their Artists*. Westport, Conn.: Greenwood Press, 1996.

Simonson, Lee. "Modern Furniture in the Department Store." *Creative Art* 3 (November 1928): xvi–xxi.

"Six Rooms on View." *Good Furniture Magazine* 19 (August 1922): 98–99.

Skillings, W. E. "Is the 'Atmosphere' Window an Economic Waste?" *Advertising and Selling* 11 (16 May 1928): 34.

Smith, Elizabeth A. T. "Arts and Architecture and the Los Angeles Vanguard." In *Blueprints for Modern Living: History and Legacy of the Case Study Houses*, ed. Elizabeth A. T. Smith, 145–65. Exhibition catalog. Cambridge, Mass.: MIT Press, 1989.

Solon, Leon V. "The Viennese Method for Artistic Display: New York Galleries of the Wiener-Werkstaette of America." *Architectural Record* 53 (March 1923): 266–71.

"Some Christmas Cards of Artistic Merit." *Arts and Decoration* 18 (December 1922): 29.

Spewack, Samuel. *The Skyscraper Murder*. New York: Macauley, 1928.

Sprackling, Helen. "An Apartment in the Twentieth-Century Manner." *House Beautiful* 68 (November 1930): 484–86.

Staggs-Flinchum, Janis. "A Glimpse into the Showroom of the Wiener Werkstätte of America, 1922–23." In *The International Twentieth Century Arts Fair*, 26–35. Exhibition catalog. New York: Haughton's, 1999.

Starr, Kevin. *The Dream Endures: California Enters the 1940s*. New York: Oxford University Press, 1997.

———. *Endangered Dreams and the Great Depression in California*. New York: Oxford University Press, 1996.

Stern, Robert A. M., Gregory Gilmartin, and Thomas Mellins. *New York 1930: Architecture and Urbanism between the Two World Wars*. New York: Rizzoli, 1987.

Storey, Walter Rendell. "American Furniture Design To-Day." *Creative Art* 6 (April 1930): 251–57.

———. "The Roots of Modern Design." *Design* 37 (March 1936): 3–7, 38.

"Straight Lines and Stream-Lines." *Arts and Decoration* 40 (January 1934): 38–41.

Susswein, Rita. "The AUDAC Exhibition at the Brooklyn Museum." *Parnassus* 3 (May 1931): 14–15.

"A Symposium on Modernism in Decoration, by a Group of Well-Known Decorators." *House Beautiful* 65 (March 1929): 306–7, 362, 364–65.

Tallmadge, Thomas E. "Will This Modernism Last?" *House Beautiful* 65 (January 1929): 44–45, 88.

Teague, Walter Dorwin. "This Modern Style—If Any." *Advertising and Selling* 10 (4 April 1928): 23–24, 70–71.

Thieme, Ulrich, and Felix Becker, eds. "Karl König." In *Allgemeines Lexikon der bildenden Künstler von der Antike bis zur Gegenwart*, vol. 21, 157–58. Leipzig: E. A. Seemann, 1935.

Thompson, Helen G. "Outlines for Living." *Arts and Decoration* 40 (November 1933): 6–9.

———. "With Notebook and Pencil—." *Arts and Decoration* 39 (August 1933): 6–9.

Toker, Franklin. *Fallingwater Rising: Frank Lloyd Wright, E. J. Kaufmann, and America's Most Extraordinary House*. New York: Alfred A. Knopf, 2003.

Trapp, Kenneth R., ed. *The Arts and Crafts Movement in California: Living the Good Life*. Exhibition catalog. Oakland: The Oakland Museum/New York: Abbeville Press, 1993.

Trow's New York City Directory. New York: R. L. Polk, 1916.

Troy, Nancy J. *Modernism and the Decorative Arts in France: Art Nouveau to Le Corbusier*. New Haven: Yale University Press, 1991.

Twombly, Robert C. *Frank Lloyd Wright: An Interpretive Biography*. New York: Harper and Row, 1973.

"Urbanity of 'The Follies.'" *Arts and Decoration* 11 (October 1919): 302.

"Various Countries Exhibit Modern Art." *American Architect* 133 (June 1928): 823–27.

"The Vestal Bill." *Good Furniture and Decoration* 35 (December 1930): 333–34, 337.

Vogelgesang, Shepard. "Contemporary Interior Design Advances." *Good Furniture Magazine* 32 (May 1929): 229–34.

Wagner, Otto. *Moderne Architektur*, 3rd ed. Vienna: Anton Schroll, 1902. Reprinted as *Modern Architecture: A Guidebook for His Students to This Field of Art*, trans. Harry Francis Mallgrave. Santa Monica, Calif.: The Getty Center for the History of Art and the Humanities, 1988.

Wagner-Rieger, Renate. "Karl König." In *Österreichisches Biographisches Lexikon, 1815–1950*, 36–37. Vienna: Böhlau, 1969.

Wainright, Shirley B. "The Modern Home and Its Decoration." In *Studio Yearbook 1930*, 59–84. London: The Studio, 1930.

Wank, Eugene Miller. "The Washington Square Players: Experiment toward Professionalism." Ph.D. dissertation, University of Oregon, 1973.

Weber, Kem. "Why Should the American Furniture Buyer, Manufacturer and Designer Go to Europe?" *Good Furniture Magazine* 25 (November 1925): 261.

Welzig, Maria. *Josef Frank, 1885–1967: Das architektonische Werk*. Vienna: Böhlau, 1998.

Westheim, Paul. "Architekturen von Otto Salvisberg—Berlin." *Moderne Bauformen* 3 (1914): 113–40.

———. "Das Lindenhaus von Otto Salvisberg." *Tonindustrie-Zeitung* 140 (1914): 1.

———. *Neuere Arbeiten von O. R. Salvisberg*. Berlin: Hübsch, 1927.

"Where Are Our Moderns?" *Good Furniture and Decoration* 34 (March 1930): 115.

"Where Beauty Is Created." *Arts and Decoration* 33 (May 1930): 68.

Willensky, Elliot, and Norval White. *AIA Guide to New York City*. San Diego: Harcourt Brace Jovanovich, 1988.

Wilson, Kristina. "Exhibiting Modern Times: American Modernism, Popular Culture, and the Art Exhibit, 1925–1935." Ph.D. dissertation, Yale University, 2001.

———. *Livable Modernism: Interior Decoration and Design during the Great Depression*. Exhibition catalog. New Haven: Yale University Art Gallery/Yale University Press, 2004.

Wilson, Richard Guy, Dianne H. Pilgrim, and Dickran Tahsijan, eds. *The Machine Age in America, 1918–1941*. Exhibition catalog. New York: The Brooklyn Museum/Harry N. Abrams, 1986.

Witt-Dörring, Christian, Eva Mang, and Karl Mang, eds. *Neues Wohnen: Wiener Innenraumgestaltung, 1918–1938*. Exhibition catalog. Vienna: Österreichisches Museum für angewandte Kunst, 1980.

Wlach, Oskar. "Oskar Wlach, Bewerbung für die Aufnahme in die Liste der Sachverständigen für Architektur und Hochbaufach." 18 June 1924. Copy in possession of the author.

———. "Professional Career of Dr. Oskar Wlach." April 1958. Copy in possession of the author.

Wolfe, Elsie de. *The House in Good Taste*. New York: Century, 1913.

Wright, Frank Lloyd. *Frank Lloyd Wright, Chicago*, vol. 8, *Sonderheft der Architektur des XX. Jahrhunderts*. Berlin: Ernst Wasmuth, 1911.

———. *Modern Architecture: Being the Kahn Lectures for 1930*. Princeton, N.J.: Princeton University Press, 1931.

Young, Grace Alexandra. "Modernists' Dilemma: A Quest for Contemporary Furniture Puts You at the Mercy of Your Own Judgment." *Arts and Decoration* 41 (June 1934): 18–23.

Ziffer, Alfred. *Bruno Paul*. Munich: Klinkhardt and Biermann, 1992.

"Zu den Bauten von Otto Rudolf Salvisberg." *Moderne Bauformen* 2 (1925): 33–71.

Zweig, Stefan. *Die Welt von Gestern: Erinnerungen eines Europäers*. Frankfurt am Main: S. Fischer, 1953.

Index

Illustration Credits

From *Architectural Forum* 71 (December 1939): 433 (figs. 132, 133); from *Architectural Forum* 78 (June 1943): 97 (figs. 139, 140); from *Der Architekt / Die bildenden Künste* 1, no. 12 (1916/1918): 146 (fig. 22), 147 (fig. 26); The Art Institute of Chicago, Photography by Robert Hashimoto (figs. 59, 89); from *Arts and Decoration* 5 (May 1915): 269 (fig. 18); John P. Axelrod, Boston, Photography by Clive Russ (figs. 81, 83); Bildarchiv der Österreichischen Nationalbibliothek, Vienna (fig. 1); from *California Arts and Architecture* 58 (October 1941): 3 (fig. 142); from E. Clute, *The Treatment of Interiors*, New York: Pencil Point Press, 1926 (figs. 43, 46); from *Creative Art* 4 (April 1929) (fig. 85); © DESIGNbase, Northampton, Mass. (fig. 152); from P. T. Frankl, *The Arts and Decoration Home Study Course Covering the Modern Movement as Applied to Interior Decoration and Kindred Subjects*, New York: Arts and Decoration, 1928, part 5 (fig. 71); from P. T. Frankl, *Form and Re-Form: A Practical Handbook of Modern Interiors*, New York: Harper and Brothers, 1930 (fig. 78); from P. T. Frankl, *New Dimensions: The Decorative Arts of Today in Words and Pictures*, New York: Payson and Clarke, 1928 (figs. 29, 45, 48, 51, 64, 72, 75, 76); from P. T. Frankl, *Space for Living: Creative Interior Decoration and Design*, New York: Doubleday, Doran, 1938 (fig. 106); Collection Paulette Frankl (figs. 6, 8, 9, 13, 14, 16, 17, 20, 28, 30, 32, 33, 35–38, 40–42, 60, 62, 64, 65, 67, 68, 70, 74, 77, 84, 93, 96, 101, 102, 104, 105, 107–31, 134–38, 144–48, 150, 151, 159, 160, 163, 164); from *Good Furniture and Decoration* 34 (April 1930): 204 (fig. 95); from *House and Home* 2 (October 1952): 92 (fig. 162); from *House Beautiful* 66 (1929): 580 (fig. 50); from *House Beautiful* 92 (June 1950): 105 (fig. 153); Indianapolis Museum of Art (fig. 79); from *Innen-Dekoration* 26 (1915): 66 (fig. 11); from *Innen-Dekoration* 29 (1918): 29 (fig. 24), 33 (fig. 27), 36 (fig. 23), 41 (fig. 25); from *Innen-Dekoration* 39 (1928): 60 (fig. 54); Institut für Geschichte und Theorie der Architektur, Eidgenössische Technische Hochschule, Zurich, Nachlass Otto Rudolf Salvisberg (fig. 10); from *Interiors* 107 (September 1947): 91 (fig. 149); from R. L. Leonard and C. A. Glassgold, eds., *Annual of American Design*, New York: Ives Washburn, 1930 (figs. 87, 88, 92, 94); Library of Congress, Prints and Photographs Division, Washington, D.C., LC-USZ62-83263 (fig. 12); from E. McCoy, *Modern California Houses*, New York: Reinhold, 1962 (fig. 161); The Metropolitan Museum of Art, New York, Collection of John C. Waddell, Photographs © The Metropolitan Museum of Art (figs. 52, 100); The Minneapolis Institute of Arts, The Modernism Collection, Gift of Norwest Bank, Minn. (figs. 55, 86); Museum of Fine Arts, Boston, Collection of John P. Axelrod, Photograph © 2004 Museum of Fine Arts, Boston (fig. 53); © The New Yorker Collection 1928, Julian de Miskey from cartoonbank.com, All Rights Reserved (fig. 49); from E. A. Park, *New Backgrounds for a New Age*, New York: Harcourt, Brace, 1927 (fig. 44); from *Printing Art* 24 (February 1915): 488 (fig. 15); Private collection (figs. 2–7, 31, 34, 39, 47, 103); Sollo:Rago Modern Auctions, Lambertville, N.J. (figs. 143, 154); Sotheby's, New York (frontispiece, figs. 61, 73, 82, 90, 141); Theater Collection, New Public Library at Lincoln Center (fig. 21); © Virginia Museum of Fine Arts, Richmond, Va., Photography by Katherine Wetzel (fig. 66); from *Vogue*, 15 November 1915, 68, Courtesy Condé Nast Publications, Inc., New York (fig. 19); Richard Wright, Chicago, Photography by Brian Franczyk (figs. 56–58, 69, 80, 82, 91, 97–99, 155–58)

Christopher Long is associate professor of architectural history and theory at the University of Texas at Austin. He was a contributing author to *Josef Frank: Architect and Designer* (Yale).